Working Fathers

Books Authored or Coauthored by James A. Levine

Who Will Raise the Children? New Options for Fathers (and Mothers)

Day Care and the Public Schools

School Age Child Care: An Action Manual

Fatherhood U.S.A.

Getting Men Involved: Strategies for Early Childhood Programs

New Expectations: Community Strategies for Responsible Fatherhood

Working Fathers

New Strategies for Balancing Work and Family

James A. Levine and Todd L. Pittinsky

Addison-Wesley Publishing Company, Inc.

Reading, Massachusetts   Menlo Park, California   New York
Don Mills, Ontario   Harlow, England   Amsterdam   Bonn
Sydney   Singapore   Tokyo   Madrid   San Juan
Paris   Seoul   Milan   Mexico City   Taipei

Flexible Work Option Request form is used by permission of Work/Family Directions.

Many of the designations used by manufacturers and sellers to distinguish their products are claimed as trademarks. Where those designations appear in this book and Addison-Wesley was aware of a trademark claim, the designations have been printed in initial capital letters.

DaddyStress® and The Fatherhood Project® are registered trademarks of James A. Levine.

Managing Smart® is a registered trademark of the Families and Work Institute and Work/Family Directions.

Levine, James A.
    Working fathers : new strategies for balancing work and family / James A. Levine and Todd L. Pittinsky.
        p.   cm.
    Includes bibliographical references and index.
    ISBN 0-201-14938-9 (alk. paper)
        1. Fathers--United States--Psychology. 2. Fathers--United States--Employment. 3. Work and family--United States--Psychological aspects. I. Pittinsky, Todd L. II. Title.
    HQ756.L474   1997
    306.874'2--dc21   97-2067
                                         CIP

Jacket design by Jean Seal

Text design by Greta D. Sibley

Set in 11-point Minion by Greta D. Sibley

123456789-MA-0100999897

First printing, June 1997

For Joan
   —JAL

For Bernard and Janet Serbin Pittinsky
   —TLP

Contents

Acknowledgments

From Jim and Todd: This book could not have been written without the support of many colleagues. The Families and Work Institute (FWI) and its cofounders Ellen Galinsky and Dana Friedman, provided the home for our research, and The Ford Foundation, represented by June Zeitlin, provided the initial funding for our study of working fathers. A consortium of corporate sponsors supported the Institute's 1992 National Study of the Changing Workforce, including the study's founding cosponsor, Salt River Project, and study cosponsors, Allstate Insurance Company; American Express Company; AT&T; Commonwealth Fund; DuPont Company; General Mills Foundation; IBM Corporation; Johnson & Johnson; Levi Strauss & Co., Inc.; Mobil Corporation; Motorola, Inc.; The Rockefeller Foundation; Salt River Project; and Xerox Corporation. Additional support was provided by Philip Morris, Inc. and Ceridian Corporation.

Many companies generously opened their doors and many people gave generously of their time over the years to be interviewed for the research that fed into this book. Although it is not possible to acknowledge them all directly, they all made this book possible.

A talented and dedicated team of research assistants helped

complete this project on a seemingly impossible timetable. For their good work and good cheer, thanks to Amy Warren, Marla Winnick, Jean Halloran, Erik Diamant, Keith Winnick, Roy Bahat, Andres Saenz, and Eleanor Antoine.

At FWI, Terry Bond, Dana Friedman, Ellen Galinsky, Arlene Johnson, Ed Pitt, and Cali Williams provided constructive and timely content review critical to the completion of this work. Melissa Rowland and Debbie Lowe played bigger roles in keeping the infrastructure of our work going than they will ever appreciate, as did Arielle Eckstut and Daniel Greenberg of James Levine Communications.

Outside of FWI, Michael Lamb and Joe Pleck were very generous in letting us draw on our work together over the last fifteen years. Pat Hersch, Jack Hailey, and Graeme Russell provided especially useful critiques.

Addison-Wesley's Bill Patrick saw the potential to make this a bigger project than our initial proposal suggested and helped us find our voice. Editor Sharon Broll skillfully helped us rearrange the pieces and Amanda Bichsel Cook helped shepherd things to the right places. Elizabeth Carduff, Jennifer Prost, Debbie Yautz, Michele Hanson, Debbie McKenna, Laura Ayr, Jeanne-Marie Hudson, and Andy Corbett have been energetic and extremely responsive in shaping the plan to get this book to as wide an audience as possible.

From Jim: Thanks to Jessica and Joshua, for making it so interesting and fulfilling to be a working father. And special thanks to two people who made this project not only possible, but fun. My wife, Joan, gave me the support and space to focus on it intensely, cheered me along, and never complained about my temporary leave of absence from our time together. Without her I never could have made this deadline. Todd Pittinsky, once again, contributed his extraordinary intelligence, critical thinking, organizational and editorial skill, and mastery of print and on-line research tools. This is the second book we've worked on together, and I hope there will be many more.

From Todd: My contribution to this project would not have been possible without the generous assistance and support of several individuals and organizations, in addition to those listed above.

Acknowledgments

I gratefully acknowledge the guidance in this and other endeavors provided by Rosabeth Moss Kanter of the Harvard Business School and my coauthor, James A. Levine. I am indebted to them not only for their encouragement and substantive guidance, but perhaps most profoundly for the lessons they teach as role models: the power of talent and commitment, compassion and hard work, to change our world. My thanks to the Harvard Business School and Graduate School of Arts and Sciences for their generous commitment to and support of graduate student education and research. In particular, I thank Professor J. Richard Hackman for his intellectual challenges and insight. Finally, I acknowledge a contribution for which it is difficult to find the proper words, the support of family and friends, especially: Janet and Bernard; Matthew and Scott; and Larry, Jill, and Harris.

Introduction

I t is 1:15 P.M. on a balmy day in June 1996, and I am on the thirty-sixth floor of Merrill Lynch & Company's headquarters in the World Financial Center, the waterfront spire at the edge of Wall Street. In this gray-walled, no-nonsense conference room, forty men from different areas of the company—traders, attorneys, information-systems guys, managers—have gathered to talk. Not about emerging markets, which might be expected, but about an emerging issue with unexpected consequences for both their work and family lives: fatherhood.

The lunchtime seminar I am conducting on DaddyStress/Daddy Success was supposed to end fifteen minutes ago, but no one has stirred from his seat. Bernadette Fusaro, the HR manager in charge, seems to have forgotten that she asked me to confine this to one hour. These men, ranging in age from late twenties to mid-fifties, are totally engrossed in sorting out the dilemmas of being a "working father."

"We'll have to stop in another fifteen minutes," I say. "I promised the company I'd let you guys go back to work! I'll stay around afterward for anybody who wants to talk, for as long as you can." After I finish, six men stay to talk for another fifteen minutes.

I have been researching and working with fathers for more than two decades, but fifteen years ago, even ten, I never would have imagined this scene. A Fortune 500 company in a notoriously competitive business sponsoring a workshop on fatherhood? Men actually attending—and staying—because they thought it was important to them both as fathers and as employees?

During the 1980s I had conducted seminars on dual-career parenting with my colleague, Ellen Galinsky, cofounder and president of the Families and Work Institute. But when we arrived at companies like Time-Warner (then Time-Life), the employee–parent most likely to show up was mom. A few guys were sprinkled in the audiences, but they would rarely ask questions. Not that they didn't have questions. But the fathers would typically wait until the workshop was over, until the women had drifted out, and then approach me with their concerns.

I first got a sense that something important about fatherhood was emerging in 1990. Thanks to a grant from The Ford Foundation, I began to explore what life was like for men as they tried to balance their commitments to work and family. Much had been written, of course, about working mothers. What about working fathers?

I wasn't sure I would actually get any companies to enroll in our study, but when senior management at Apple Computer quickly agreed to participate, it was a good sign. Still, as I strode into Apple's San Jose, California, headquarters in October 1990, I was nervous. Would anyone actually show up for the focus groups I was supposed to lead? In this notoriously workaholic culture, would any man take time from pressing deadlines for an open-ended conversation about work and family life? Employee excitement was palpable, fueled by then-surging sales of the Macintosh and announcements that the company was developing new technology that would change the face of computing. I imagined myself reporting back to The Ford Foundation, "Sorry, no one showed up. So much for working fathers."

But when I got to the fourth floor of the main administration building, Debbie Biondollillo, then vice president for human resources, greeted me with enthusiasm. How long could I stay? So many men had responded to the e-mail announcement of my research—second on the daily posting, right behind Apple's current stock price—that she hoped I would be willing to add some extra sessions.

During what turned into a two-and-a-half-day stay, the men did indeed come, usually in groups of about ten, and many didn't want to leave. They talked and lingered beyond our schedule because they wanted to talk more. This wasn't some Men's Movement retreat, a sweat lodge in the middle of the woods where New Age men bared their souls about unfinished business with their fathers. This was the heart of Silicon Valley, as competitive as it gets, with engineers and marketing managers and number crunchers (and later, at a nearby manufacturing facility, with guys working the line and running forklifts) opening up about the tension between the two most important dimensions of their lives: being there for their families and succeeding at work.

For me, listening to these men was an "aha" experience. Here were dads talking about pick-ups at child care, overnight travel assignments, and supervisors who needed to "get a life."

In interviews at other companies, big and small, I began to hear similar stories. I also began to listen and probe in informal research settings—the everyday situations that are rich with easily overlooked details. How did my Dominican-American taxi driver, the one with a rosary and pictures of his kids on the dashboard, ever have time to see his family, given his twelve-hour shifts? While checking on lost luggage at the airport in Seattle, I overheard the clerk talking with colleagues about his six-day-old's infection and wondered how he would manage bringing his new identity as a father to work everyday.

Meanwhile, a combination of research data from the Families and Work Institute (FWI) and other sources began to confirm the national significance of what I was hearing from individuals and small groups: *More* men were feeling *more* conflict between work and family life than anybody had thought, but they were reluctant to talk about it. Men did want to succeed as providers; it was crucial to their identity as men and as fathers. But they wanted something more: an involvement and relationship with their children. Combining both was enormously difficult, as the realities facing working mothers made clear, and they were increasingly stressed out about it.

During the course of my research, it became obvious that I wasn't the only one learning from these focus groups. Fathers seemed to benefit from the chance to talk with one another. It was reassuring just to know that other guys were experienceing the same conflicts, and it was even more helpful for employees and supervisors to pick up a few tactics on how best to cope. So I decided to turn my research into a seminar called "DaddyStress/Daddy Success: How Fathers and Managers Can Deal Effectively with Work-Family Conflict."

I did not advertise the DaddyStress/Daddy Success seminar, just included it in the repertoire of presentations I make on fatherhood to all sorts of groups. But by the mid-1990s, companies like Merrill Lynch, American Express, IBM, and Time-Warner—companies that a decade earlier would have given no thought to the working fathers in their ranks—were asking for that presentation. The same demographic data that I had read were inevitably pushing them to realize that working parents come in two flavors— mothers and fathers—and that *for the sake of their business* they needed to start paying attention to both.

∾

This book is designed to give you—business people (male and female) and parents (fathers and mothers)—a new understanding of working fathers. "So," my publisher asked early on, "which section of the bookstore should we put it in, parenting or business? Is it a book for fathers or a book for managers? Is it a book about parenting or a book about work?" Actually, it's a book about both dimensions of men's lives. And it's a book for women in their roles as parents and workers, whether managers or employees.

Books for fathers typically omit attention to the workplace, as if the workplace does not have any impact on them as parents. Books about work typically omit attention to men as fathers, as if men leave their parent selves at home when they go to work. To date, it is only books for and about working mothers that have acknowledged and sought an integration between these two key dimensions of identity.

But work and family are interdependent spheres for fathers, just as they are for mothers. Men don't shelve their father-part at work, or their worker-part at home. Each aspect of their life deeply affects the other. Until we get beyond the fragmentation of work and family as separate spheres for both men and women, our society will never be able to adequately address one of the biggest challenges of contemporary life: how to balance the continuing need for workplace productivity with the continuing need to care for our families. Whoever you are, whatever shelf you have found this book on, it will both address dimensions of experience and challenge you to understand their integration in a new way.

It is somewhat rare to combine social analysis and how-to advice, as this book does. The combination is deliberate. One of the limitations of books of purely social commentary is that they are long on analysis and short on action. They tend to illuminate a problem and then stop short of addressing what readers most want to know: "What can I do right now?" One of the limitations of pure how-to books is that they are long on lists of tips, but short on providing a framework to help the reader understand a problem in a new way. I have combined both elements, much as I do in my DaddyStress/Daddy Success seminars.

This book is organized into three parts, each designed to reframe your thinking about working fathers and their place in balancing the new work–family equation.

Part I, "DaddyStress/Daddy Success" explains working fathers as a hitherto unacknowledged component of the changing workforce—how and why they are experiencing more work–family conflict, and why paying attention to them matters for both business productivity and the quality of family life. I focus on working fathers not to minimize or obscure the needs of working mothers but, quite the opposite, to advance both their interests. To explain this seeming paradox, let me refer you to a drawing now found in many introductory psychology textbooks.

This "reversible figure" drawing was first used in 1899 by psychologist Joseph Jastrow to demonstrate that (1) what we see is determined by a combination of what's out there (the available data) *and* what we expect to see (the schema already in our minds), and (2) it is very difficult to see two competing representations at the same time. Whether you see a rabbit or a duck depends on whether you expect to see a rabbit or a duck. In either case, once you are focused on one version of the picture, it is almost impossible to see the other at the same time.

Most current discussions of work and family life are so focused on the working mother rabbit that they cannot see the working father duck. Part I of this book is designed to *temporarily* change your angle of vision so that you can see the working father. My ultimate goal is not to keep you fixated on the working father, but to get you to see both the working mother and the working father at the same time. As the drawing suggests, that means creating either an entirely new picture or an entirely new way of looking at the picture, one that recognizes that the two coexist. Women won't be able to advance at work and men will not be able to have a fuller presence in family life unless we keep working fathers in focus in the work–family picture.

Part II, "Strategies for Work," recognizes that men do not leave their "father self" at home when they go to work. It explains what can be done as fathers or as workers—whether employee, manager, or executive—to create a supportive workplace. It shows what is being done right now by companies taking the lead. And it shows how father-friendliness can benefit the business bottom line and also advance the cause of women who are seeking to create a truly family-friendly workplace.

Part III, "Strategies for Home," recognizes that men do not leave their "work self" when they are with their families. It explains how to make sure that fathers are emotionally connected to their children when they are home and when they travel. Moreover, it rethinks the quality time issue in terms of relationships in and outside the family. Paradoxically, staying connected to your children may not require spending more time with your children, but investing more time in staying connected to your wife *and* to other important people in your child's life—child-care providers, teachers, doctors, coaches, and so on.

This book offers insights and strategies for several different audiences:

- **Working Fathers** We show you how your concerns of balancing work and family life compare with those of other men throughout America. We give you a new way of thinking about the challenge, and provide proven, practical strategies for dealing effectively with the tug you're feeling between the two areas of life you care about most: your family and your work.

- **Working Mothers** For too many years, you've been waging the battle to create family-friendly workplaces with only half an army. We give a new perspective on the experiences of your husbands and sons, and new ideas on changing the workplace. We show you how attention to working fathers can, in the long term, help eliminate the "mommy track." And we help you enlist a new set of recruits at work and at home.

- **Managers** Whether you're in human resources, mid-level management at the operational level, or line management, you are dealing with the day-to-day realities of (employees stressed by) downsizing, competition, and changing family needs. We show you how to recognize and respond to your working fathers in ways that create a more family-friendly workplace for all employed parents, while supporting your bottom line.

- **Executives and Consultants** Workforce 2000 is different from what you may think. If you're struggling with the diversity issue and don't know how to deal with stalled change efforts and lack of acceptance from some white males, we show you how and why work–family and diversity initiatives already underway in many businesses can be strengthened by addressing fathers, a too-long ignored component of the changing work force.

∾

When reporters call my office, they often ask me to comment on the current "revolution" in men's work and family lives. My research shows that we are in the midst of an *evolution*, not a revolution—an evolution largely driven by changes in women's roles and economic opportunities.

This evolution needs to be carefully cultivated. As an increasing number of fathers tries to balance commitments to work and family life, more than a million American fathers are unemployed or underemployed. Millions are disengaged from their children through divorce or desertion. At The Fatherhood Project, which I have directed since 1981, we work on examining and developing ways to support the involvement of all men—married, unmarried, or divorced—in the lives of their children. Much of our work is focused on low-income communities and the creation of father-friendly practices in organizations that deal with families on a day-to-day basis—hospitals, health clinics, preschools and child-care programs, schools, social service agencies, and religious and spiritual organizations.

Our goal here is to contribute to this evolution by reframing the understanding of work and family life in America, by opening up a new set of conversations between fathers and their employers, as well as between fathers and mothers. The group this book focuses on—working fathers—is no small group. In 1995, there were just over 25 million fathers in the United States with a child under 18 in their household; 96 percent of them were employed. In 1994, there were over 69 million children under 18 years of age in the United States; 69 percent of them lived with two parents and another 3 percent lived with their father only. By paying serious attention to both working mothers and working fathers we can transform today's work–family challenge into win–win solutions for America's business and America's families.*

---

*A Note on Language: We use the term *working mothers* to refer to women's participation in the paid labor force. We underscore here that women and men taking care of children at home are indeed working very hard. As a matter of literary style *we*, the authors, have chosen to use the pronoun *I* for the remainder of this book.

Part 1

DaddyStress / Daddy Success

Chapter 1

DaddyStress
The Invisible Dilemma

On a frigid January morning in Rochester, New York, a hundred executives of Bausch & Lomb—the worldwide health and eye-care company that generates $1.9 billion a year on products that include the disinfecting solution for my contact lenses —are gathered in the cafeteria for my breakfast seminar on the changing work force. They do not realize that they are about to take a test.

"You've all heard of the SAT," I say, "the Scholastic Aptitude Test. Some of you probably took it in a high school cafeteria not unlike this one, anywhere from ten to thirty years ago. It was supposed to assess how well prepared you were for college."

"Today I'm going to administer the W.A.T.—the Workforce 2000 Aptitude Test. Don't worry, it's not nearly as long as the SAT— it will probably take less than five minutes, and you don't need a number two pencil. It's designed to assess how well prepared you are for the changing work force that has been forecast by the Hudson Institute's landmark report, *Workforce 2000*."

"The test consists of a series of twenty slides, all pictures of people who are or could be members of the changing work force. As I display them, jot down the categories of workers you see. When we're done, I'll ask you to call out your answers."

As I flip through the slides, the assembled executives concentrate intently. A test-taking mentality has taken over; they want to get things "right," especially in front of their peers. Interestingly, all of them will "fail" the test in exactly the same way, as do most audiences to whom I show the slides.

After the last slide, I turn up the houselights and walk around the room full of men and women, asking those with eagerly raised hands to tell us what they saw.

"African-Americans."

"Women."

"Hispanics."

"Working mothers."

"Elderly."

"Asians."

"People with disabilities."

Not one person identifies fathers as a distinct category. The twenty slides are evenly distributed by gender, with a good mix of age and race. Although two-thirds of the people in the room are parents, nobody thinks to mention fathers.

What is going on? What is going on is emblematic of a shortcoming of almost every discussion to date of the changing nature of the American work force. It is an omission in almost all discussions of diversity. Like most people who take the W.A.T., like most who try to understand *Workforce 2000*, this group of executives focuses exclusively on people's external attributes: race, age, gender, and ability. They look at skin color and see the increase of African-Americans, Hispanics, and Asians. They look at hair that is gray, white, or thinning and see "older workers." They look at a wheelchair and see workers with disabilities. And when they look at women they often imagine children at home and see "working mothers."

Race, age, gender, ability—all are critical dimensions of diversity, all worthy of the attention they have begun to receive. But diversity is more than skin deep—not just the external attributes of the workforce are changing. Over the last twenty years—at the same time our society has seen a dramatic increase in the labor force participation of working mothers, workers of color, and workers with physical disabilities—men's internal values have been changing. On the outside, the fathers who will comprise *Workforce 2000* may look like the men of the last generation or two. On the inside, they are often very different people, with different motivations and aspirations, leading different lives.

Like their own fathers, these men want to be good breadwinners. The provider role is still crucial to their identity as men and as fathers. But they no longer define being a *good father* almost exclusively in terms of the ability to provide economically. Being a good father has another, equally vital component, a dimension that many want with their children and felt lacking in their relationships with their own fathers: "having a close relationship with their children," or "being involved with their children's lives." It is not that they are *better* fathers than previous generation's, or that men of previous generations failed to value closeness, but that the economics of family life and expectations about fatherhood have changed.

Because it is internal, men's work–family conflict is often invisible—not only when executives look at the slides in the W.A.T., but also when they look at their colleagues and employees.

THE INVISIBLE DILEMMA

It is time for the second part of the test at Bausch & Lomb. I ask the audience to write down two numbers. First, I ask, "What percentage of working mothers experience a significant amount of conflict between work and family life?"

"Eighty percent," says a woman in a blue suit at the back.

"Sixty percent," says a man in the first row.

"One hundred and twenty percent!" snaps the woman next to him, arousing laughter throughout the room.

As with most groups, the estimates average about 80 percent. Four out of five working mothers must be feeling a strong tear between job and family life. Conflict has become the defining characteristic of today's working mother.

Next I ask, "What percentage of working fathers experiences a significant amount of conflict between work and family life?"

"Zero," says the feisty woman in the front row, causing another roll of laughter.

"Zero? Give me a break. How about twenty?" blurts a dark-haired man at the right edge of the room.

"It's gotta be more like fifty," says a man toward the back.

As with most groups, the average estimates for women are two to four times higher than those for men. In fact, however, the experiences of men and women are much closer than most people realize.

When companies have actually surveyed their male employees about work–family conflict—which they have only recently started to do—their level of work–family conflict turns out to be as great as for the female employees. In the mid-1980s, when Merck & Co. surveyed its employees, it found that "40 percent of men and 37 percent of women [with teenage children] experienced high work–family conflict." In 1987, when a public utility surveyed it's 1600 employees, "36 percent of fathers (compared to 37 percent of mothers) reported 'a lot of stress' in balancing their work and family lives." A survey of 1,200 employees in a Minneapolis company found "higher percentages of fathers than mothers reported difficulties with child care (72 v. 65 percent) and general 'dual-career problems' (70 v. 63 percent)." The following year, in 1988, an employee survey at DuPont revealed that comparable numbers of men and women were concerned about work-family issues. And in 1984, while AT&T was in the midst of its court-ordered breakup into regional companies, a survey of its mostly male top managers and executives "discovered that their kids caused these employees more stress and worry than anything else, including their careers."

But those were company-specific studies, done by some of the most progressive corporations in the world. What about a totally random sample of the U.S. work force as a whole? Could it possibly be that fathers, on average, experience as much work–family conflict as mothers?

The Families and Work Institute (FWI) had a unique opportunity to find out through its 1993 *National Study of the Changing Workforce,* which surveyed a representative sample of the American population. The study is the most comprehensive of its kind since the U.S. Department of 1977 *Labor's Quality of Employment Survey.* When FWI looked at work–family conflict in dual-earner families where both parents work full time, it found no significant differences between mothers and fathers. Nearly one-fifth report "a lot of conflict," and two-fifths report "some conflict," for a total of 60.6 percent.*

In fact, it did not matter to fathers whether mothers worked full time, part time, or not at all. If conflict level was determined only by time and resources, one would expect significantly lower levels of conflict among men in families where mom stays at home. But 56 percent of fathers in those "traditional families" still report feeling some or a lot of conflict: 16 percent "a lot of conflict" and 40 percent "some conflict." DaddyStress, it turns out, is not confined to men in "harried" dual-earner families.

Most revealing, when FWI researchers compared work–family conflict among mothers and fathers in *all* family forms, there still were no significant differences: 58 percent of all working parents experience significant conflict balancing their work and family/personal lives; 16 percent of working parents are at the highest end of conflict. In addition, fathers of different socioeconomic classes do not report different levels of work–family conflict. This is a widespread phenomenon among American men, not one restricted to the so-called "yuppie" fathers.

For many people, *working mother* has come to symbolize con-

---

* When we report findings from the Families and Work Institute's *National Study of the Changing Workforce,* mother (or father) refers to a woman (or man) with at least one child under the age of eighteen living in her (his) household, for whom she (he) has all or partial responsibility. When we refer to work–family conflict, we refer to one of the variables researchers use to explain the intersection between people's work and family lives; other important variables that researchers use include stress and coping effectiveness.

flict. When a woman works outside the home, our society assumes she must feel a constant tug-of-war between her "job self" and her "parent self." But *working father* is a redundancy, isn't it? Saying that "fathers work" is like saying "fathers father." The prevailing assumption is that men do not feel that tug-of-war between their "job selves" and their "parent selves."

But if those assumptions were ever right, as we head into the twenty-first century they are definitely out of date. The experiences of men and women struggling to provide and care for their families—in many ways so profoundly different—are similar in important ways. For the majority of American men, an internal shift in values has created what I call the *invisible dilemma* of DaddyStress, a largely unrecognized conflict between their double duties of work and family that they feel they should not expose. Understanding DaddyStress—what men want, what they do, how they feel—may lead to an important new common ground for men and women, beyond the gender divides that have characterized so much public and private discourse over the last twenty years.

WHAT TODAY'S FATHERS WANT

Put simply, what fathers increasingly want is the ability to both provide for *and* spend time with their children. Although work is an unquestionably powerful source of male identity and satisfaction, family is equally strong. A 1991 Gallup poll found that a majority of American men—59 percent—derive "a greater sense of satisfaction from caring for their family than from a job well done at work." In 1992, a national survey conducted by the Roper Organization for *Playboy* magazine found men "evenly split about whether the main focus of their life is job (31%) or family (33%)," with the other third saying "both equally." Two years later, in 1993, a nationally representative study by University of Illinois psychologist Joseph Pleck concluded that men now "seek their primary emotional, personal, and spiritual gratification from the family setting." By 1996, a Consumer

Survey Center poll of men in their thirties and forties done for Levi Strauss & Co. discovered that 84 percent of baby boomer men say that "success" means being a good father, while 72 percent cite having a close partnership with a spouse or significant other. Poll after poll—and I have cited only a few—turns up similar results.

Does this mean that men—especially fathers—are slackening their interest in work and career? Absolutely not. Analysis of FWI's *National Study of the Changing Workforce* indicates that the men with the strongest aspirations to advance, the men who are most eager for increased challenge and responsibility, are fathers in the primary child-rearing years. Of dads with children under eighteen, 64 percent want more responsibility, while only 55 percent of men without children (or with children over eighteen) want more responsibility.

This high level of simultaneous commitment to both work and family is different from a pattern observed as recently as 1983 by Fernando Bartolome of the Harvard Business School, who found many male managers taking what he termed the *mañana* approach, continually putting off family concerns until "tomorrow." But by 1994, when a Families and Work Institute/Whirlpool Foundation survey asked a representative sample of U.S. men, 'What makes you feel successful at home,' the most frequent response was good family relationships and spending time together, followed by "financial security" and "being able to afford things."

The integration of work and family is not only what more and more of today's fathers want; it is also what women are looking for in their marriage partners, according to a 1993 *Parents* magazine survey of its readers. In the same year, when *Child* magazine asked its readers to rank the characteristics of a "good father," both mothers and fathers gave first place to "being involved with my children's daily life," followed closely by "being able to support my family financially."

In fact, most of the U.S. population now agrees with this double-duty definition of the good father, according to the Family Research Council (FRC), a conservative Washington think tank headed by Gary Bauer, former domestic policy advisor in the

Reagan White House. A survey conducted for FRC by the Roper Oganization in 1993 found that 76 percent of adults said that mothers and fathers should be "equally responsible" for "infant care and feeding" or for "taking care of a child who is sick or injured." When it comes to "tucking a child in bed," the number in favor of equal care jumped to 94 percent, and "helping with homework" rated 96 percent. But when it comes to earning an income, a large percentage still expects the father to be primary breadwinner. Although the same survey found that 58 percent of adults feel responsibility should be shared equally, 39 percent said breadwinning should be the primary responsibility of the father, and 3 percent said they did not know.

What these data suggest about today's families—and about today's working fathers in particular—is both profound and largely ignored. "[T]he questions about juggling home and family life are always asked as if there were only one sex on the planet," say Rosalind Barnett, research scholar at the Radcliffe Institute, and journalist Caryl Rivers. "Men, it is assumed, . . . have built-in, watertight doors that separate each part of their lives. The man at work, we believe, never sits at his desk worrying about his kids."

Not true, according to an emerging body of research, as well as to earlier research that has not received as much attention as it deserves. Since men don't often express their emotions about parenthood (or much else) as readily as women, it's easy to assume that they don't have strong feelings on these issues. But according to a multiyear study of a random sample of three hundred dual-earner couples conducted by Barnett for the National Institutes of Mental Health, men feel just as much anxiety on the job because they are fathers as women do because they are mothers: "[G]nawing concern about the children—such as worry over their safety or their choice of friends or about the financial burden they impose—can cause either parent to suffer stress-related health problems." In fact, a man's experience as a *parent*—not as an employee—was the strongest predictor of whether he would have stress-related physical symptoms. In terms of men's mental health, the roles of worker, spouse, and parent had equal significance.

That men have such strong physical and emotional reactions when concerned about their children's well-being was actually revealed about twenty years ago in a fascinating study conducted by Michael Lamb, now chief of the section on social and emotional development at the National Institutes for Child Health and Development. Mothers and fathers watched and listened to a videotape of a crying baby, followed by a videotape of a smiling and cooing baby. "While they watched," Lamb explains, "we monitored parents' blood pressure, heart rate, and galvanic skin response. We found that crying babies elicited accelerated rates on all three measures, while a comfortable baby elicited a deceleration. There was no difference in reaction between mothers and fathers. For both fathers and mothers, the changes seemed to be preparing the body for behavioral responses to the baby. Deceleration leads people to continue what they are doing, whereas acceleration is an indication of anger or the body being aroused and prepared for action—presumably the action of going to the baby to relieve the distress. The same patterns in males and females suggest that both have a basic physiological response to these important signals. We repeated this test in three or four different studies with babies of different ages—preterm babies, full-terms babies, and so on. And again, the physiological responses of fathers and mothers were indistinguishable."

New research reveals that, as children age, working fathers continue to have strong reactions about the care of their children. Among the biggest worries of fathers today is how their children are faring in child care while they are at work. That's not what researcher Kirby Deater-Deckard at Vanderbilt University and her colleagues expected to find when they interviewed 589 dual-income married couples in Boston, Richmond, and Atlanta. They assumed fathers would be less emotionally affected than mothers by leaving their children in day care. But when they controlled for a host of other variables that might affect paternal stress—including the children's age, sex, and ethnicity, the number of children in the family, per capita income, parents' age and education, even attitudes toward traditional gender roles in the family—they discovered that fathers feel as much, and sometimes more, anxiety about separating from their preschoolers in day care as mothers do. Furthermore, fathers who are more satisfied with their child-care arrangements feel less stressed at work, more satisfied in their role as parents, and more satisfied with their lives in general, according to FWI's *National Study of the Changing Workforce.*

Stress over child care, long a major worry for the 23 percent of the mothers in the work force who are single parents, is increasingly being shared by the 4 percent of working fathers who are single parents. Some are men like Stuart Browy of Columbia, South Carolina, who now has what he calls the "3 P.M. syndrome" under reasonable control, thanks to support from his employer, National Cash Register. "My eleven- and thirteen-year-old sons call me at my office just to let me know they are safe." But others, like Alan Smith, a single father in the rural town of Brimfield, Massachusetts, struggle with their employers. Smith's day job with the U.S. Postal Service was eliminated, and he was told he had to work nights. "I told them I could not work nights because I had a ten-year-old son and I am a single parent. I cannot afford child care on one income, plus I would not be able to be a parent for my son. Being with my son two days a week is not a good way to be a parent. They said they don't care. The topper is, they hired temps to do my day job. I just don't know where to turn."

Whether in single- or dual-parent families, one of the common denominators among working fathers is feeling torn by two emotions: guilt for not spending more time with their children and worry about being able to make a living. Jack Simonetti, professor of management at the University of Toledo, and his colleagues, surveyed 330 middle-class baby-boomer parents in 1993. Contrary to prevailing opinion, the study revealed that working mothers do not have a monopoly on guilt: 47 percent of fathers said they do not spend enough "quality time" with their children. And when they are unable to spend more time with their families, 78 percent of the men say they feel guilty "often/always" or "sometimes," compared to 76 percent of the women, who expressed more confidence in the time they spent with their children. It's a double bind, expressed aptly by Chris Celentino, a bankruptcy attorney and partner in a San Diego, California, law firm. "You work longer hours because of the fear that you're not providing enough. Then there's the guilt that you're not spending enough time with your family. It goes around and around. You work harder for stability, and it gives you less stability than you think."

"There's always conflict," says Stephen Roache, a father of two sons (ages eight and ten) who works as director of finance for the Harlem School of the Arts. "I often feel guilty because I probably missed a Boy Scout meeting or whatever. My older son is in Boy Scouts, softball, and basketball. My younger son is in piano and Jack and Jill, a group for African-American boys. On a typical day I'm up at 6:30 A.M., shower, make breakfast, fix lunches, and get them out to the bus stop. My wife presses their clothes before she leaves for work. I'm home by about 8 P.M. At the end of the day I get a half an hour with them before they go to bed. On weekends I take one of my sons to piano and Cub Scouts. I just need a day to do what I want, to read a book, read the *Times* cover to cover. I love what I do, but if I'm going to make any more money it will be at the same pace. There's no getting around that in this day and age."

RETHINKING THE SECOND SHIFT

So what if men *feel* torn between being with and providing for their children? So what if they experience much of the same anxiety, worry, and guilt felt by working mothers? After all, what men actually *do* in their families pales in comparison to women, doesn't it? Most working mothers not only are employed, but are doing most of the child care and housework, working a virtual "second shift" at home, a phenomenon documented in a 1989 book of that name by my colleague and friend, Arlie Hochschild, professor of sociology at the University of California at Berkeley, with Anne Machung.

"The second shift" has become a widely used catchphrase, a shorthand way of distilling the gulf between the experience of working mothers and fathers. But in fact, *the second shift*—certainly the popular simplification—is not an accurate way of describing what mothers or fathers really do at the end of the 1990s. And it's not just that the domestic labor gap between men and women has been closing over the last decade. In navigating through the territory of men's and women's experiences in the 1980s, Hochschild was not only using an already outdated map, but looking at only part of it.

At the beginning of her book, Hochschild cited a then nearly twenty-five-year-old study in which Alexander Szalai and his colleagues "found that working women averaged three hours a day on housework while men averaged seventeen minutes; women spent fifty minutes a day of time exclusively with their children; men spent twelve minutes. On the other side of the coin, working fathers watched television an hour longer than their working wives, and slept a half hour longer each night." Although *The Second Shift* went on to explain—in a more sophisticated and sympathetic way than any previous work—the complex interplay of beliefs about gender roles that shapes the behavior of mothers and fathers in all families, a reductionist version traveled far and wide. And even today, the twelve-minute figure, drawn from 1964 data, lives on, regularly popping up in attempts by academics, politicians, and the media to explain a wide variety of social phenomenon.

For example, in a 1991 article on New Age guru Robert Bly, the *Atlanta Journal and Constitution* writes, "But the stoic emotionally stunted John Wayne-style Warrior is the only role model held up for American men, Mr. Bly says, and fathers aren't available to explain otherwise. Most Western men work away from the home; statistics show they spend, on average, about 12 minutes a day with their children."

In a 1994 article on whether African-American men are "in crisis," the *San Francisco Chronicle* reports psychologists who say the problems of manhood "transcend race and social class," citing as evidence "a study showing that the average man living at home spends 12 minutes a day with his children."

A February 1996 article in *The Arizona Republic* on juvenile crime cited author E. Timothy Burns's work *From Risk to Resiliency*. Burns wrote that in the 1930s family members spent an average three to four hours each day interacting with each other. "Today," he says, "fathers in middle-class families spend about 12 minutes a day interacting with their children."

The twelve-minute figure even had wings, and made it across the ocean to the British Parliament. In a 1993 story, "New Man Still a Myth," The Press Association Newsfile announced the publication of *The Century Gap*, a book by Labour MP Harriet Harman, which used the Szalai study to argue that "women's entry into the workforce has not been matched by men's entry into the home.... 'New Man' may have appeared in the commercial breaks, but he has yet to put in a sustained appearance at home. . . . working women average three hours a day on homework, working men seventeen minutes; working mothers spend an average of fifty minutes a day exclusively with their children, working fathers twelve minutes."

Although it was taken as the gospel of inequality, the twelve-minute figure did not actually hold up to closer scrutiny by Joseph Pleck of the University of Illinois at Champagne–Urbana, one of the most respected students of men's and women's time use in the country. *The Second Shift* was anchored in Alexander Szalai's 1965–66 study of a national random sample of 1,243 working parents which reported that on average, working mothers were spending three hours and fifty minutes a day on housework and child care, compared to twenty-nine minutes for the average working father. But Pleck noticed that Hochschild's report omitted Szalai's calculations for time spent on weekend days, when both parents spend more time in family roles, and for time spent on housework activities such as "shopping, administrative services, repairs, and waiting in line." When Pleck factored in Szalai's missing data, he found that in 1965–66 "employed fathers actually spent an average of ninety-one minutes per day in housework and child care combined," or more than three times the twenty-nine minutes reported in The Second Shift. So even in 1966, the twelve-minute figure does not appear to have been an accurate estimate.

Of course, Pleck's analysis of the 1965–66 data still revealed a glaring differential between the share of child care and household work done by mothers and fathers at that time. If a ratio of 8:1 was outrageous, 2.5:1 was far from equal.

Has anything changed during the last thirty years in what men are actually doing to account for the experience of work–family conflict reported by today's working fathers?

The answer is yes. For one, social scientists have been looking more carefully at a larger work and family map, one that includes the time parents spend in paid work and commuting, and that distinguishes among different types of family responsibilities. According to the FWI's 1993 *National Study of the Changing Workforce,* fathers who work full time put in about six hours a week more at their paid jobs than do mothers who work full time. Employed mothers who work full time report actually working 41.6 hours at their main job and 42.2 hours at all jobs. In contrast, employed fathers who work full time report working 47.1 hours at their main jobs and 48.2 hours at all jobs.

This gap in actual hours worked, 5.5 hours at their main job and 6 hours a week for all jobs, is likely further increased when commuting times for job-related activities are figured in; the *National Study* finds that men report spending an extra hour a week commuting. Based on a thirty-five-hour work week, the average working father is still putting in an extra day of paid work a week compared to his full-time working spouse. The paid-work gap is even greater when dad works full time and mom works part time; a common arrangement in families with young children. In 1993, 96.5 percent of employed fathers were working at full-time jobs, compared to 74.1 percent of employed mothers.

At home the gap goes just the other way, because on average fathers still do less housework and child care than mothers. But over the last three decades, men's participation in these areas has increased substantially in both proportional and absolute terms.

In 1960, for every hour dad put in, mom put in four; in 1981, for every hour he put in, she put in two; by the early 1990s, for every hour he put in, she put in one and a half. Pleck's 1996 analysis of the data available to date shows that the differential has been more than cut in half, especially for parents of young children. Fathers are available for their younger children between 2.8 to 4.9 hours on weekdays and 9.8 hours on Sunday, which represents nearly two-thirds (65.6 percent) of the time that mothers are available. When it comes to direct interaction—through play, caretaking, or just hanging out together—fathers of young children spend, on average, 1.9 hours on weekdays and 6.5 hours on Sundays, just over two-fifths (43.5 percent) of what mothers do. With teenagers, an eleven-year study of a random sample of 584 two-parent families conducted by sociologist Kathleen Mullan Harris of the University of North Carolina at Chapel Hill found that teens do activities with their fathers almost as often as with their mothers.

The household gap is closing not just because fathers are doing more at home, but because mothers are doing more in the workplace and less at home. But combined with the added hours that fathers continue to spend at their paid work, the total number of hours that mothers and fathers spend providing for and caring for their families is converging.

That is exactly what Rosalind Barnett found in her study of dual-earner couples. "Altogether women spend more time on household chores (about 3.7 hours a day) compared to the men (about three hours a day). . . . On average, the men worked for pay 48.5 hours a week, compared to forty-two hours for their wives. . . . So while women do more of the housework (roughly 55 percent), this picture is a lot closer to equality than it is to the second shift scenario."

"The good news," says Barnett, "is that in dual-earner couples, women are no longer alone in working a second shift. The bad news is that everyone is working very long hours. . . . Nobody is doing much time in the easy chair."

Barnett's findings confirm the impression I get when I interview working fathers and working mothers. No matter how large or small their employer, or whether they are self-employed, both parents seem to be working very hard, tugged in different directions as they try to care for their children financially, physically, and emotionally. This seems to be a belief shared by most people in the United States. In 1992, when the *Mass Mutual Family Values Survey* asked what "fathers today struggle with most," adults in America identified work–family conflict as the central dilemma in men's lives: 39 percent chose "making ends meet," the exact same percentage that selected "finding quality time for their families." Only a very small percentage saw fathers as putting a higher value in self-absorption such as "finding time to relax" (5 percent), "succeeding in their careers" (6 percent), or "finding opportunities for romance" (1 percent).

Yet even as the work–family conflict of mothers and fathers continues to converge, the "second shift" phenomenon—the fact and feeling of "doing it all"—is surely a reality for many women.

One reason is that, no matter how much time mothers and fathers spend at their jobs or at home, it is still mothers, on average, who take the responsibility for worrying about what has to get done, when, and by whom. And it is mental energy, not just physical energy, that goes into caring for anybody or anything. As a corollary, the types of jobs at home that women are more likely to end up doing are those that are least discretionary. They are the often unpleasant chores—cleaning the bathrooms, scrubbing the kitchen floor—that have to get done and often can't be postponed until later.

Still, as I listen to the stories of working mothers, I often hear what starts as resentment slide into an acknowledgment and appreciation for how hard their husbands are working and how stressed they feel. At first glance, Ruby Jordan's story could be read as one more bit of data confirming a "second shift" story. Ruby worked as an attorney for the Queens, New York, District Attorney's office while her husband, Samuel, and his partners were trying to establish their own small law firm. Ruby had primary responsibility for their young daughter, Sarah. "When I was working we tried to work it out, but I did it all. I'd leave the office and say, 'Now I have to start my second job.' Everything would be falling on me. He doesn't cook. He'll change the diapers. He can dress the baby, but I have to lay it out. Everything else is left up to me."

But soon she is talking with sympathy and pride about her husband's Jamaican roots that emphasize the family. "Every day he's out by 5:30 or 6:00 A.M. He feels he has to do it for the family, for us to get a home, have adequate schooling. He's torn between spending time with the business and at the same time spending time at home. It hasn't been giving back as much as we expected. We haven't been able to get a house, travel. He gets the brunt of it. Actually, there are days when I say, 'Leave it, close it down!' He would do phenomenally in a law firm. People have been talking to him about judgeship, other options. He's still hesitant to walk away. It's like walking away from a marriage, even though it's at its worst point now." In fact, Ruby later says she does not really want him to walk away from the firm or from the service he gives to their church and community. "He's a strong Christian, a deacon in the Baptist church. He's got a huge responsibility there."

WHY DADDYSTRESS STAYS INVISIBLE

Why does the invisible dilemma remain invisible? What keeps the experience of working fathers so far removed from corporate discussions of diversity, *Workforce 2000*, human resource planning, work–family, and work–life? If concern about their role as father is so significant to men, why haven't we heard more about it?

Samuel Jordan may feel the conflicts that Ruby observes, but he is not likely to talk about it, any more than Allen Morton, who works for the Urban League in Westchester, New York. According to Allen's wife, Patsy, "Some days he's totally exhausted and can't stand it. He would say he's got 'too much going on,' but he wouldn't call it stress, maybe a man thing."

It is indeed a "man thing" not to talk about work–family conflict. Most men carry it in silence, as "real men" have been taught to handle emotional conflicts all their lives. "As a gender, we find it hard to admit when we're lost driving on the freeway, so it's especially difficult when we're lost about one of the most important areas of our lives," says Michael Kimmel, professor of sociology at the State University of New York at Stony Brook and one of the nation's leading authorities on men and masculinity.

A female attorney writing in the *New Jersey Law Journal* reports: "A court reporter told me that at a deposition she attended recently, both opposing male attorneys asked her separately if she could come up with an excuse why she couldnt stay after 5 P.M. They both had to leave by then to pick up their kids, but were too afraid of losing face with their opponent to make the request themselves."

But the experience of working fathers is kept invisible by another set of forces. If the principal culprit in the cover-up is men themselves, supporting roles are played by social science experts, and the media, and women.

Men get some cues from the workplace. According to a female executive at a family-friendly company, "I could easily go in and request part-time work, and no one would think badly of me. But if I were a man making that request, I'd get ridiculed."

Colleagues, coworkers, and bosses view a family photo on a man's desk as a sign of stability and commitment—he's got someone to provide for—rather than as a picture of real people whose real needs could tear him away from his desk. According to Kimmel, "They might question your loyalty if you say you're trying to figure out ways to balance work and family, so you wind up feeling very alone."

One man told me he can't bring himself to ask for a change in the weekly staff meeting which ends at 5:30 P.M., even though he needs to pick up his daughter at day care by 5:30 P.M. Why not? Because at work he'd seen an excellent temp lose the opportunity for a permanent position by saying she wanted to get home in time for dinner with her large family each night. "I live in fear," this man says, "that speaking out about my domestic responsibilities could work against me as well."

Still another reason for men's silence is that they have often seen their male colleagues lionized for heroic work efforts that defy family needs. The front page of one corporate newsletter told of an engineer who worked for seventy-two consecutive hours—three days straight—to make sure the project was delivered on schedule.

More often the message is implicit. Until recently, one very progressive company routinely scheduled its semiannual sales and marketing conference on the third weekend in June—Father's Day.

Charles Rodgers, principal at WFD (formerly known as Work/Family Directions), a Boston-based consulting organization that works with many Fortune 500 companies, tells the story of an all-male focus group at a client firm. "One guy was expecting his second child. He said, 'Maybe I'll take this paternity leave the company offers.' Almost to a man, the other guys said, 'No, no. You don't take paternity leave. You take a combination of vacation and sick leave.' The prevailing wisdom was: Don't stand out."

Not standing out is a pattern in men's behavior now being confirmed by Catalyst, the research and advisory organization focused on women's advancement at work, in a study of two manufacturing and two service organizations in the midst of implementing flexible work arrangements. According to Catalyst vice president Marcia Brumit Kropf, "Men feel that they can access only certain types of flexible arrangements. And they do not feel that they can access them around fathering. For instance, consider reduced hours. Men in our first-round focus groups in all four organizations said that they felt that they could probably ask for it if they were sick, for an illness for themselves, perhaps for family members, but that they did not feel that they could ask for it for most work–family issues. Men in these groups are visibly uncomfortable talking about their work–family dilemmas. They worry about its visibility. And unsupportive corporate cultures."

Given all these cultural cues, it is not surprising that men keep quiet about their family needs. What has been surprising, however, in my research at corporations is the types of coping strategies some fathers use—many familiar to working mothers—to keep their dilemma invisible.

"Avoid the supervisor" is a frequent ploy. One marketing manager parks in a back lot so that at 5:30 P.M., when he has to drive to the day-care center, he won't have to walk in front of his boss's office. Even though he gets in to work at 8 A.M., he wants to minimize any perception that he is uncommitted. More commonly, men wait until just after their supervisors leave to go home.

"Dash for day care" is another strategy. As part of an eight-person team working a line that inspects and packs pharmaceuticals, a factory worker in New Jersey has perfected his technique. Like Superman changing back into Clark Kent, he removes his white jumpsuit in the thirty seconds it takes to travel from the plant floor to the locker room and, unless there is ice on his windshield, can be speeding down the highway to the child-care center within another thirty seconds. "I can't be late," he says. "They fine you $10 when you're late, and we just can't afford it."

The "another meeting" ploy is a white lie that I found more widespread than I had expected. Meetings are so important in many companies that the only way some men feel they can break away from work, even at 6 P.M., is by saying, "I've got to go to another meeting." As one father put it with an ironic grin, "I don't have to tell them it's a meeting with my family."

It is not just fear of compromising their jobs that leads men to keep their dual responsibilities invisible. From fear of compromising their myth of masculinity, some men hide their responsibilities from their best buddies and, to some extent, from themselves.

John, for example, who lays pipe on the 6 A.M. to 2 P.M. shift for a large utility company in the Southwest, gets home by 3 P.M. every day so that his wife, Beverly, can go to work behind the cosmetics counter at a local department store. At home, John takes care of his two children, ages six and eight, when they come home from the nearby elementary school. He supervises homework, monitors their play with friends, prepares dinner, and gets them ready for bed. Though it's a role that he enjoys, it is not something he talks about with his mates in the yard as they change out of boots and coveralls. John explains that he keeps quiet because he does not want to be accused of being a "Mr. Mom." Even though several of the other guys he works with have similar sets of child-care responsibilities, they trade stories about working on their cars or yards, which they do while keeping an eye out for their children down the street.

The way Beverly talks about John sheds light on how women participate in the cover-up that keeps men's dual responsibilities invisible. At the department store, Beverly tells her coworkers that John "watches the kids" until she gets home, leaving the impression that he plays a secondary or back-up role in child care. The fact is, John is as involved as Beverly with all of the minute-to-minute decisions and details that go into serving dinner ("I don't want that yukky stuff"), supervising playtime ("Daddy, Timmy hit me"), or preparing children for bedtime ("Not yet, my favorite show is still on"). But as Arlie Hochschild elucidated so clearly in *The Second Shift*, each family constructs its own "gender ideology," a set of beliefs about appropriate maternal and paternal roles—what they think *should* be the case—that often flies in the face of their own lived reality. Like John's, the family story that Beverly tells publicly is not "wrong"; it just omits telling details about their daily life. It maintains their mutual sense of who they are and who they want to be. And like many other public family stories told by men and women in warehouses and convenience marts, locker rooms, and supermarkets, it preserves the privacy of a gradually changing story about working fathers.

There is, of course, another public story of family life, conveyed not in the course of day-to-day conversations but designed for widespread dissemination. It is the story written by "experts" and transmitted widely by the media, creating a standard against which we often hold our own family experiences. Again and again, the story is told and translated in a way that highlights the work–family conflict experienced by working mothers and that minimizes what working fathers actually do and feel. In the 1970s, for example, a study by Boston University psychologist Freda Rebelsky found that men spent only thirty-seven seconds a day in vocal interaction with their newborns. The study did not claim to examine men's participation in caring for their infants, including nonverbal communication. But when translated by the popular media, thirty-seven seconds became an emblem signifying how little men contribute to child care, just as *The Second Shift*'s twelve minutes would do in the 1990s.

The success of the second shift metaphor has made it difficult for students of family life, and the media, to tell the public story of the changing American family in a way that presents the emerging story of fatherhood. The gradual evolution in men's roles lacks the drama that reporters often think they need to keep their readers interested. In a superstar culture, what grabs media attention are the superstar fatherhood stories. When the president of American Express resigns to spend more time with his family, it is page-one news in *The Wall Street Journal*; but how many fathers are earning at that level or can go on to lucrative consulting gigs? And when the media isn't covering superstars, they continue to look for the extremes of fatherhood. Feature after feature appears about at-home dads, a small number at one end of the spectrum, while a barrage of stories about "deadbeat dads," reinforces the stereotype at the other extreme that most men are fleeing from their children.

Meanwhile, one of the main challenges playing out in men's lives is the unsensational but very real day-to-day attempt to combine making a living with being there for their kids. "Women still assume primary responsibility for family life," says Dana Friedman, founding copresident of the Families and Work Institute. "But the most important conclusion of research comparing men and women is that work–family conflict is related to family roles and responsibilities. When men take more responsibility for their children, they experience the same conflicts as women. To think about work–family conflict as a women's issue is much too narrow a view. This is an issue that goes beyond gender."

Chapter 2

Daddy Success
The Payoff for Fathers, Mothers, Companies, and Kids

W hy does it matter that men succeed at combining work and family life? Because supporting men in being good fathers is good for men, good for children, good for women—*and* good for business. The family benefits may seem intuitive, but a converging body of research is now pointing to the dividends for business: Good dads make good workers, and good workplaces help men be better dads.

This news about working fathers has largely gone unnoticed, waiting in the background while one of the most significant demographic and social trends of the last thirty years—the rise of the "working mother"—has commanded attention.

Was she here to stay? In 1987, more than half of mothers of children under five were in the paid labor force. A front-page headline in *USA Today* on March 21, 1987, announced, "New Moms in the Workforce 'Now the Norm.'"

Was she hurting her kids by leaving them in day care? When Pennsylvania State University psychologist Jay Belsky released a 1988 literature review concluding that twenty or more hours of out-of-home care a week put infants at risk for insecure attachment to their mothers and greater levels of aggressiveness, he triggered a storm of controversy—and more than one suggestion that if anybody was harming children it was guilt-inducing researchers, not working mothers. Five years later, when Belsky and his colleagues re-examined the issue and modified their earlier findings, a front-page story in *The New York Times* announced, "Study Shows Day Care Not Harmful to Children."

The controversy about working mothers has hardly been put to rest. As recently as April 1996, a *Commentary* magazine cover story by David Gelertner argued, point blank, that mothers should stay home. But staying home was something America's mothers seemed less and less likely to do, and other research suggested it actually was good for children to have working mothers. Ellen Galinsky of the Families and Work Institute (FWI) found that whether mom *chose* to work outside the home or to stay at home was one of the key factors in child outcomes. Researchers Grace Baruch and Rosalind Barnett, my colleagues at the Wellesley College Center for Research on Women, found that managing multiple roles actually contributed to women's mental health and, therefore, benefited their children. Psychologist Faye Crosby of Smith College used the term "juggling" to describe women's attempts to balance work and family life, emphasizing not the deficit but their energy and skill.

The focus on working mothers begged a question that went largely unasked: What were the consequences for families—and for business—when fathers worked? That work typically took fathers away from their children for more than eight hours a day was an unquestionable "fact of life." It was what men did and had always done. Whether men *chose* to work was not an issue: They wanted to work and they had to work. It was through their work, through being good economic providers, that they established their very identities and helped care for their families. It did not occur to anyone that business could or should do anything—other than give them a paycheck—to support men as fathers. After all, why would it matter? Work and family were seen as separate spheres.

Although most eyes were focused on working mothers, advances in several fields began to offer a new understanding of working fathers. Research in child and family development, which had almost exclusively focused on mothers, began to document the vital role that fathers play in children's lives. Research on work and family began to see them as interdependent spheres and to demonstrate the importance to business of supporting their employee's family life. Research on effective management began to notice the overlap between the skills developed and used within the family and those required in the rapidly changing workplace. All are converging to yield a new way of understanding fathers and work: Good dads make good workers, and a supportive workplace helps men be better dads.

DISCOVERING WORKING FATHERS

One hundred and fifty years ago, the notion that a father's work life could be separated from his family life would have been considered preposterous. It was transparent that the nature of his work would affect how he treated his children *and* that his relationship with his children would affect his ability to be productive at work. The two were inextricably linked.

In an agrarian economy, men and women worked long days together in the fields or with the animals, and their children worked right alongside them. When they came inside at dusk, they did not leave work behind. According to Bradley Googins, director of the Center for Work and Family at Boston University, "Little if any space was reserved for what we would call the living room or family room. Work was performed within the living structure, and it was not until the mid-eighteenth century that the craft shop that was separate from the home began to emerge." Even as late as 1860, "nearly 60 percent of the labor force earned their living as farmers. By 1910, however, less than one-third of the labor force was engaged in farming." The industrialization of America during the intervening years, says Googins:

> reshape[d] every institution, value, and custom associ-
> ated with work. . . . The workplace would now be defined

by the factory, which would capture a large group of citizens and introduce the workday, work structure, and work habits that would mold the common perceptions about work in America. . . . The life of a factory worker, closed off from the outside, tied to a production schedule, and often routinized by the partialized task or role, was in great contrast to that of his father's generation, which was independent, "master of the earth," and close to the family.

Not only did work and family come to be viewed as separate spheres, but also as separately gendered spheres with federal and state laws designed to "protect" wives and mothers from horrible working conditions. Enforcing the Protective Labor Law in 1908, the U.S. Supreme Court court ruled, in *Muller* v. *Oregon*, "Long hours of labor [work] are dangerous for women primarily because of their special physical organization." Similarly, they demonstrated—with evidence from nine different authorities—that the "evil effect of overwork before as well as after marriage upon childbirth is marked and disastrous." By 1912, thirty-four states had enacted measures to restrict women's working hours.

During the late 1930s, in the aftermath of the Great Depression, social scientists studied the impact of a father's job loss on the family. But by the 1950s, with the postwar economy growing, fathers had largely dropped out of the family research picture. The 1958 publication of *The Changing American Parent*, the most authoritative book in the field, was based on interviews with 350 mothers and not a single father. Even in 1969, when the *American Journal of Orthopsychiatry* published a pioneering article, "Father's Participation in Infant Care," the researchers admitted in a footnote that their work was based exclusively on interviews with mothers who were at home caring for their infants. Presumably, the fathers were too busy at work to be interviewed.

To determine the impact of fathers on their children's development, most researchers studied *paternal absence*—meaning that dad was divorced or dead.

A father at work was not considered absent in the same way that even part-time working mothers are today, even if he worked seventy hours a week or traveled all the time. If dad was present as an economic provider, nobody thought to ask how he was connected to his kids or whether it mattered if he was physically or emotionally absent.

A sprinkling of studies did ask whether a father's late-shift schedule could have a negative affect on his children. According to Cornell psychologists Urie Bronfenbrenner and Nan Crouter:

> One 1965 study found that fathers working "on the late afternoon shift rarely saw their school-age children during the work week. The job of discipline fell to the mother, and the shortage of time shared by both parents produced conflicts over what to do with that time." In 1969 another study showed that when fathers worked on the night shift, their daughters scored significantly lower in tests of academic achievement.

These were important findings, suggesting that a dad's time at work—and not just his income—affected his family. But such findings were quickly lost in the growing avalanche of research about working mothers.

During World War II, the nation built publicly subsidized daycare centers so "Rosie the Riveter" could support the boys "over there." No small irony, then, that a generation later academic research was asking whether working mothers were harming their children, their families, and America's future. But under the pressure of women's labor force participation, and with more women scholars designing the studies, a new research paradigm for studying working mothers emerged. "For years, social scientists have focused on women in the workplace and whether employment is good or bad for women," says Maureen Perry-Jenkins, then assistant professor of family studies at the University of Illinois. "This view is too simplistic." From her study of forty-three dual-earner families with wives working full time, Perry-Jenkins discovered, "It's not the job so much that matters to a woman's psychological well-being and to family relationships. It's how women feel about themselves, their work, and their roles in the family that has great significance." And how women feel about their work, it turns out, has less to do with the amount of time on the job than with the nature of the jobs— whether or not the work is interesting and challenging, whether or not they are given autonomy, and whether or not they are treated with respect by supervisors.

The new research on working mothers has enormous implications for understanding the impact of work on fathers and their children. If "whether mom is employed" is too narrow a focus, so is "whether dad is unemployed." For both mothers and fathers it is far more important to understand the nature of their work and how they feel about it.

That's just the question a new generation of scholars is trying to answer. Research by Stewart Friedman, professor at the Wharton School of Business at the University of Pennsylvania, is now revealing that "kids are the unseen stakeholders in the American workplace" and that fathers' work is an unseen and underappreciated influence on children's development. Along with Drexel University professors Jeffrey Greenhaus and Saroj Parasuraman, Friedman is studying more than 800 working mothers *and* fathers who have managerial or professional jobs. In ages four to seventeen, they find "fewer behavioral problems" such as shyness, withdrawal, and aggressiveness among children whose mothers "have control over how, where, and when their work gets done" and among children whose fathers "say they are satisfied with their work." Moreover, they find that "the amount of time parents spend working isn't linked to their children's behavior. What does have an impact is how much parents' work tensions taint home life. Parents whose jobs don't distract them from family when they are home, or interfere with their psychological involvement with their children, have better-behaved kids."

Does this new research mean that the quantity of time parents spend at work is irrelevant? Of course not. Research by Ohio State University psychologists Toby Parcel and Elizabeth Menaghan,

authors of *Parents' Jobs and Children's Lives*, both confirms the
Wharton findings about how work is organized and shows that the
amount of time fathers spend at work still matters. "If mom is more
satisfied at the job, she is more likely to create a home environment
that is beneficial to the kids," says Parcel. "Home environment in
turn has an effect on children's cognition and behavior problems.
We haven't studied this for fathers, but the same could very well be
true." However, Parcel and Menaghan found clear evidence that both
underemployment and overemployment for fathers have a negative
effect on their three- to six-year-old children. Low work hours,
which take more of a toll on men's self-esteem than on women's, are
associated with increased behavior problems—whining, hitting, acting out, and poor peer relations. But fathers working *sustained* overtime—not just putting in occasional long hours—have a negative
effect on children's language development. The same is true for
mothers. "If you think about the possibility of both parents working sustained overtime," says Parcel, "it could compound the effect."

What is it about what happens *during* the time that fathers
work that may be as important as *how much* time they work?
Research finds it not just quantity of time that affects dads, but how
they are treated on the job that effects their parenting. When University of Illinois psychologists Karen Thomas-Grimm and Maureen
Perry-Jenkins studied fifty-nine blue-collar fathers with children
between the ages of eight and twelve, they discovered that how they
were treated at work affected how they parent. Dads who aren't
treated well at work have lower self-esteem and tend to be harsher
and more stringent disciplinarians. Dads with more autonomy and
control over their work—and with supportive supervisors—had
higher self-esteem, which, says Perry-Jenkins, "is carried home and is
apparent in greater acceptance of kids and less stringent disciplinary
techniques." Similar findings about young children were reported
when Boston University psychologist Frances K. Grossman and her
colleagues studied twenty-three fathers and their first-born five-year-
olds. Dads with more autonomy and satisfaction on the job played
longer and had a better quality of interaction with their children.

Why does it matter if the nature of a dad's worklife affects the nature and quality of his relationship with his kids? Because the involvement of fathers with their children is proving to have important influences at every stage of child development, from infancy through adolescence. Consider just a few highlights of research across the child's life cycle.

- At six months of age, babies with actively involved fathers score higher on the Bailey Test of Mental and Motor Development. Is this a momentary indicator with no long-term payoff? Research suggests not. At age three, premature infants whose fathers spend more time playing with them have better cognitive outcomes, whether or not the father is living in the same household. And if their fathers are involved during the first eight weeks of life, children manage stress better during their school years.

- In the preschool years, dads' involvement with their school-age children also yields continuing dividends in intellectual and social development. A sense of competence in daughters—especially in mathematics—is linked to a close and warm relationship with their fathers. Boys with nurturant fathers are more likely to internalize their dad's modes of problem solving. And both boys and girls with involved fathers demonstrate a greater ability to take initiative and direct themselves.

- In adolescence, dads' involvement reduces the risk of drug use, juvenile delinquency, and teen pregnancy, while increasing the amount of education completed by teens when they reach their early twenties.

Whether researchers look at cognitive development, sex-role development, or psychosocial development, "children seem better off when their relationship with their father is close and warm," according to Michael Lamb, chief of the section on social and emotional development at the National Institutes of Child Health and Human Development. That may seem like common sense for today's fathers, since that's the sort of relationship most men want to have with their children. What is not so apparent, says Lamb, is that the nature and extent of fathers' connection to their children is greatly influenced by how "other important people"—like employers and colleagues at work—"perceive and evaluate the father-child relationship."

Men take their work home with them in more ways than one. The way the workplace treats them (whether it is supportive or not) has an impact on how they behave as fathers. And, as we shall see, the opposite holds as well: When men are supported in helping their children to grow, they are better able to help grow the business bottom line.

WHY GOOD DADS MAKE BETTER WORKERS

"Until very recently," said Cornell University psychologists Urie Bronfenbrenner and Nan Crouter in a 1982 research review, "researchers have treated the job situation of mothers and fathers as separate worlds having no relation to each other and, presumably, leading to rather different results. For mothers, it was the fact of being employed that was thought to be damaging to the child, whereas for fathers it was being unemployed that was seen as the destructive force."

For most of the twentieth century, the social sciences perpetuated the schism between work and family. "There was a sociology of work and a sociology of the family, a psychology of occupations and a psychology of marital relations, says professor Lotte Bailyn of MIT's Sloan School of Management. When Bradley Googins closely observed the interplay between work and family life inside a Fortune 500 company, one supervisor said "Family—what has that got to do with work? That is totally separate and belongs outside of here." In a prescient 1977 monograph titled *Work and Family in the United States,* sociologist Rosabeth Moss Kanter, who would go on to become one of the first women tenured as a full professor at the Harvard Business School, warned that treating work and family as separate spheres would be bad for families *and* bad for business.

By the mid-1980s, the need to reduce the tension between work and family life was so great that "work–family" had become an industry. In 1983, Fran Sussner Rodgers founded Work/Family Directions out of a small office with five employees and one very large client, IBM. By 1996 Work/Family Directions, now known as "WFD", had become the largest consulting group in the field, an organization of about 350 employees serving 150 of the largest corporations in America and generating annual revenues of $65 million. In 1989, pooling the studies they had been conducting throughout the 1980s, Ellen Galinsky and Dana Friedman established the Families and Work Institute as a national center dedicated to producing reliable, research-based information for organizations that were trying to balance "the changing needs of America's workforce with the continuing need for business productivity." In its first seven years, FWI released more than one hundred studies and reports, most of them grabbing national media attention. Meanwhile, a bevy of weekly and monthly work–family newsletters was published to serve what had become a new field; consulting firms like Touche Ross added "work and family" practices; and the positions of "work–family" or "work-life specialist" became staples of human resource departments.

Implicitly, if not explicitly, most of the research in the work–family field has been concerned with working mothers. But when companies do study both male and female employees they find, almost inevitably, that responding to the family needs of working mothers *and* working fathers contributes to the bottom line.

A 1992 study at St. Paul Companies found that "staff who believed work was causing problems in their personal lives were much more likely to make mistakes than those who had few job-related personal problems (30 percent compared with 19 percent)." Chicago-based Fel-Pro, which manufactures gaskets for the automobile industry, found that the more employees used family-supportive benefits, "the more they exhibited initiative, teamwork, flexibility, and openness to total quality efforts," and the more likely they were to suggest product or process improvements. A study released by DuPont in October 1995 found that employees who use work-life programs are 45 percent more likely to "go the extra mile" to assure that DuPont succeeds. There was a direct correlation between a supportive work environment as defined by the company's work-life programs and increased employee commitment.

Multicompany studies bear these findings out. In a 1996 survey of 800 organizations by William Mercer, Inc., a New York City–based consulting firm, 69 percent of the 347 respondents who were able to quantify the return on investment for work-life programs said the return was equal to or greater than the cost; 47 percent observed an increase in productivity, only 1 percent observed a decrease; and 36 percent did not know if productivity had changed. According to Mercer's Richard Federico, "when people are less stressed, they tend to produce better."

And they are more likely to remain loyal to their companies, reducing the cost of turnover which, "including recruitment, training, and less visible expenses such as delays, break-in costs of new workers, and ripple effects on coworkers, costs between 93 percent and 150 percent of a departing employee's salary—and up to 200 percent of salary for a highly skilled or senior person.

According to the FWI's *National Study of the Changing Workforce*, "Employees who experience work–family conflict are three times as likely to think about quitting their jobs as those who do not (43 percent compared to 14 percent)." According to a 1995 survey of 1,000 managers and executives by Manchester Partners International, the "lack of balance between their work and personal lives" was one of the top six reasons why four out of ten managers were being terminated, voluntarily resigning their posts, or being given poor performance reviews.

Conversely, when employees feel they are being helped to create some balance, their staying power increases dramatically. When IBM asked a group of employees to assess the factors that influenced their decision to stay with the company, work–family balance ranked five overall, and second among the company's top performers. According to NationsBank Chairman Hugh McColl, the bank's turnover rate is 50 percent less among the 35,000 employees who have taken advantage of programs designed to help balance work and family life. When First Tennessee National Corp. started treating family issues as part of business strategy, it found that "supervisors rated by their subordinates as supportive of work–family balance retained employees twice as long as the bank average and kept 7 percent more retail customers . . . [contributing] to a 55 percent profit gain over two years, to $106 million." Mike Dedek, a father of three who works as a software engineer at Lexis-Nexis, explains, "My dedication to this company is primarily due to their family friendliness. I've stayed at the same company for seven years and probably will for my entire career, if they want to keep me around."

Even more startling, FWI's evaluation of work–family programs at Johnson & Johnson found that "policies on leave were very significant in employees' decisions to stay, even if they had not personally used them."

Why should feeling that the workplace makes it possible to be a good father be so important to men? My colleague Rosalind Barnett is appalled that it seems necessary to ask. "[Fatherhood] is one of the most important relationships a human being will ever have. How did we get to a point of having to explain why men's relationships with kids are so important?"

Nevertheless, in her study of dual-earner couples for the National Institutes of Mental Health, Barnett began to tease out one set of relationships between business productivity and fatherhood. According to the American Medical Association, stress underlies 80 percent of all physical ailments. In the same way that family life can be a source of stress, it can also provide a buffer from work stress— good relations with their children actually can reduce the risk that men will have health problems. Barnett found that "being a father who is deeply involved with his children is good for a man's health. The men in our study who had the fewest worries about their relationships with their children also had the fewest health problems. Those who had the most troubled relationships with their children had the most health problems. . . . Our research definitively shows that family issues are a major factor in men's health and productivity, and that failures to address them will have disastrous consequences not only for public health in this country but for our ability to effectively compete in world markets."

HOW FATHERING SKILLS WILL HELP THE TWENTY-FIRST CENTURY BUSINESS

When it comes to coaching businesses on how to develop and sustain a competitive advantage in the marketplace, Peter Senge of MIT's Sloan School of Management is unquestionably one of the most influential business consultants of the decade. His best-seller, *The Fifth Discipline*, helped define the *learning organization* as what businesses will have to become to survive and grow in the twenty-first century. As Senge puts it, learning organizations are workplaces "where people continually expand their capacities to create the results they truly desire, where collective aspiration is set free, and where people are continually learning how to learn together."

Senge consults to AT&T, Procter & Gamble, Ford, Digital, and many other Fortune 500 companies. He commands $15,000 or more just for lecturing about his innovative way of thinking. So what knowledge is most sought by those who attend his programs on leadership and mastery? Of the five disciplines of the learning organization, which are they most curious about: systems thinking, personal mastery, mental models, shared vision, or team learning?

You may be surprised to learn that Senge says that "finding balance between my work and my family"is cited by attendees as their number-one priority.

Senge's contribution to the discussion of work and family life is one of the least discussed, but most profound, aspects of his work. Reacting to a 1990 *Fortune* cover story, "Why Grade A Executives Get an F as Parents," Senge found most revealing not what the article pointed to—long hours and personal characteristics such as perfectionism and impatience—but what it didn't say. "Nothing was mentioned about how the executives' organizations contributed to their problems as parents or what they might do to improve matters. It seems that the author, like most of the rest of us, simply accepts the fact that work inevitably conflicts with family life, and that the organization has no part to play in improving imbalances between work and family."

In a chapter from *The Fifth Discipline,* titled "Ending the War between Work and Family," Senge explains:

> The disciplines of the learning organization will, I believe, end the taboo that has surrounded the topic of balancing work and family, and has kept it off the corporate agenda. The learning organization cannot support personal mastery without supporting personal mastery in all aspects of life. It cannot foster shared vision without calling forth personal visions, and personal visions are always multifaceted—they always include deeply felt desires for our personal, professional, organizational, and family lives. Lastly, the artificial boundary between work and family is anathema to systems thinking. There is a natural connection between a person's work life and all other aspects of life. We live only one life, but for a long time our organizations have operated as if this simple fact could be ignored, as if we had two separate lives.

Senge's work is important not just because his holistic vision sees beyond the artificial work–family divide. Senge highlights the family as a learning organization and the importance of the skills developed in family life for the business enterprise. Senge draws on the words of Bill O'Brien of Hanover Insurance to explain the "potential synergy that can exist between learning organizations, learning individuals, and learning families." As O'Brien puts it,

It's ironic that we spend so much time and money trying to devise clever programs for developing leadership in our organizations and ignore a structure that already exists, and which is ideal for the job. The more I understand the real skills of leadership in a learning organization, the more I become convinced that these are the skills of effective parenting. Leading in a learning organization involves supporting people in clarifying and pursuing their own visions, "moral suasion," helping people discover underlying causes of problems, and empowering them to make choices. What could be a better description of effective parenting? The fact that many parents don't succeed especially well simply shows that we haven't created the learning environment for parenting, just as we've not created the learning environment for developing leaders.

Sounds logical as theory, but do the skills developed in a family *really* lead to business success? Look no further than at the remarkable business success of female entrepreneurs to get a glimmer of an answer. According to a 1996 report of the Joint Economic Committee of the U.S. Congress, in the last fifteen years the number of women-owned businesses in the United States has quadrupled, jumping from 2 million to 8 million. For most of the last decade, women have been starting new businesses at a greater rate than men, and in 1994, for the first time ever, women-owned businesses employed more people than did the Fortune 500 firms. Moreover, 75 percent of these female entrepreneurs are married, compared to 57 percent of all women in the United States.

Some of these female entrepreneurs honed their business skills in the corporate world and are seeking an alternative to the so-called "mommy track." But others have been out of the paid work force—by choice or default—to take care of their children. What skills could they have been using or developing during the years at home taking care of kids?

How about juggling multiple assignments? Establishing priorities. Communicating clearly. Providing "customer" service. Identifying and coaching talents and strengths. Saying "no" and setting limits. Creating networks of support. And dozens of other skills that are now required by modern business, 80 percent of which is now in the service sector, not in the manufacturing sector.

Success in business, like success in family life, is a process. Work and family are not separate worlds requiring completely different skills, but different worlds requiring many of the same skills applied in different context. In the best of cases, work and family will complement each other: Being a parent can be a training ground for being a learning manager, and being a learning manager can prepare one for parenting.

Some managers seem intuitively to recognize the interdependence of work and family. At Corning Inc., for example, I was privileged to work with Ed O'Brien, consistently ranked as one of the best managers in the company, no matter what the assignment. In 1986, O'Brien was assigned to take charge of Corning's somewhat lackluster Education and Training Division; by 1991 he had turned it into a leading profit center, selling services to other Corning divisions. Central to O'Brien's success was his realization that the division was failing to tap the talent pool of men and women who wanted to succeed at raising their families and to succeed at work. Recognizing this, O'Brien let people define their own schedules, and he took advantage of what they had learned at home, as parents, to drive his customer-service-oriented business.

Now business researchers are beginning to tease out what makes a good manager, and how the best managers seem to do what O'Brien instinctively did. At Merck, Perry Christensen and his colleagues began drawing attention to the "value of family experiences for the corporate setting. For example, the dilemmas of a single-parent father raising children can provide skills and attributes like project planning, values clarification, and setting priorities for a short amount of time." At MIT's Sloan School of Management, Professor Lotte Bailyn and her colleagues are documenting the work practices of what they call "integrated" individuals—men and women "who are able, despite the cultural imperative to the contrary, to link [the work and family spheres;] . . . they used skills more often associated with the private, domestic sphere of life, such as sharing, nurturing, collaborating, and attending to the emotional context of situations."

Psychologist and family researchers, also are examining the ways in which the experience of parenthood can develop skills applicable to the workplace. Harvard University psychologist William Pollack has been looking specifically at the connection between the skills of being a good father and a good manager or leader. The psychological skills "most closely related to success as a manager and as a father were affiliation (capacity for enjoying connection to and cooperation with other people) and autonomy (capacity for enjoying independent decision making and action)." Pollack says, "Modern leaders, male and female, need creative vision, emotional flexibility, independent decision making capacity, along with the ability to work within systems, creative networks, and teams. They must also be able to rally support and achieve results in the midst of almost constant organizational change. My consulting experience and research have shown that, for men, those very skills are the ones most successfully learned and mastered by the well-adapted father."

Emory University psychologist John Snarey studied 240 fathers over a forty-year period and found that involved fathers are more likely to have career success—as well as happy marriages—by midlife. In his book, *How Fathers Care for the Next Generation,* Snarey finds that by midlife, devoted dads on average were more likely to thrive in their careers. Devoted dads in the study went on to become involved in care-giving activities outside the home, as managers, mentors, coaches, or community leaders. Why? Because, according to Snarey, "Parenting provides skills and a perspective you might not get elsewhere. Fatherhood can build mentoring skills which can later be used in the workplace when the father is in a manager role, supervising younger employees. You can build on what they do well, rather than shoving things down their throat."

Peter Senge predicts that in the coming years, business will have to look for "the synergy between productive family life and productive work life. The old world of sharp boundaries between work and family is falling away. A new world of blurred boundaries is here, and it is a world that only a few organizations are facing up to."

BENEFITS FOR FATHERS AND MOTHERS

When men succeed at work and at home, the dividends show up not just in the development of children and the health of companies, but in the development of fathers and the well-being of mothers.

Thirty years ago, in his classic book about life-span development, *Childhood and Society*, Erik Erikson argued that our preoccupation with the responsibility of adults for children's development has blinded us to a full appreciation of how children stimulate adult development. Erikson says of fathers, "Mature man needs to be needed, and maturity needs guidance as well as encouragement from what has been produced and must be taken care of."

Since then, a body of scholarship has documented some of the specific ways in which father involvement benefits fathers themselves. Contrary to stereotypical belief, men's sense of personal happiness and satisfaction is more strongly linked to their family roles than to their work roles. "What is perhaps most surprising," says Joseph Pleck, is the persistence of the "view that men are obsessed by their work and oblivious to their families. . . . Overall, the picture emerging from recent literature on men in family roles is of men who are deeply connected to their families and whose subjective well-being is significantly related to the quality of these connections."

Snarey's longitudinal study found that men's involvment with their children did affect their occupational success—positively. "Greater childrearing participation does not generally translate into lower occupational mobility for fathers. In fact, contrary to the speculation that family participation will hinder men's careers, fathers who cared for their children's intellectual development and their adolescent's social development were more likely to advance in their occupations."

Keeping with Erikson's notion that parenting provides a foundation for generativity at midlife, Snarey also concluded that "fathers who participate strongly in childrearing are also more likely to become societally generative at midlife." And such fathers are more likely to support the opportunity for their wives to succeed in the workplace.

For decades economists, policy analysts, and legal theorists have argued that men's increased involvement in childrearing is a necessary prerequisite of women's economic equity. In its 1981 report, "Child Care and Equal Opportunity for Women," the U.S. Commission on Civil Rights asserted, "As long as private lives and public institutions are organized around the premise that child care is an exclusively female responsibility, equal opportunity will be unattainable." A decade later, *Beyond Rhetoric,* the final report of the National Commission on Children, a group established by Congress and President Reagan to "create a blueprint of a national policy for America's children and families" concluded, "Parenting is not an issue solely for women. . . . Opportunities for personal growth and development should be equally available to men and women in our society, and the privileges and responsibilities should also be shared."

In 1994, shortly after accepting a position on the Supreme Court of the United States—the second woman in history to do so—Justice Ruth Bader Ginsburg was asked what made her agree to a flexible schedule for law clerk David Post, who was attending Georgetown University at night. His wife, an economist, had a demanding job, and Post cared for the children before and after school. "This is my dream of the way the world should be," said Justice Ginsburg. "I was so pleased to see that there are indeed men who are doing a parent's work, who do not regard that as strange. People like David, I hope, will be role models for other men who may be fearful they won't succeed in their profession if they spend time caring for their children, or are concerned they will be thought of as less than a man if family is of prime importance."

How possible is it to create a father-friendly workplace outside the hallowed walls of the U.S. Supreme Court, where the boss does not happen to be one of the twentieth century's leading advocates for equal opportunity for women and men?

As the next section shows, wherever you work, there are steps you can take—as a father or a mother, manager or employee—to start creating the father-friendly workplace.

Part 2

Strategies for Work

Chapter 3

Creating the Father-Friendly Workplace

I n 1986, a relatively new magazine called *Working Mother* published a cover story, "The 30 Best Companies for Working Mothers," that had an impact far beyond its then-200,000 readers. By 1995, though the magazine's readership had grown only to 600,000— about 5 percent of the 21 million Americans who read *TV Guide* each week, or 8.5 percent of the 7 million who read *Business Week*—the release of the "Best Companies" list had become a media event in its own right, covered widely by the press and eagerly anticipated by the business community. Vice President Al Gore considered the list so important for making a statement about family friendliness that he was the featured guest speaker when the 1996 awards were given out, two months before the presidential election, in New York's fabled Rainbow Room.

The *Working Mother* awards gave the American business community and the media that watched it so carefully a new vocabulary, an index that changed the discussion of the business enterprise. What did it mean to be a *best company* for moms? The four criteria were:

1. Pay above average within the industry and geographic area
2. Opportunities to advance

3. Child care

4. Other family-friendly benefits such as financial aid for adoption

In 1996, workplace flexibility was added as a fifth yardstick.

Companies vying for female talent wanted in on the list from the get-go. In 1988, *Working Mother*'s list of thirty companies jumped to "The 50 Best Companies for Working Mothers," because so many companies wanted to be recognized. In 1990 it grew to "The 75 Best." Faced with a torrent of applications, in 1992 *Working Mother* decided to cap the list at "The 100 Best Companies for Working Mothers" in order to maintain the sense of competition for elite status. Meanwhile, the list had become such an icon in American business that *The Wall Street Journal* ran a front page story on the behind-the-scenes jockeying to make "the list." Even if they did not make the list, many companies began trying to position themselves as family friendly.

Without doubt, the *Working Mother* list has had positive effects. As a mass of working mothers entered or returned to the work force during the last decade, it provided a new type of scorecard. In order for businesses to keep their competitive edge, an army of Total Quality Management (TQM) consultants was advising businesses to pay more attention to their "internal customers," otherwise known as employees. The *Working Mother* list helped focus attention on the specific needs of a specific group of employees whose talents, skills, and needs could no longer be ignored.

There is a danger of hype here, of course. As *The Wall Street Journal*'s work–family columnist, Sue Shellenbarger, put it, "If the river of press releases crossing journalists' desks in the United States were to be taken at face value, the American workplace is becoming a very family-friendly place indeed. . . . But the work–family publicity explosion reflects not so much a solution to an epidemic of work–family conflict, it reflects the basis of the problem. To many companies, fashioning a family-friendly image is nothing more than that—an issue of image, not substance."

And there has been another danger. Focusing attention on the real and extensive needs of working mothers has reinforced the notion that it is mothers, and mothers alone, who experience work–family conflict. It subtly reinforces the notion that men do not—or should not—experience work–family conflict, which perpetuates an increasingly dysfunctional status quo. If men did experience work–family conflict, it was something that they should keep invisible. As the national media made clear, this was a women's issue.

WHY FAMILY FRIENDLY ISN'T ENOUGH

In fact, as we have seen in Chapters 1 and 2, work–family conflict is an issue for men, with far more impact on fathers and their families than most people realize.

How can we move to include men in the largely single-sex discussion of family friendliness? Is there a need for special attention to father friendliness, for a list of the "best companies for working fathers?" If so, can we recognize men without compromising or jeopardizing the gains that have been made for women? Or, to avoid getting trapped in a polarized discussion about the relative needs of mothers and fathers, should we set our sights on the needs of working *parents*?

These are questions my colleagues and I grapple with frequently. *Working parents* and *family friendly* are both explicitly gender-neutral terms, but have tended to be interpreted by many as code words for *working mothers* and *mother friendly*.

Interestingly, efforts to support the family at work have not always been friendly to women. In 1932 the "married persons clause" of the Economy Act—instituted to ensure "one job per family"— stipulated that "married persons were to be discharged if their spouses were also government employees." In effect, this meant women. "This legislation was eventually repealed, but by 1939 'married person's clauses' had been proposed in twenty-six states, 1,505 married women had been discharged, and 186 had resigned to protect their spouse's positions." As recently as 1962, forty states and the

District of Columbia had laws that set maximum daily or weekly hours for women. Only in 1964, with Title VII of the Civil Rights Act, did the law of the land prohibit discrimination on the basis of sex with respect to "compensation, terms, conditions, or privileges of employment."

What should be done in the late 1990s, when working mother and workplace family friendliness have become so inextricably linked?

According to Arlene Johnson, vice president of FWI:

> The challenge today is to communicate family friendliness in a way that men feel they have equal access, while at the same time communicating to women that they are at no-fault for their careers. How to recognize the different needs of men and women and at the same time make these gender neutral is something most companies haven't mastered. To look at fathers separately within the organization has some risks, just as looking at women has risks. You start to see family friendliness as a men's or women's issue and lose the perspective of it as an organizational issue.

Remember the reversible figure in the introduction which people alternately see as a rabbit or a duck, but do not see as both at the same time? Getting to the point of seeing work–family issues as organizational issues—and of creating true equal opportunity for women—will require some separate attention to fathers, at least for the short term, in ways that do not detract from the needs of mothers.

Faith Wohl, who spent more than a decade guiding the family-friendly initiative at DuPont, the chemicals manufacturing giant, puts it this way:

> We cannot provide solutions to work/family balance issues by altering the behavior and treatment of women alone. The degree to which men are now experiencing first hand the impact of the responsibility for caring for children along with the scheduling conflicts presented by working wives suggests that the business world is going

to have to make significant changes in the design of work and the demands of the workplace.

But Wohl's recognition of men contains a dilemma. Aren't family-friendly benefits focused on women because they are, in fact, needed more by women? Yes. And no.

"The politically correct statement that work and family issues are not just women's issues, while accurate, often obscures very important gender differences," say Charles Rodgers and Fran Sussner Rodgers, the husband–wife team who are principal and chairman, respectively, of WFD. "Women still bear the major share of the responsibilities of the care of children and the household. . . . To take advantage of the talents and education of women, we must acknowledge this reality. However, in the long run, creating workplaces where men feel free to assume greater family roles, and where all employees have a way of contributing which is consistent with their personal circumstances, will be the greatest contribution to the work and family field."

The long run needs to start now. To be clear, my long-term term goal is the creation of workplaces that are truly family friendly—that respond to the needs of working parents, regardless of gender. But in a society that has defined work–family so exclusively as a women's issue, reaching that goal will require a transitional stage in which specific attention is paid to fathers as working parents. Only through purposely highlighting the issue will our society be able to break perspective and begin to move forward, including both working mothers *and* working fathers in the creation of the family-friendly workplace.

WHAT FATHER FRIENDLY MEANS

When I told my friend Sam that I was writing about the father-friendly workplace, he said, "Oh, you mean companies where they offer paternity leave?"

"Well, not quite," I replied.

"Oh. You're going to write about the companies that offer *paid* paternity leave?" he ventured.

"Well, yes," I replied, "and no." Sam looked puzzled.

Why was I downplaying the importance of paternity leave? Although it can be a part of the father-friendly workplace, paternity leave—or any one specific program or policy—leads to much too narrow a picture of father friendliness.

But I was not surprised that Sam zoomed in on paternity leave right away. It is what most people think of, in part because the media has so consistently made paternity leave the focus of any discussion of fathers and the changing workplace. It is as if there is a telephoto lens that automatically goes from its widest angle to its narrowest, without anybody noticing.

Consider what happened on August 14, 1991, when ABC's *Nightline* did a show about fatherhood that asked, "What happens when a baby boomer's newfound sense of family crashes head-on into his fierce ambition?" The show focused on two dads. Jeff Coulter, a former Microsoft sales executive, alleged he had been fired for trying to get home at night before his son and daughter went to bed, even though he worked more than fifty hours a week. Les Sotsky, a partner with Washington's largest law firm, Arnold & Porter, was on a four-day-per-week schedule—though still working the equivalent of a full-time job—so that he could spend more time with his daughter, Sophie. Neither father had taken or requested an extended paternity leave that would interrupt his career. Each was just trying to carve out some time for his family during the normal work week, which is what most men want to do.

But when *Nightline* correspondent Chris Wallace asked for an opinion about these sorts of arrangements from the head of Korn Ferry, an executive search firm with forty-two offices around the world, Lester Korn explained how men were going to hurt their careers if they took six-month paternity leaves, which neither Coulter nor Sotsky had requested. Zoom went the lens. What could have been an interesting discussion about the challenge of finding a win–win for working fathers and their employers turned into a narrowly stereotyped view of what fathers want, and what families need. Even though a father-friendly company might offer paternity leave, father friendliness cannot be limited to paternity leave or any other specific program or policy.

Think about the faulty logic of what I call *paternity leave preoccupation*. A small percentage of fathers in any given company are new fathers. New fathers are "new fathers" for a relatively short time in the course of their parenthood. But when children are no longer infants, do they stop needing their fathers?

Father friendliness cannot be reduced to a company having a paternity leave policy, paid or unpaid, on the books. Father friendliness also cannot be limited to the same criteria that *Working Mother* uses to select its "Best Companies for Working Mothers," though it certainly would include them. Nor is a father-friendly company one that gives preferential treatment to fathers over other employees or offers benefits to dads that are not available to moms.

The father-friendly company is one that maintains a culture and programmatic mix that supports working fathers in both responsive and proactive ways. Father-friendly companies create climates where men and women realize that it is safe to bring up their needs to care for their children and families without being penalized. Even more, they foster an understanding that it makes good business sense to enable men to be good fathers, that work and family are not separate spheres for men or women, and that helping employees be good parents helps them be better workers.

CREATING A FATHER-FRIENDLY WORKPLACE

What does it take to create that sort of climate? Presented later in this chapter are the elements that go into creating a father-friendly workplace. Many of the elements apply equally for creating a mother-friendly workplace. But typically, when these elements are presented in discussions of family friendliness, they are perceived as if they are needed only by women. The focus here is on applying these elements so that men are intentionally factored in, not inadvertently filtered out.

To explain each element I use examples from a variety of businesses in different industries, each facing enormous competitive pressures. No example is meant to suggest that the entire company is father friendly, any more than any entire company is likely to be uniformly mother friendly. Even at the best companies, family friendliness is often episodic, largely dependent on relationships with an immediate supervisor. And most of the companies mentioned—even the recognized leaders in family friendliness on the *Working Mother* list—are at an early stage of awareness that "working fathers" constitute an employee group with real needs and concerns.

Consider S. C. Johnson & Son, Inc., the Racine, Wisconsin-based manufacturer of industrial and common household products, such as Johnson's Wax and Windex. Founded in 1886, this family-owned business has spent a century making a remarkable commitment to the families of its employees, which now number 3,500 in the United States and 12,000 worldwide. Indeed, in 1996 S.C. Johnson was named the "caring corporation" of the year by the national Child Care Action Campaign for its leadership in the work–family area. But until 1966, barely more than a generation ago, supporting strong families meant that when a woman married a male employee she left the company with her silver; the corporate goal was to provide one job for as many families in the community as possible.

Over the next three decades, the company not only changed its policies, but emerged as a champion of working mothers, making the *Working Mother* best companies list every year it has been published. However, it wasn't until 1995 that S. C. Johnson & Son, Inc. realized it should pay attention to working fathers for strategic business reasons. "We are in the most competitive environment we have ever been in, and the winner is going to be who gets the best people," says JoAnne Brandes, vice president and general counsel of the company's Worldwide Professional division and a 1994 "*Working Mother* of the Year." "It's not easy to attract the best and the brightest to live in Racine, Wisconsin. If we've got a culture that says we are about your family life and not just talk about mothers, that makes a heck of a difference. We were just able to recruit a critical top [male] executive from Procter & Gamble who has six kids."

Seeing what father friendliness looks like at S. C. Johnson and other companies can broaden the angle of the lens that keeps narrowing the vision of father friendliness down to paternity leave. Before looking at the elements of the father-friendly workplace, it is important to dispel several myths about the creation of the family-friendly workplace.

Myth 1: Female managers are more likely to support employees seeking a healthier balance in their work and family lives. Wrong. Analysis of FWI's *National Study of the Changing Workforce* finds both male and female employees reporting that male managers are just as accommodating of their employees' work–family needs as are female managers.

Myth 2: Older managers, especially men who climbed the career ladder with a wife at home, won't support changes. This is also wrong. My interviews with senior executives in their sixties revealed that while they did not experience significant work–family conflicts, many see them being played out in the lives of their sons and daughters. They are learning to be supportive by seeing the barriers that their own children are up against.

Myth 3: The not-for-profit sector is more family friendly than the for-profit sector. Wrong again. FWI's examination of "best practices" in the world of higher education suggests that it faces the same challenges and has as far to go as the for-profit sector.

Myth 4: Change has to come from the top and filter its way down. Wrong. In fact, change comes from a combination of forces—top-down, bottom-up, and even in organizational pockets that filter sideways into the rest of the company.

No matter the type of organization where you work, no matter what type of job you have—individual contributor, mid-level manager, executive, or consultant—you can use or adapt one or more of these elements to make your workplace more father friendly for yourself and/or for your employees.

Chris Colbern, for example, is a working father and director of payroll services at CIGNA, a Philadelphia-based insurance company. He helped create and served on a committee that explored the feasibility of flexible arrangements for the employees he supervises. After studying what other companies had done, he established a compressed schedule that better met the needs of working fathers, working mothers, and all employees.

David Mason, head of a small architecture and engineering company in St. Louis, was trying to recruit a talented job candidate, a father then employed by another firm that allowed him to work extended hours (7:30 A.M. to 5:30 P.M.) and take every other Friday off. The only way to lure the man away from his job was to agree to let him stick to his unusual schedule. Mason's experiment was so successful that he ended up switching his entire firm to the schedule: "We've found that our productivity has increased, and we've got people calling us who want to work here just because of the schedule."

You don't have to be a father or a man to help create a father-friendly workplace. At some companies the change process starts because women recognize the importance of addressing fathers. As director of human resources at DuPont in the mid-1980s, Faith Wohl, acting on insights from anecdotes she heard and her own intuitions, sponsored companywide research to systematically explore the nature of work–family issues for men as well as women. Not only did the DuPont findings lead to father-friendly changes at the company, they have become a key data source, sparking work–family initiatives and leading other companies to pay attention to working fathers.

In 1996, Donna Klein, director of work-life programs for Washington, D.C.-based Marriott International and a champion for hourly wage earners, engaged my colleagues and me at FWI to create a seminar series on effective fathering designed to reach employees no matter where they worked in the hotel—front desk, housekeeping, maintenance, sales, or management.

In this chapter I provide the elements of father friendliness, rather than a "one-size-fits-all" approach. Such approaches, while alluring in their simplicity, seldom, if ever, work. I do not offer a step-by-step approach to making the workplace more father friendly, because there is no one first step that is right for all companies. Some companies start with surveying their employees and work systematically to address their concerns from there; others forge ahead by offering a service such as an electronic parenting network, on-site child care, or support for elder care, and then discover that fathers are an important user group.

What counts most is attitude: an awareness of the need to factor working fathers into any discussion, or planning, of family friendliness, and a willingness to turn the awareness into action—starting somewhere.

Asking, Listening, and Learning

To find out what fathers are experiencing may require listening to them in new ways. That is what Arlene Johnson learned from her research at FWI:

> We were doing focus groups in a major accounting firm on family and career issues, and the men said, "We're so glad women are bringing up family issues because they are very important to us and we don't feel we can bring them up as much." This is starting to change, but men's ability to bring up this issue rides on the shirttails of women. The traditional expectation is that men will make a living and that somehow fathering will fit into that; for women the primary expectation is they will be mothers and earning a living will fit into that. Women feel permission to raise this issue and if they don't, it's raised for them. For men it's more of an issue about whether to bring it up.

"We found there was a benefit in doing separate focus groups for men and women," Johnson says. "Women's issues were so critical that men felt silenced. It's not that these issues are less important to men, but women had such a head of steam about them. Some men even say they are reluctant to ask for flexibility because they don't want to take it away from women. They don't understand that flexibility is not a fixed quantity. This all comes out of the perception that work–family policies are for women."

Unless employers ask men specifically about their family needs, they may never discover them. One of the reasons men's work–family conflict remains an "invisible dilemma" is because men are reluctant to talk about it. The perception is that *real men* avoid admitting—much less talking about—problems. And since work–family issues have tended to be defined as women's issues, men often fear being penalized should they broach them. A vicious cycle sets in: Men don't make their needs apparent, and employers continue to define work–family as a women's issue, which reinforces men's reluctance to express their needs. When employers invite men to discuss their work–family needs, make clear that it is "safe" to talk, and then listen to what they hear, they break the cycle. They discover that working fathers are a key constituency of the changing work force.

Robin Johnson, assistant professor at the Darden School of Business at the University of Virginia, finds that sometimes father friendliness can stem from a different attitude while listening to what male employees are saying during the normal course of business. While conducting research at Xerox, Johnson encountered a male employee with high performance appraisals who began receiving significantly lower evaluations from supervisors. "When asked by a human resource director why his performance might be slipping," Johnson explains, "the employee explained that he thought in part it was influenced by his family situation, as he was going through a divorce and custody difficulties."

The female human resource director responded, "So?"

Johnson explains that the woman was not unsympathetic to work–family issues; in fact, she was a champion of them at the company. "But she still needed to have someone say, 'Look what you are doing here,' and point out this and other situations where she assumed that a woman's work–family situation was 'legitimate' and important but a man's was not."

There are several different ways to begin the process of asking, listening, and learning.

Surveys of All Employees

DuPont has systematically assessed the needs of its work force for more than ten years. By making the results of its corporate surveys publicly available, DuPont has significantly advanced national attention to the work–family issues of all employees. By paying careful attention to the needs of fathers as well as mothers, it has worked to make its own workplace more father friendly.

Male Focus Groups

Running focus groups targeted to men can bring out needs that don't surface in coed groups where, as FWI's Arlene Johnson points out, men can feel as if they shouldn't talk. In 1990 when I conducted focus groups for fathers at Apple Computer, the sheer number of men who signed up—as well as the issues they presented—helped the company rethink the work–family initiative it was developing as "not-for-women-only." In 1995 the leadership at S. C. Johnson & Son had already decided it should begin addressing the needs of fathers, but focus groups validated—in a more emotionally powerful way than is often possible with surveys—the depth of men's concerns about their ability to be good fathers. Moreover, focus groups helped identify individual fathers who were interested in taking a lead role in developing the company's initiative for dads.

Mixed Gender Task Forces

Some companies establish an internal task force on work–family issues. If the group is comprised entirely of women, it runs the risk of not asking or hearing about men's concerns. Even if it has one male representative, it runs the risk of losing his participation if he feels he is there as a token. S. C. Johnson & Son carefully created a work–family task force with roughly equal participation by men and women. Although task force participation may be voluntary, companies can send out strong signals that they support and encourage broad-based participation. IBM's Workforce Diversity division even established a task force of white males that led to the 1996 announcement of a corporatewide policy of two weeks' paid paternity leave on the occasion of the birth or adoption of a child. According to Ted Childs, IBM's director of Workforce Diversity, "Change here is coming from within. We have eight task forces, one of white males. One of the issues that surfaced was the importance of being encouraged to be involved with their families."

Flexible Scheduling

Flexible use of time is the single most important element in creating a workplace that is friendly to fathers, mothers, and all employees regardless of parental status. This does not mean asking employees to work less, but giving them more control over when and where they get their jobs done.

Of course not all jobs are amenable to flexible scheduling. And when implemented, flexibility needs to be implemented for business reasons, not as an accommodation to working fathers, as work–family researchers have learned. Currently, flexibility is often perceived as an accommodation to working mothers, greatly limiting its impact and effectiveness. But when flexibility of workers' time is understood as a strategic business issue, it becomes a way to enhance competitive advantage *and* to reduce the work–family conflict experienced by fathers and mothers. This is such an important element of father friendliness—and of the change in business culture necessary to bring it about—that I devote the entire next chapter to it.

Communicating

Communicating to all employees that family friendliness is also for working fathers is a key way organizations can help their father-friendliness efforts take root.

If your company has or is trying to launch a work–family initiative, look carefully at the way the message is being communicated. Do the pictures on your brochures, fliers, and newsletters include men, or just women? Do newsletters reporting on how benefits are being used feature only stories about working mothers? Even the most progressive companies are sometimes surprised to realize that their literature promoting family friendliness inadvertently and unintentionally suggests that their policies are "for women only."

According to AT&T's spokesperson Burke Stinson, his company paid attention to my advice a few years ago to include photos of both men and women in all announcements of work–family benefits. "We tried this subtle but perhaps not-so-subtle approach," says Stinson. "It helped validate that parental leave was for both men and women and helped change the ratio of use. In 1979, unpaid parental leave was taken on a 400 to 1 female to male ratio; today it is an 18 to 1 female to male ratio. We may have contributed to the improvement in the 1980s by changing the name from maternity/paternity leave to parental leave. The realist in me says we have a long way to go, but the public relations executive in me can't help but say 'what a great improvement.'"

At Apple Computer, the data gathered from the focus groups led the company to take extra steps to communicate that fathers were included when it announced a major work–family initiative in 1991. The focus groups revealed the subtle ways in which the culture had come to lionize the work styles of young, single, mostly male engineers. A respected marketing manager was famous for "macho meetings"—a 7 A.M. meeting to start the day and an 8 P.M. meeting to end it. A newsletter lauded the heroic efforts of an engineer who had worked thirty-six hours straight to complete a project, then gone home to shower, and return to work. Not much need for sleep, much less to spend any time with his family. To start counteracting this impression, Apple announced its work–family initiative with a four-page newspaper-sized mailing to all of its 14,000 domestic employees. The top three-fourths of the back page was devoted to explaining how men were struggling with work–family dilemmas and that all programs and policies were intended for fathers as well as mothers.

The message started to get through. One month after the announcement, Jim Cutler, then one of the top 140 employees and director of Apple University, the company's internal training and organizational development division, became the first dad to take advantage of family leave. Upon the birth of baby Zachery, Cutler spent a full month at home with his wife and their two school-age children. "This felt like a unique opportunity to have the whole family together," he says. "I spent time with the baby, but, more important, I spent time with the older kids, who typically get ignored when a baby is born." Within the next two months two men who reported to Cutler took similar leaves.

Supporting Fathers from the Top

Nothing helps a corporatewide communications effort like vocal and visible support from senior leadership. Role modeling from top management also has great impact.

At Aetna, where 76 percent of the 41,000-employee work force is female, Chairman and CEO Ron Compton has continually made clear his commitment to family-friendly benefits for mothers *and* fathers. One month after a speech challenging other CEOs to "flex or break," Compton's remarks were distributed to all Aetna employees:

> In today's atmosphere of repeated downsizing, where expenses are a very real concern, . . . should "soft" programs like flexible work environments be the first to bite the dust? Absolutely not! . . . You might be interested to know that about 20 percent of those on flexible schedules are men. Because—surprise—we're finding men also are assuming child-care and aging-parent responsibilities. . . . Although Aetna has no quotas or formal goals, by the year 2000 at least twice as many of our people will be on flexible schedules. At the heart of the work–family issue—like at the heart of every other business issue—it is the imagination, the will, and the flexibility to make it work that makes the difference. As senior managers, we have to bring that imagination and good will to the table.

"I'm convinced that flexible work arrangements can help Aetna achieve superior results," Compton told his employees in 1994.

More than 5,000 of them (13 percent of the company) were using these arrangements. Case in point: Claims examiner Scott Mapston's productivity while working at home full time is 18 percent higher than the average for other claims processors. The arrangement allows him to be home after school for his seven- and nine-year-old daughters while his wife works as a waitress. He can also adjust his hours as family needs arise: "When Erin missed the bus, I brought her to school and got her there around 8:45 A.M. I haven't started working yet, but if I start at 10:00 A.M. and then work until 6:30, I will just put that on my time card."

Committing to All Workers

A father-friendly company seeks to help employees at all levels, from the executive suite to the sales floor or shop floor.

Eddie Bauer, the Redmond, Washington-based casual lifestyle retailer, has worked aggressively to make sure that its extensive range of work–family benefits is available to all of its 12,000 employees. In 1986, the company became one of the first in the country to offer paid parental leave to both mothers and fathers. In 1996, it introduced "Balance Day," a bonus day off for all employees to take care of their personal needs, whether for children, errands, or recreation. It also offers such pioneering programs as emergency care for mildly ill children, group mortgage discounts, and "Home and Healthy," which sends a registered pediatric nurse to the home of all employees with a new baby to conduct a postpartum examination between twenty-four and seventy-two hours of the mother's discharge from the hospital. "We treat the in-store people with respect," says Craig Boyes, manager of associate benefits and work/life quality. "I know I would not be here without them. This place is not a hierarchy." George Winkelmaier, a salesman at the Eddie Bauer store in Reno, Nevada, explains the company policy of letting him adjust his hours on a weekly basis has made him a better salesman and a more involved father, since he is able to take his four-year-old son to occasional balloon races in the morning, then work from noon until 9 P.M.

At the Los Angeles Department of Water and Power (LADWP), the nation's largest municipally owned utility company, men comprise 80 percent of the work force. Its Work and Family Care-Fathering Program is the most extensive in the country in both scope of service and effectiveness in reaching a broad range of employees. Since its inception in 1987, it has anually served 1,200 of the company's 9,000 employees—both mothers and fathers—with the percentage of fathers served increasing from 40 to 60 percent. The Fathering Program includes pre- and postpartum services, on-site child care, child care resource and referral, a special "Tips for Dads" information hot line, peer support groups, monthly information seminars, child support collection via payroll deduction to ensure that divorced fathers are meeting their monthly obligations, and counseling to help dads with any sort of family-related problem.

Oscar Flores, an electrical distribution mechanic who works on high-voltage power lines, started using the LADWP Fathering Program to support his wife, Pamela, even before their baby was born. He wanted to make sure everything was going well with Pamela's pregnancy, since they had tried for five years to have a child. Flores was able to take paid family-care time to go to the obstetrician with her. When the baby was nearly due, he got a company beeper, provided when fathers are within three weeks of the due date. "It gave me great peace of mind," says Flores. "Without it, it could take the dispatcher forty-five minutes to reach me in the field, another forty-five minutes for me to get back to the yard, and then I'd still have to get home." When his wife started breast feeding, Flores borrowed a breast pump for her from the company's lactation program, which teaches men how to use the pump so they can help their wives, and a video on how to operate it from the "Dad's Department" of the company's Parent Resource Library. "This is our first kid and I'm involved with every little thing," he says proudly. And LADWP wants dads to be involved, for business reasons: Babies are less likely to be sick when mothers breast-feed, leading to less absenteeism and lost productivity by mothers and fathers.

A water utility worker, Mark Lopez, who installs and takes out old meters, was disconsolate from the divorce that separated him from daily contact with his children until he got in contact with Ray Castro, director of the Fathering Program. "My heart would ache from week to week," says Lopez. "Mr. Castro said you're a good father who wants to see his kids. Ray was like Pepto Bismol. He gave me the backbone to take the reins and be assertive and a little more aggressive. Now that I have visitation I'm much happier. It's done an enormous job for me."

In 1995, the annual cost of this extensive program was $987,000. If that seems expensive, it is less than the $1 million LADWP calculated it was losing in 1985 salary and benefits costs because of child-care-related employee absence and tardiness, which did not factor in immeasurable losses in customer service. A 1995 sampling of supervisors found a "decrease in absenteeism and tardiness and an increase in morale for employees served by the program." According to Faye Washington, chief administrative officer at LADWP:

> The Fathering Program has made a distinct difference in the corporate culture. It expresses to fathers that there is more to working than just coming in and punching a clock and going home after eight hours, that we care about the quality of life they live beyond work. To those who would challenge whether we should keep this kind of program given the economy, given the downsizing, I would say we can't afford not to keep a program like this: As a company we are experiencing lower absenteeism, higher morale, and higher productivity. The cost is minimal given the value it produces.

Rewarding Performance, Not Face Time

Appraising employees on what they get done, rather than on how many face-time hours they put in at the office, is a key element in creating the father-friendly workplace.

Hewlett-Packard, a high-technology manufacturer based in

Menlo Park, California, has made flexible schedules for as many employees as possible a core element of its business strategy. "I get paid for the results I produce, not when I produce them," says Ted Tucker, a program manager in the Corporate Quality Group whose official schedule includes every other Friday off to be with his kids. Tucker's performance, like that of all HP employees, is assessed with a 360-degree process that gives him feedback from his manager, peers, customers, and subordinates. Employees who work off-site are evaluated on their ability to work independently yet communicate with their team to meet goals.

Although many companies profess to want to reward performance instead of face time, many report difficulties doing so. One way is to assess managers on their support of work–family balance for employees. HP's 360-degree assessment process allows for that feedback. First Union of Charlotte, North Carolina, the nation's sixth largest bank, now surveys its employees on that dimension of their managers' performance.

Making Work Teams Father Friendly

Diverse workplaces, from hospitals to consulting organizations, have increasingly embraced teams—groups of employees working collaboratively, often with control over many of their own work arrangements—as a source of workplace productivity.

In 1993, after First Tennessee Bank reorganized its work force into teams, an account record processing group rearranged its schedule to better serve customer needs and to give team members an extra day off a month. Customer service turnaround time was cut in half—from eight days to four—and the team's quality score in customer service jumped by 60 percent.

Does working as part of a team always improve men's and women's ability to balance their work and family lives? My research suggests that there is great potential for teams to help working fathers *if* the teams have the right skills *and* are supported in the right ways.

Stan Brown is a team leader in the Worldwide Spare Parts Commodity Group of Texas Instruments, the second largest semiconducter and peripherals producer in the country. He has three preschool-age children. Stan's wife works full time. "The team system," he explains, "was originally put in place for travel reasons, so that a traveling employee would not halt the work flow of others. What we have found is that it works extremely well for work–family situations as well." On mornings when he needs to stay home with a sick child, Stan uses e-mail to notify all of the relevant people that he will be at home for the day. Next, he updates his voice mail, letting callers know who they can reach as a back-up. Stan's back-up is another employee at the company at the same level who knows enough about his job to field questions and priority requests. Team members know how to pass time-sensitive calls along to him at home, which Stan does not mind at all. In fact, he finds that he is able to get a great deal of work done at home on these days.

Communicating your needs as a working father and team member are critical to team performance. Consider the experience at a Florida-based office of KPMG Peat Marwick LLP, where a four-person management consulting team was hard at work on a crash deadline for an important project—coming in early, leaving late, working on weekends. Unknown to the other team members, one man had a pregnant wife, and there were some complications, explains team leader James Horan, southeast area partner in charge of international services. "Well, that individual began letting the team down. He started coming in late, leaving early, even disappearing for chunks of the day without articulating why. Other team members began complaining."

Horan wondered why a previously high-performing employee had slipped so much. "The real cause and the real danger was the secrecy," Horan explains. "He was afraid to articulate the problem to the team."

Horan asked this employee into his office one afternoon and probed. The young man articulated the problems he was facing at home. "I could tell this was an extremely difficult situation for him, because he was a good performer and wanted to do right by the team. As it was unfolding, it was not a good situation for anyone. We did not have a solution."

Horan decided the only answer was to put another person onto the team for this project. "From a manager's perspective," he says, "it is infinitely better to have someone saying that for a short time he will be able to give only 70 percent—that is something a manager can deal with. But a manager is really in trouble if someone he or she is counting on to give 125 percent comes through with only 75 percent. That spells trouble for the individual, the team, and, perhaps most important, the client. Nobody wins."

As Horan recounts the details of the story, he explains, "I remembered that after my first child was born, I disappeared to Columbia, South America, two days after the birth. Yes, the work was important, but with hindsight I am not sure that I made the right move."

If teams lack strong leadership or strong group process skills, performance problems driven by conflicting work and family needs may not surface, and the performance of the individual and the team may suffer. According to Laura Avakian, vice president of human resources at Boston's Beth Israel Hospital, which relies heavily on a team-based approach, the key to promoting father friendliness in teams is for the leader to "foster team environments that legitimate discussion of work–family need. It's just too important and too risky to leave it to chance."

Father-Friendly Child Care

A father-friendly company works proactively to make sure that the fathers using its on-site child-care or other family services feel as welcome as working mothers.

At Ben & Jerry's, the creative ice cream maker, policies at the child-care center, which serves four hundred employees and other community members, are designed to include dads from day one. "We require both parents to come in for the initial meeting," says

Beth Wallace, former director of the Ben & Jerry's Children's Center. "Its important that we get dad's perspective. Fathers often think they have less of a role and that's not true. We want to hear from them." Because the company runs three shifts around the clock and the center is open only from 7 A.M. to 6 P.M., the staff will schedule interviews during non-standard hours as necessary.

Sponsors of company-based child-care programs indicate that dads are now as likely to drop off or pick up their children as moms. But father-friendly programs promote the participation of dads during the day as well. At Ben and Jerry's, the center is as open and flexible as possible to make sure that workers get special time with their kids. One dad on the second shift (3:30 to 11 P.M.) brings his three- and five-year-olds in at 2 P.M. so he can spend an hour playing "in their world." At John Hancock's state-of-the-art child-care center, electrical journeyman Ed Falanga is able to have regular lunch dates with his five-year-old son, Anthony: "I try to make it to lunch with him at least once a week, especially on the days when I know I'll be working overtime." Hancock's Assistant Controller Pat Gill, whose wife also works full time, is a regular user of Hancock's Kids-to-Go program, an activity program for summer and holidays when school's out. Gill brings his two children to work on those days, and the company does the rest. "It's $20 per day per child, but it's really convenient and the kids love it," he says. "Besides, there's an unforeseen benefit—we get to spend 45 minutes together in the car each way with no distractions, no TV, no friends coming over."

BE&K, an engineering construction company based in Birmingham, Alabama, established a state-of-the-art on-site child-care facility because the three founders—all fathers—thought it would benefit their 1,200 employees, most of whom are men. Moreover, the company establishes mobile child-care units to assist workers in its construction sites. Dads who use BeKare take great pride in what they typically refer to as "their center" and find that using it links them to an informal parents' network. "We get to know one another, and then we can talk about our kids through the day," says systems analyst Steve Stewart, whose three-and-a-half-year-old daughter uses the BeKare center. Stewart is a member of the parent involvement committee that meets monthly with the director and teachers. "The average longevity of a person in my position with other companies is about two years," he says. "Here, because of the benefits, it's seven to eight years."

Indeed, companies intent on making their day care father friendly do it not just to be socially responsible. They know there is a bottom-line benefit when working fathers—like working mothers—don't have to worry about who is caring for their children. Explaining why Patagonia , the clothing retailer based in Ventura, California, offers an on-site child care center as well as paid maternity and paternity leave, founder and co-owner Yvon Chouinard says, "I want [my employees] focused, and if they are distracted by guilt, they can't focus. We don't provide these benefits because we're nice."

A 1994 survey of fathers with children enrolled in corporate-sponsored worksite child-care centers by Montgomery, Alabama-based KinderCare found that 68 percent of the fathers surveyed reported an increase in job productivity, 73 percent said it was easier to concentrate on the job, and 74 percent said they were less anxious than if their children had been in child care farther away. Moreover, most of the fathers surveyed spent an average of 30 minutes each week visiting their child, mostly at lunch time. So while on-site child care reduced DaddyStress, it also increased the time kids had to be with their fathers by approximately twenty-five hours a year, even before factoring in the added time these working fathers spend commuting with their kids.

Fatherhood as a Guiding Value

Can a small business in a ferociously competitive field afford to help men be involved fathers, even if it means reducing the company's billable hours in the short term? Yes—it can even thrive and grow while it commits to valuing family and organizes its work to preserve that commitment.

Rodgers, Joseph, O'Donnell & Quinn, a San Francisco law firm, was founded in 1981 by seven men and three women who broke out of a large San Francisco firm to establish a company that allowed for a life beyond legal practice. Founding partner Neil O'Donnell agreed to go only if his partners allowed him to work half-time for four months during the crucial start-up period in order to be home with his newborn daughter. In 1996, partner Alan Samelson, father of children aged three and eight, cut back to 80-percent time because he was finding it difficult to strike a balance between family and work at 100-percent time. His new schedule allows him to help with carpooling in the morning, get home earlier, and not work weekends. And he appreciates being around his children more because "kids don't respond on demand to your schedule. Like the other morning, my son told me something shocking while he was getting ready for school, which led to an important conversation. Kids are known for blurting something important out at unusual times. You don't get the opportunity to hear these things if you leave before they wake up and if you return after they go to bed.

"It's not just me that has to deal with a pay cut," says Samelson. "The firm's billing hours are cut as well. There has to be a mutual recognition among the partners to sacrifice income. Basically, the commitment here to families is strong enough that people will sacrifice money for it."

But it is a commitment that pays off in the firm's ability to recruit and retain top flight attorneys. "We usually hire young lawyers who have already worked for a year or two," says Neil O'Donnell. "Often their experience has been that they have worked incredibly hard in the large law firm for a period of time and then they have said, 'I have to do something else in my life.' We work very hard, but we always make sure that people have time for other things in their lives."

The same philosophy underlies the success of Pearson, Crahan, Fletcher & England, a twenty-year-old full-service advertising agency in Indianapolis. Its thirty-five employees and annual capitalized billings of $25 million make it one of the two or three largest ad agencies in the state of Indiana. "Being a dad was more important than having a career," says founding partner Larry Fletcher, "but you had to have a career to pay the bills." That's the inner tension most men struggle with constantly. Most small service-oriented businesses with a commitment to families struggle with another. "We need people here most of the time," says Fletcher. "But at the same time, we want people to be with their families." Fletcher and his colleagues found no magic formula for managing the tension successfully other than to work together and be flexible. "We are a small enough group. We have a formal structure, but we all work together. We can tell if the work is getting done. We're constantly asking how we can readjust so it's a win–win. If you put people in a position where they can't win at home, then they aren't going to do the job here."

Ron Pearson, president of the firm, coached his son's baseball team and served for many years as president of Big Brothers of Greater Indianapolis. Instead of detracting from the business, his community service helped land the firm's biggest client. Fletcher "coached Little League, which I am terrible at, but at least I was out there being a dad. I was active in the band parents' association while my kids were going through school. Owners and partners are busy guys, but we got my account load to less than eighty hours a week, and I cut my travel time so I could be in town more." Art director Jeff Lovell, who has custody of his three teenagers, keeps an unorthodox schedule, coming in late because he has to get his kids off to school, working until midnight or all weekend when he doesn't have his kids. "I just let the company know what is going on," he says. "It's just a lot of trust. I would not be able to stay with the company if they didn't trust me to get the work done."

That trust builds loyalty and longevity. "People know very much that family comes first," says Pearson. "That's why we have a lot of people who have been here a long time. I would feel sad if I couldn't say there are people who have become more involved with their own families because they have seen that sort of thing happen here."

Using Communication Tools to Support Working Fathers

Communication tools—including e-mail, Internet connections, and in-house parenting forums—can all be creatively applied to help support working fathers.

Electronic mail, which is becoming ubiquitous as a way to foster workplace communication, is a terrific tool for encouraging dads to ask for advice and get assistance from other parents.

At Eastman Kodak, the Rochester, New York-based photochemical corporation, an internal study revealed that, beyond any programs and policies, there was a need for better communication. "We had people inside the company—mothers and fathers—struggling with basic problems," says Adam Baker, a human relations specialist at Kodak. "The idea was to put these parents in touch with one another. This way, any larger issues would come to the surface and could be brought to the attention of the policymakers."

Kodak's Working Parent's League (WPL) was started in 1991 by twelve parents who put out a newsletter on the electronic mail system. It quickly garnered another 400 members and a huge response; in the first two weeks of February 1992, more than 8,000 notices were posted about everything from babysitters to used high chairs. Right away the League drew out fathers like product engineer Bill Baum, who joined a WPL committee to explore the possibility of establishing an on-site day care center. "I keep making the point that this is a family issue, not a woman's issue," he says.

Texas Instruments, the Dallas-based semiconductor and peripherals manufacturer with 35,000 employees, has a similar on-line Parents Network where employees can exchange information and experiences or sign on to specific discussion areas such as Young Children, Older Children, and Twin/Multiple. Ching-Yu Hung, a member of the company's technical staff and father of two, refers to himself as a "quiet listener" who has gathered information on ear infections, getting children to sleep, high-chair recalls, and what to do with children at amusement parks. "I save, print, and rush the information to my stay-at-home wife," he says. "Just hearing parents exchange questions and tips gives me a sense of support. [It's] made life easier for my family."

According to Gary Garcia, a Texas Instruments senior auditor and father of twenty-month-old Nicholas, "I may only want 20 percent of the messages everyday, but it is worth it to me to have access to this 20 percent. When it came time to get a car seat, I looked up that category. You hear about people's experiences. It's better than *Consumer Reports* because it's people's own stories. *Consumer Reports* may not tell you if it is difficult to buckle the buckle, but a parent who has used it will. A few weeks ago, my wife needed to bring Nick on a plane to visit her mother. There was a whole series of e-mail I got about how to prepare for a flight with a baby—how to prepare him mentally, what to bring, what to do before getting on the plane. We learned to go extra early so he could become familiar with surroundings. And we then went for a walk around the airport to make him tired so he would be less cranky and would fall asleep on the plane. We also learned to bring a new toy he had never seen before to keep his attention on the plane. The messages made it a better experience for us all, especially for other passengers on the flight."

Offering Workplace Education and Support for Fathers

Old-fashioned, face-to-face seminars also go a long way to creating a father-friendly culture. Aside from their e-mail parenting networks, both Texas Instruments and Eastman Kodak offer regular parenting seminars for fathers, as do the Los Angeles Department of Water and Power and a slowly increasing number of organizations, including the U.S. Army.

For some companies, offering educational programs is one way to begin communicating that family friendly means father friendly. That's the route taken by S. C. Johnson & Son, Inc.. "Sixty-five percent of our workforce is male, and of that over half are dads," says Mary Kay S. Carr, director of diversity. "We offer a lot of things that are beneficial to moms and dads, but we wanted to find something that would help dads in particular." In late 1995, when the company announced a lunchtime program for fathers to be presented by trainers from the Kansas City-based National Center on Fathering, more than a hundred men showed up. And even more turned out for a follow-up evening session in early 1996.

Bryan Jennings, a 33-year-old chemical process operator,

works second shift, from 3 to 11 P.M, then goes home to care for his three children, ages 3, 4, and 15, while his wife works third shift. "We all get to the breaking point," says Jennings. "I feel that if my family knows I'm stressed out, then I've failed them. As men, we need this type of support. I've met . . . fathers like myself that have experienced the same everyday trials and tribulations. Many of the guys in the group all work here in the plant. That's what calms the spirit, to hear that you're not in this situation alone."

"We know that an awful lot of our work force is made up of dads. Dads are dealing with the same challenges as working moms," Carr says. "How do I get to my child's soccer game and get this project done? We have single dads who have to go home and make dinner for their children. By providing them with resources, we can help our fathers be both better dads and better employees. This and other work/life initiatives help set us apart from other companies and help us recruit the best talent."

Beyond attracting talented workers, workplace-based educational programs for dads may help support the organizational mission by strengthening families. That's what the U.S. Army is finding out at the Fort Hood, Texas, base that serves 48,000 soldiers, making it the largest military installation in the world. In 1993, Chaplain Jon Tidball was getting used to the same story: A couple would come in for counseling, the man brought in kicking and screaming by his wife who threatened divorce unless he started paying attention to her and the children when he got home from work. "You'll do everything for Uncle Sam, for your job and your country," the wives would say, "but you won't lift a finger for your children."

"At first the guys put up an argument," says Chaplain Tidball. "'Honey, I'm tired when I get home.'" And they are. Most of the soldiers start work at 5:00 or 5:30 A.M. with several hours of physical exertion, and do not get off until twelve hours later. If enlisted, they are sick of taking orders all day; if officers, they are tired of giving orders all day. If they went into the field for a month or more, they felt they had gotten behind the power curve at home and lost touch with their children. Any way you look at it, they were discouraged.

"But," says Tidball, "after we talk the lights start coming on and some of them start to cry. They don't want to miss their children's growing up and repeat what they had with their own parents. They're worried about breaking the habit they're in, about how they're going to get out from behind the eight ball."

Instead of confining his services to individual counseling, Tidball decided to offer a half-day seminar on effective fathering to the seven hundred men in his battalion. But he quickly discovered the men "didn't want to *hear me* talk about fatherhood. *They* wanted to talk about fatherhood, about what was happening, about what had happened to them and what had discouraged them in their own attempts to be good fathers, about the lack of support from their wives, about how to deal with discipline. It was kind of a pent-up flood. Men just opened up."

The seminar turned into a continuing series of brown-bag lunches, explains Tidball, "with guys helping one another. I'd find guys at the motor pool talking about what's going on with their family and giving each other marriage counseling." In accordance with military procedure, Tidball conducted "after actions," evaluations that solicit anonymous feedback from participants. By passing along copies of the evaluations to his supervisors, and by briefing his commander and other chaplains on what he was doing, he got the Fort Hood Fathering Program funded as a regular part of base operations. "I got their attention," says Tidball, "by showing a problem for military readiness and deployability that we have not addressed: The parenting influence is gone."

Encouraging Fathers' Participation in their Children's Schools

A ten-year study involving 20,000 students and their families conducted by Temple University psychologist Laurence Steinberg concluded that one of the two most critical influences on the decline of school performance by American students was not problem schools or poor curricula, but parent disengagement from school life. (The other influence was peers who denigrate academic success.)

This finding has a clear implication: Companies looking for ways to improve the education of the public schools that will supply 90 percent of their future employees need only look at the work schedules of their current employees. According to Fran Sussner Rodgers, chairman of WFD, 60 percent of parents have a hard time being involved with their children's schools because of their work schedules.

The father-friendly company makes it possible for fathers (and mothers) to take time to participate in their children's schools without feeling that they are falling down on their jobs.

Hemmings Motor News, a privately held publishing company headquartered in Bennington, Vermont, offers Education Participation and Community Service Days, two paid days off per year to all regular full-time and part-time benefit-eligible staff.

Employees elect whether to use their days to participate at a local school or to volunteer for another type of community program. Fathers and mothers at the company use the days to attend their children's school for a day; to meet the teachers and students and obtain a better understanding of the school curriculum, classes, and daily activities; to teach or speak at schools about career opportunities as they relate to their work, hobby or special interests; and to assist teachers for the day, either in the classroom or on an academic field trip. This benefit is not limited to parents, signaling the company's strong support of community involvment.

Hemming even formed a subteam charged with responsibility for increasing staff participation. In 1995, twenty-five employees, approximately one-fourth of employees at the company, took advantage of this benefit. The subteam has been working with area schools inviting them to identify opportunities for staff involvement. It also conducts regular brown-bag lunchtime meetings during which they discuss parenting and educational issues, as well as brainstorm new ways for staff participation.

In addition, the Hemming Employee Assistance Program—a program that provides fully paid counseling sessions for employees, spouses, and dependent children—can be used by employees to assist in solving educational and developmental problems experienced by their children.

"The goal of these programs," explains Hemming's Mary Cossin, "is to strengthen the school system by encouraging father and mother involvement."

Supporting Fathers Who Need to Stay Home When a Child Is Ill

According to the American Medical Association, working parents face a sick-child crisis between six and nine times a year, with the average length of illness ranging from one day to a week. A survey of more than 1,000 working parents conducted by Bruskin/ Goldring Research for Whitehall-Robins Healthcare found that one of the most stressful child-care situations parents face is leaving a sick child with a sitter. In many of these cases, a child is too sick to be sent to school or preschool or the child-care center. In most cases it is mom who stays home because, as you will see in the next chapter on changing your corporate culture, moms, dads, and their employers tend to assume the culture won't approve of dad staying home.

But a father-friendly company recognizes that in most American families, both mothers and fathers are working. And it makes it possible for those mothers and fathers to work out the sick-care arrangements that are best for them and their child—sometimes with mom staying home, sometimes with dad.

John Hancock, the nation's eighth largest life insurer, offers up to three paid family days a year so employees can stay home with a sick child or other family member. Hancock business economist Adam Seitchik, even though he cannot meet all his son's requests— a note posted on the wall, dictated by a three-year-old son and written out by his nursery school teacher says, "Dear Daddy, Please don't go to work. I want you to play with me. Love, Evan"—says, "it makes me feel good to know that my employer allows me to be there for him. When Evan has been sick and Pam is in school, they have made it easy for me to be there."

Offering Information on College Financing

Even as they try to find the time to be with their preschool and school-age children at home, working fathers are terribly aware of the need to figure out how they will pay for tuition when their children grow and want to go to college. Of course, this is a concern of working mothers, but companies that offer information for planning in this area get an especially strong response from dads.

GTE Corporation, one of the world's largest publicly held telecommunications companies, headquartered in Stamford, Connecticut, offers a Saturday College Planning Seminar for employees and their families. "College planning is such an important topic that it really needs full-day attention," says Randy MacDonald, senior vice president of human resources and administration, who conceived and oversaw the program. "In addition, it was extremely important to us that we develop a time and format that involves the high-school kids who will be ultimately living the decisions."

Parents clearly agree—more than 1,200 GTE employees, spouses, and children at close to forty GTE sites nationwide attended the September 1996 seminar. The seminar links college admissions and financial planning experts with GTE employee families to help them plan a range of aspects of children's college education, from college admissions and financial aid to managing social changes. It includes talks, a case study, financial aid advice, SAT workshops, and several panels, including a panel of current college students who field questions from children and the parents. Parents are given resource materials covering many of the session topics.

According to MacDonald, "We recognize that our employees are often working a lot more hours than they have in the past and the College Entrance Planning Seminar allows us an opportunity to give them something beyond the normal benefits, to give them an opportunity to focus on the right things for their families."

Brian B. Taylor, director of corporate tax for GTE Corporation, describes his family's "first college-planning adventure" as the older son, Devin, gets close to the college-application process: "GTE's program underscored many important facts about the college-planning process which will come in handy with our younger son, Kyle, as well, when it gets to be his turn." But GTE's program does something more than transmit information. "The program seemed to have a calming effect on Devin," Taylor observes, "and the program has initiated a cycle of interest and discussion between Devin, my wife, Jacquelyn, and myself, which can only be helpful to this process. Devin's attendance at the seminar stimulated his interest, and he seems more motivated than before the seminar to discuss the process. The student panel at the seminar offered insights into the opportunities and potential pitfalls of campus life in a way that Jackie and I could never accomplish."

GTE supports their employees' goal of promoting the education of their college-aged children in several other ways, including several scholarship programs and a 401K plan that permits parents to draw down against their accounts to pay for college if they so choose. GTE will also provide its employees an 800 number to the AYCO Company, where GTE employees can call to have financial-aid questions answered during the time parents work on the forms.

"The college planning seminar is a great way to involve dads in work–family offerings," explains Sandy Robertson, an associate practice leader for organization effectiveness. "We had a great turn-out of fathers, despite a Nor'easter storm!"

Paid Paternity Leave

I warned against defining father friendliness solely in terms of paternity leave, but hardly mean to suggest it is not important. To be realistic, though, men are unlikely to take advantage of leave for any substantial length of time unless it is paid, at least in part. Among other reasons, which I present in Chapter 5, that's because neither dads nor moms want, nor can afford, to sacrifice what is typically the larger household income.

Where paternity leave is paid—at high-profile family-friendly companies like Lotus Development and Patagonia—it is more widely used by men. But pay has proven to make a big difference at organizations that are smaller and less well known, too. In February 1990, Sacramento became the first county in California to offer paid parental leave to its employees. Within one year, members of the 1,700-person county sheriff's department were its most frequent users, with slightly more than half of the fifty-two leaves taken by men. Under county policy, employees with at least one year of continuous employment are eligible for 160 hours of parental leave over four months.

Wayne and Pam Irey, both employed by the sheriff's department, took their leaves sequentially after daughter Shelby was born in September 1990. While Pam added the new parental leave to her disability and accumulated vacation days to take a long stretch at home, Wayne took the first part of his leave during the Christmas holidays when family members were visiting.

Deputy Sheriff Bob Lozito, who works on the Critical Incident Negotiations Team, dealing with everything from hostages to potential suicide, took off two weeks straight when his son Michael was born. After that he chopped up the extra hours according to his somewhat unpredictable schedule. "Taking the leave gave me some very happy, unanticipated experiences. I went to our baby's first doctor's appointment and saw the weighing, saw what percentiles he's in, and got to ask my own questions," he recalls.

Fostering Responsible Fatherhood in the Community

The father-friendly workplace impacts not only on the homes of its employees, but on its community. Given the large numbers of children growing up in homes without resident fathers, it is an especially important opportunity for social responsibility and charitable giving to make it possible for male employees to serve their communities.

In Hattiesburg, Mississippi, the Willmut Gas Company has taken a lead role in supporting the Positive Male Role Program of the Head Start centers of the Pinebelt Association for Community Enhancement. Most of the parents in PACE Head Start are poor young women working in low-paying industries—poultry cleaning, sewing factories, and textile mills. Their jobs are very time-consuming, often requiring twelve-hour shifts, and leaving little time for children and their needs. If there is a man in the household, it is usually not the father: Of 466 families enrolled, only 75 have the biological father living at home. The scarcity of men in the lives of PACE children and the problems facing young black men in Mississippi—drug addiction, legal entanglements, and low-paying work, if any—prompted parent involvement coordinator Gaye Newsome and executive director Peggy Butler to initiate a program that would provide positive contacts with men. Johnny Tatum, president of Willmut Gas, not only responded enthusiastically on behalf of his own employees—giving them time off during the week to volunteer at the centers—but helped rally other businesses, churches, and the local U.S. Army base to participate in the program.

For the Calvert Group, a money management firm in Bethesda, Maryland, that specializes in socially responsible investments, valuing families, and enabling the 150 employees to spend time in community service are both strong parts of the corporate culture. Employees receive a $1,000 bonus on the birth of a baby, two weeks' parental leave, and company subsidy of half their annual child-care expense. Moreover, all employees get and are actively encouraged to take advantage of twelve days a year of community leave to coach sports or provide service to their communities. "We screen companies for their employee practices so we have to practice what we preach," says Evelyne Steward, Calvert's vice president of human resources. "We recognize our employees as one of our assets. What do you do with your assets? You take care of them. It is not just to be nice; it is to make our business successful."

And by so doing, to help their communities succeed. Bill Williams, training director for the company, explains that "one of the programs in which I am active is a local schools speaker series. I go for a morning or afternoon to an area school and talk with kids of different ages about my career to help get them thinking about different jobs and the skills they require and rewards they bring." Calvert also brings kids into the company through a year-long co-op program with a local high school, through which participating students are assigned a volunteering employee whom they shadow, learning valuable details about job and industry.

At the company, most of the community involvement projects come up through a standing group of employees that meets regularly to help shape them. Although there is a staff person formally involved in coordinating, it is very much the employees who bring up the ideas to the company, rather than the other way around. This means that programs well-reflect the interests, concerns, and commitments of the men and women in the company.

Williams observes a number of benefits for the company, in addition to those for the community. "The programs really contribute to employees taking pride not only in the company, but in what they do. Sometimes it's too easy, even in a job you love, to get caught up in some of the mundane details and demands of the work. Explaining your work to someone else—particularly a young person—reminds you and makes it fresh for you. And that's exciting."

Not Romanticizing Working Fathers

Just as a focus on working mothers has inadvertently tended to reinforce work and family as an exclusively women's issue, attention to working fathers runs the risk of unintentionally obscuring the fact that the needs of America's working mothers have not yet been adequately addressed. It is crucial to keep the needs of all working parents in perspective.

These days, the media loves dads whose high-profile positions are matched only by their high-profile paternity. *The Des Moines Register*, for example, ran a long feature in 1994 when David Lyons, director of the Iowa Department of Economic Development, began bringing his one-month-old daughter, Maureen, to the office.

> With one hand, he's taking notes on a legal pad. With the other, he's holding Maureen. A burp cloth hides part of his power tie. Welcome to the office of Iowa's top eco-

nomic development official. The crib in the corner office and the pacifier resting on the stack of government documents make for a clear illustration of just how pervasive the work–family balancing act has become. A few times a week, Lyons brings in his newborn daughter for a couple of hours while her mother, a lawyer on maternity leave, rests or runs errands. Her father reads memos out loud to her, holds her during staff meetings, and walks her in her snugly sack while he reads reports.

Each time I read stories like this I am of two minds. I am delighted to think that they will promote a greater awareness of men's work/family needs and of their interest in caring for their children. But I am also afraid that they will deflect attention from the needs of millions of working mothers who receive little special consideration when their children are born, much less permission to bring them to the office.

In 1995, when Congressman Bill Orton, Utah, started bringing his baby, Will, to the House of Representatives in Washington, D.C., a few times a week, the media was all over him. *People* did a double-page photo spread. *CNN Cable News* interviewed him. And papers including *The Boston Globe, Chicago Tribune, The Detroit Free Press,* and *Los Angeles Times* sent reporters to do features. Quite understandably, all the attention garnered backlash as well as praise. In response to one of *The Washington Post*'s two stories, one woman wrote in Letters to the Editor, "Leave it to a man to do something women have been forbidden to do in the working environment, and, of course, his actions are tolerated—not even questioned. . . . Rep. Orton's actions are a slap in the face to every working mother."

Representative Orton was not trying to insult women but, at age 46, was trying to get to spend time with the child he and his wife feared they would never have. "If I didn't figure out a way to spend time with the baby during the day, I'd never see him," said Orton. But the strong reactions his story drew suggest that any company trying to move to create a more father-friendly environment by drawing attention and extending support to working fathers should be careful not to flaunt the attention shown. Focusing on fathers is a short-term tactic to achieve a long-term goal: support for all working parents, regardless of gender. It's important to attend to working fathers but lose sight of or to slight working mothers.

Chapter 4

Breaking the Culture Collusion

After reading the last chapter, filled with snapshots of father-friendly workplaces, you might be thinking, "They look great, but my workplace is nothing like that." In this chapter, I'll address what most dads—and moms—see as the greatest obstacle to making their workplace father friendly: corporate culture.

One aspect of culture, more than any other, makes it difficult to balance work and family life: the inflexibility of work schedules. Yet creating more flexible scheduling is not only good for fathers and their families, but also good for the business bottom line. And with the right strategies, flexible scheduling can be negotiated and managed in more business situations than you may realize.

What keeps the workplace from being more father friendly? What keeps men from pushing for the sorts of changes they want? The most common response from both fathers and mothers is, "The corporate culture won't support it."

Leading experts agree. According to Ellen Bankert and Bradley Googins of the Boston University Center on Work and Family Life, there is often more than meets the eye at a company with a state-of-the-art child-care center at corporate headquarters or a showcase of awards for its work–family programs:

Spend some time . . . talking to employees and you begin to see another side of today's family-friendly company. In their eyes, fifty- and sixty-hour weeks seem to be the norm. Everyone talks about judging people on output, but face time is more important than ever, especially given the recent round of layoffs. . . . On paper, there is a growing list of programs and policies that appear to signal a commitment to a healthy balance between work and personal life, but the culture is anything but balanced. . . . What's particularly problematic is that many employers believe that their family-friendly programs have resolved the range of work–family problems that beset today's working family. But the real set of work–family issues such as time, flexibility, balance, and even values of respect and commitment cannot be addressed by the current programs; they require fundamental changes in culture.

CORPORATE CULTURE

Culture is defined—in the words of David Nadler and Michael Tushman in their classic business text, *Strategic Organization Design*—as "a set of values, beliefs, and norms (that is, expected behaviors) that are held in common by people in a group." Culture is the most important yet most elusive dimension of work. It's not what is written down in the policies and procedures manuals, although it includes those elements. It is the medium we work in, as transparent yet ever present as water is to the fish in the ocean. It includes all the messages, assumptions, values, and norms about how time should and should not be spent.

Since culture results from the continuing interactions of individual employees, managers, and executives then, to borrow from the name of a popular chain of toy stores, "culture are us." And it follows that workplace culture can change only through a combination of factors—not just executive orders, policies, or programs, but the accumulation over time of a series of small steps taken by individual men and women as managers and employees.

According to the Managing Smart model developed jointly by the Families and Work Institute and WFD, culture can most effectively be made more family friendly through a partnership between managers, staff members, and the company. In my experience, when it comes to making the culture more father friendly, all three partners are often constrained by assumptions and fears—by what they think the culture is or needs to be, rather than what it really is or could be.

BLAMING THE CULTURE

Quite often fathers limit their own capacity to create change by unknowingly participating in a game I call *blame the culture*, which usually takes three to play: an employer, a father, and a mother. They all collude, without realizing it, in perpetuating workplace cultures that conform to everybody's expectations. The result is a continuous, self-perpetuating cycle: Fathers consider the culture and assume it is supportive, at best, of working mothers; companies look at lack of male participation in work–family programs as evidence that balancing work and family life is a woman's issue; and women feel they must take work–family issues on alone at the company, even though at home they need or want the support and involvement of their husbands.

To show you what I mean, consider a common occurrence at my DaddyStress/Daddy Success seminars. Whenever I start talking about the specific steps it takes to create a more father-friendly environment, somebody throws up a familiar roadblock: "Oh, but they don't allow that here."

"Who is *they*?" I ask curiously.

"What do you mean, who is *they*?"

"I mean, who is *they*? Is *they* the chairman of your company? The CEO? COO? The CFO? Is *they* your divisional manager? Is *they* your direct supervisor? Is *they* your colleagues? Is it someone who works down the hall? Who is *they*?"

I confront the group not to be antagonistic, but to expose the *blaming the culture* dynamic that more than any other, stands in the way of creating a more father-friendly workplace. It's a game of collusion played out not just in dad's workplace, but at mom's workplace, and at home between husbands and wives. No matter where the game is set in motion, it starts a self-perpetuating cycle that cannot end until at least one player refuses to play, refuses to keep the collusive system going.

Here's how *blame the culture* works in real life, in one of its many variants. Six-year-old Sarah has had a mysterious tummyache at school for the last couple of days, and the school nurse thinks maybe she should stay home for a day. It's not a major emergency, but something worth paying attention to; if it doesn't go away in a couple of days, Sarah should see a doctor.

When dad thinks about staying home with Sarah tomorrow, he factors in not only the pile of work he has to crunch through by the end of the week, and the meetings he has lined up, but how *they* will react. *They* won't like it.

When mom looks at her options, she factors in not only her own work commitments, but her understanding of the values and room for flexibility at both dad's and her jobs. She has learned to assume that at his workplace, *they* don't like it when employees are out. An absence at her workplace may inconvenience her colleagues, but the notion that *they* don't allow it does not resonate as fully. After all, she's a working mother; *they* understand and even expect her to encounter these work–family dilemmas. When she says she has to stay home tomorrow, nobody will question whether her husband can stay home instead. If someone did, she would explain that where he works, *they* are not as understanding.

For many mothers, of course, the workplace is not accommodating; *they* are not particularly understanding. I do not mean to suggest that women have it easier than men. Notice, however, that in this exchange *they* have never been spoken to. And since they have never been spoken to, they are firmly in place next week, when Sarah is back in school. Since dad did not go home to be with Sarah, there has been no change in the message to other fathers at his company: *They* still don't allow that for fathers. Since mom stayed at home, she reinforces the implicit message at her company: *They* do tolerate it, in some cases sanction it, for mothers.

In reality, of course, it's more complex. Mom may want to be at home with Sarah or feel more strongly than dad that she should be home. Dad may be under particular pressure to complete a project at a time when mom has more slack. But I have been amazed to find that even when dad is the one who takes care of Sarah, he is sometimes so worried about *them* that he explains his absence by saying he is sick, not his child. At a recent meeting in New York, for example, a colleague named Doris explained that she had only been able to fly in from Chicago that morning because her husband, Fred, was staying home with their son Timmy, who woke up vomiting in the middle of the night. "But," she said somewhat sheepishly, "Fred called in to say that *he* was sick." It wasn't that Fred was at any risk of losing a day's pay for being home with Timmy; he was a senior in-house lawyer at a Fortune 500 corporation. Doris explained, "They're not that used to fathers taking off for their kids where he works."

Once again, the invisible *they*—a stand-in for corporate culture—reared its head. Even though Fred stayed home, the game of collusion was still being played—between Fred and his company and between Fred and Doris. *He* did not feel comfortable challenging what he thought was a cultural norm. And *she* did not feel comfortable asking him to challenge it.

Blame the culture is rarely a game played just by fathers. Whenever a dad plays, there is usually a mom playing, who may not realize she is a silent partner. When I was explaining this dynamic at a lecture, a woman in the audience literally gasped out loud, saying, "My goodness, that's exactly what I do." She had instructed their school-age children that if they had a problem after school, they should call her office, not daddy's. Why? In part, perhaps, because she felt guilty about working or wanted to hold on to her identification as the primary parent. But she realized that she also assumed, for no particularly good reason at all, that at dad's business *they* would not condone those types of nonbusiness interruptions.

It's often hard to pin down where *blame the culture* starts—at work or at home—but it really doesn't matter. What matters is that the game is played in both places and that the assumptions made in both places are interlocking. Mothers and fathers continue to play this game together, reinforcing the very stereotypes that have become dysfunctional for both of them. Collusion at the company breeds collusion in the family, which breeds collusion at the company—his and hers. Round and round it goes, trapping all the players in what can be no more than an illusion.

Some challenge the notion of corporate culture as the primary culprit. According to Burke Stinson, spokesperson for AT&T, "I don't believe much in corporate culture. The inhibitor to being a good partner or dad is really in the personality of the individual. It is up to men to look within themselves—do they really want to be a good father or husband or do they continue to be driven by career ambitions? The answer has often been 'me first.' It is more challenging to deal with this attitude than with corporate culture."

Is personal responsibility all there is to it? Does culture play no role? Stinson is right that it is harder to look within than to blame without, but it's important not to completely blame individual fathers or mothers. None of us works in total isolation. Culture does have an impact—an enormous impact—on what we feel permitted to do at the workplace or anyplace. And when it comes to balancing work and family life, research consistently confirms the importance of workplace culture on individual behavior. According to Arlene Johnson, vice president of FWI, "Managers' attitudes and the general work environment have been shown to be even more important than specific policies in helping staff balance work and personal responsibilities." FWI's *National Study of the Changing Workforce* found, "The more unsupportive the supervisor, the more conflict the employee (and the spouse) feels."

So how do employees know if a supervisor is unsupportive? It's usually apparent when you have a "boss from hell" or, at the other extreme, when you have a boss who is "super supportive", and makes it clear that he or she expects you to take care of family needs. But when it is not clear—and this is true more often than not—fathers often assume the boss and coworkers will be unsupportive. So they play it safe, not asking for what they need, but doing what they think the boss wants. That way they can protect their jobs and their family's financial well-being, even if it creates other types of family stress.

Let's go back to the predictable "they don't allow that here" impasse in my DaddyStress/Daddy Success seminars. The group usually decides with much laughter that *they* is not the chairman or the CFO or anybody else they can actually name. Then I ask for a volunteer to do a role-playing exercise.

"Pretend I'm *they*," I say, "but not in some abstract way. Pretend I'm your immediate supervisor, and you need to make a request to stay at home with your daughter. Of course, you'll make up any work you miss. What would you say? How would you say it? What would you do if I did not meet your request?"

All the guys in the group start to fidget. Their eyes, which had been riveted to me, start to wander, looking around the room to see who is raising his hand to volunteer, since it is certainly not they! This reveals just how uncomfortable many men are about asking these questions.

But when a volunteer does comes forward, it often becomes clear to the group that the feared repercussions do not exist. At Merrill Lynch, for example, a volunteer said to me, "I see exactly what you're getting at. Before we do this exercise, let me tell you about a similar situation just two weeks ago. We needed someone to stay home with my son who wasn't feeling well. I didn't want to bring it up with my boss, so my wife took the day off. The next day my boss just happened to ask me how things were, and I mentioned that Barbara was at home keeping Teddy supplied with chicken soup and ginger ale. She immediately offered, 'Why don't you work at home?' I never had any sense before that she was concerned about my family. But it made me realize that for no reason I had been afraid to ask."

To break the *blame the culture* cycle, fathers "need to deal with the guts problem," says Perry Christensen, former director of Human Resources Strategy and Planning at Merck, who has wide knowledge of other companies as member of the Conference Board's Work and Family Research Council. Is creating change only a matter of fathers standing up for themselves?

When I ask Christensen what he means by "guts," he reels off a list of factors that are—we can't get away from it—deeply ingrained in corporate culture. "First of all, managers aren't very good managers so they opt to use commitment levels that they measure by face time. The only distinguishing factors are the length of hours you put in; that creates a barrier for men as well as women." He also points to the double standard. "We want to treat everyone equitably and fairly, but there is still the perception that this is just for women." This brings us back to the dilemma of change: Personal responsibility and corporate culture are intertwined. When corporate culture changes, individuals will change, but the corporate culture can't change unless individuals change.

Whats the way out of this loop? The best way I have found is to recognize up front that individuals have responsibility to change their environments *and* that organizations also have responsibility to change their environments, which so profoundly influence individuals. The most important dimension of cultural change and where there is the most potential for individuals and organizations to find common ground is by challenging assumptions about time usage that are deeply woven into the corporate culture. What families need to stay healthy is what businesses need to be productive: greater flexibility.

FLEXIBILITY FOR WORKING FATHERS (AND MOTHERS)

What do working fathers want most to help reduce the stress of balancing work and family life? More time? More money? Actually, neither. What dads want is more *control* over their work time—not less work, but more discretion over when they perform their work.

Lack of control over work schedules is the primary source of job stress for working fathers, just as it is for working mothers. That's one of the surprising findings of Rosalind Barnett's study for the National Institutes of Mental Health. Even in this period of downsizing, "Adequate compensation and job security were not major stresses for dual-earner couples. Much more stressful were issues of variety and control. Having to do dull, monotonous work and having to work under time pressure with conflicting demands were the most trying of job conditions for both men and women." It makes sense, then, that sociologist Scott Coltrane of the University of California at Riverside found that the primary factor in the ability of mothers and fathers to reduce work–family conflict and to share household tasks was the ability to schedule their work hours with some degree of flexibility.

Interest in flexibility is not new, but the extent to which employees see it as critical to their job satisfaction keeps rising. In a 1988 survey, Gallup found that 23 percent of women and 16 percent of men said that flexible hours were "essential" in a job. One year later, a Roper Organization poll for Virginia Slims found that 40 percent of men and 42 percent of women said that more flexible work hours would make them "much more or somewhat more satisfied with their jobs." In 1992, an American Management Association survey of 5,000 employees found that the number-one issue for 87 percent of respondents was more flexibility in the workplace. And when FWI conducted its *National Study of the Changing Workforce*, it found that while mothers and fathers would both like to reduce their total work time by 15 percent, what each wanted more than a reduction in hours was more control over the hours they work.

For the most part, employers have viewed flexibility as an accommodation to working mothers. That's actually one of the reasons Hewlett-Packard began pioneering it in this country in 1972. But increasingly companies are finding that giving workers more control over their time is an important factor in recruiting and retaining fathers, and in boosting overall worker productivity. Nowhere is the evidence for this more clear than at DuPont, where 75 percent of employees are male.

In 1984 and 1985, in its first survey to identify the work–family concerns of its employees, DuPont found that child care was an issue affecting the majority of *all* its employees with children under thirteen. According to Faith Wohl, then director of human resources at DuPont, the data redefined child care for top management "as more than a female 'concern.'" By 1988, just four years later, DuPont had "found startling changes in attitudes of male employees," according to Wohl. "Men now indicate that concern about children and child care is affecting them on the job on a day-to-day basis, is presenting them with difficulties comparable to those reported by women, and is having an impact on their career expectations and aspirations."

By 1995, DuPont's workplace flexibility program, which allows a wide range of scheduling options, had been used by 41 percent of its 100,000 domestic employees. Employees using or aware of the flexibility program were the most committed in the company and the least likely to feel overwhelmed or burnt out. They were 45 percent more likely to "strongly agree that they will expend extra effort on the company's behalf" and 33 percent more likely to report "feeling supported by the company." "We don't do this because it is the nice thing to do," says a DuPont senior executive. "We do it because it is a direct business benefit."

And it is becoming a business imperative. For Hewlett-Packard, giving as many workers as possible control of their time has become a core business strategy for moving into the twenty-first century. Hewlett-Packard's CEO, Lew Platt, a former single parent and a vocal champion of flexibility, says, "The idea that it's possible to be a dedicated employee—and work something different from an eight-hour-per-day/five-day workweek—is gathering momentum. . . . I don't want to imply that any employee has an inalienable right to work whatever hours are most convenient, because the requirements of the business and our customers may not make every work option feasible. But we are learning that there's more than one way to be successful."

Case in point: Ted Tucker, a program manager in Hewlett-Packard's Corporate Quality Group, has a job that requires so much travel that he is away from his wife and two sons, ages five and nine,

50 percent of the time. When he learned through an e-mail message about corporatewide opportunities for flexible scheduling, Tucker put in a request to reschedule his hours to allow him to take every other Friday off.

> "When you're leaving on a Monday you often have so much preparation to do that you don't really have the Sunday free for your family. Having two days in a row for the family, Friday and Saturday, is very important. I use the Friday morning to bike to school with my younger son. Then my wife and I have about three-and-a-half hours to ourselves—we don't have any other time during the week when things are just quiet. Then in the afternoon I do one of two things. Either I do errands that would usually take up my time during the weekend and take time away from the family, or I do things with my children because they have half-days on Fridays. We'll go to the driving range and play golf, go bowling, or fly a kite. We'll go to an amusement park or to the zoo, places that are sometimes easier to go to during the week than the weekends. When you travel a lot you can become a kind of occasional player in the household. These Fridays allow us a time to catch up."

An unusual arrangement? Of the forty people in Tucker's department, ten are using variable work schedules, most for family reasons.

Other highly competitive companies are now moving in the same direction. In 1994, after employees at Nabisco, Inc. headquarters in New Jersey chose control over time as their number-one worry, the company began offering flexible schedules to attract top talent and keep it from drifting to nearby companies such as Warner-Lambert, IBM, and AT&T. Meanwhile, AT&T's Global Business Communications Systems was learning through exit analyses that "28 percent of management associates left the company because workplace schedules were inflexible and 38 percent cited an inability to balance work and family."

Although most who take advantage of flexible schedules are working mothers, fathers are using them to an extent not generally acknowledged. When flexible schedules were introduced in two federal agencies in Washington, D.C., in 1980, nearly half the fathers changed their schedules and spent more time with their children. At White Plains, New York-based Nynex, which provides phone service for the northeastern United States, men use full-time flexible options such as compressed hours as often as women do. And at CIGNA, a 1994 survey of 1,500 employees nationwide found that 41.1 percent of male employees were taking advantage of at least one of the company's flexible work arrangements. That was less than the 52.5 percent of female employees, but still higher than the company expected. "We were surprised at the sheer number of men using the program," says Marjorie Stein, vice president of corporate employee relations, "but not at all disappointed." In fact, of all the company's programs, flextime was the most popular.

Creating flexibility for mothers, fathers, and all workers is increasingly a key bottom-line business strategy, according to Charles Rodgers, a principal at Boston-based WFD, which advises 150 major corporate clients, "The way you manage people with family responsibilities ten years ago is the way you have to manage all people, regardless of family responsibility, if you want them to meet your business goals. Both men and women are becoming increasingly frustrated over control conditions of how, when, and where they do their work. Companies that haven't figured out how to give people more autonomy are going to pay a price. There's not much of a gender gap here."

WHY MORE MEN DON'T FLEX

Hewitt Associates, a consulting firm in Lincolnshire, Illinois, has found the percentage of companies offering some sort of flexible work options creeping steadily upward from 58 percent in 1992 to 60 percent in 1993 to 66 percent in 1995. It's hard to interpret these figures, though, because "just about every company has someone working flextime on an ad hoc basis," says Karol L. Rose, a principal of Kwasha Lipton. "When companies say, 'Oh, we have flextime, we have telecommuting,' what they mean is, 'We have an individual working here who does this.' They don't mean they have an integrated system."

But there is, indeed, still a wide gap in the use of flexibility. Companies offer it far more than employees use it, and men are still much less likely to take advantage of it than women. To a great extent, that's because in most families women still take the lead responsibility for child and elder care; they earn less, on average, than men and are far more likely to work part time in order to manage child care. As discussed, our research also suggests that men, to a greater extent than women, are reluctant to take advantage of flexibility because of their perception of workplace culture.

Another part of the problem, as one recent multicompany study discovered, is a gap between what companies offer and what employees are aware of. When it comes to working fathers, this gap is exacerbated by the perception that flexible scheduling is sanctioned only for working mothers. Chicago lawyer Cheryl Heisler, who founded Lawternatives, a consulting firm for lawyers seeking to change careers, says many men "want to be there for the big and not-so-big events, the Little League game, or helping out their spouse." But the man who asks to take advantage of flexible scheduling is "not as highly valued or his commitment is questioned."

Lotte Bailyn, professor of organizational psychology and management at MIT's Sloan School of Management, says, "It's more difficult for men to ask for flexibility. It's seen as suspect. You're not a real man. A real man doesn't need flexibility. Are men not helping more at home because of gender issues? Are men not helping more because the workplace is so inflexible? This is a very vicious cycle we're in."

My research shows that some men have so thoroughly internalized the assumption that work–family benefits are designed for women that they do not even realize they can use them even when they are available. That is precisely what happened at NationsBank. "I never thought those kinds of programs were something I needed to pay attention to," says Henry Stillwell, a vice president who worked in trust administration at the bank's Houston office. When Stillwell's wife started a new job several hours away from home, leaving him with all the before- and after-school child care, he went to his boss and resigned. "I really walked in and resigned because I wasn't aware of any kind of program that we had," he says. "Not that it wasn't disseminated. It was that I figured it wasn't going to affect me. So I thought my only solution was to resign and get the house sold as quickly as possible and just move down to where she was and find myself something."

Stillwell's boss surprised him by offering him a flexible schedule, even allowing him to cut back from forty to thirty hours a week and to remove from his client list those customers who might have a problem with Stillwell not being accessible at the office everyday. "I was able to take care of my children," he says, "and the bank was able to retain my services. I will always be appreciative."

STRATEGIES FOR INCREASING FLEXIBILITY

How can fathers and employers stop playing the game of collusion and gain more control over their work time, which, more than any other single factor, can reduce their DaddyStress? Here are a set of principles, followed by a set of tactics for both employees and managers, to guide the change process.

Principles of Flexible Scheduling

These principles will help you to think in a fresh way about your workplace culture and lead you to assess whether you are trapped by assumptions about the use of time that are limiting both business productivity and family friendliness. They provide the backdrop for the tactics to actually implement the sort of flexibility that is the cornerstone of the father-friendly (and mother-friendly) workplace.

Flex For Competitive Business Advantage

If you think of rearranging schedules as *only* a matter of meeting family needs, you are working from the wrong paradigm. You are thinking of whatever the company lets an employee do as an *accommodation*, rather than as a way of doing business that lends you and your firm a competitive advantage.

Some of the smartest companies in the United States are learning to put employees' family needs at the core of their strategic planning, instead of at its periphery, as something to be worked around. Merck, for example, is trying to use work–family dilemmas to identify work inefficiencies and then create what Perry Christensen calls a "win–win for the employee and the company." As director of HR for Merck's Canadian subsidiary in 1991, Christensen sponsored focus groups on work–life issues. He asked what the company did that helped or hindered employees in their work–family balance: "We identified that the salespeople had received computers and were being asked to do all sorts of reports. Since they didn't want to cut into their sales time, they ended up doing the reports on evenings or weekends, which cut into their family time. We cut the reports from twenty-seven to twelve on a quarterly basis. As a result the sales force had an increase of time selling to doctors and time with their families."

Similar results were produced at Merck's 6,000-employee West Point, Pennsylvania, research and manufacturing facility. Maintaining safety at this 4.7-million-square-foot complex is a round-the-clock job for the fifteen members of the Command Center in the Site Protection Department. Two-person teams used to inspect fire systems and respond to spills and other emergencies in three 8-hour shifts per day. This required all staff to work overtime or for the Command Center to bring in workers to cover unfilled shifts. Then employees came up with a plan to increase coverage and reduce staff while enabling all staff to have more time for their families. How? "We eliminated an entire shift," says Joseph Salvia, director of site facilities engineering. "We switched to two 12-hour shifts and a rotation in which employees worked three days one week and four days the next. Instead of two 40-hour work weeks, each salaried employee worked the equivalent of eighty-four hours in two weeks. But employees got three days off one week and four days off the next. Productivity increased with the elimination of the transition time for one entire shift, morale improved, and we've got more people interested in working here. It's a training-level job, not something where you want to work too long. But now people see it as giving them more time for their personal lives."After switching to the new schedule, engineer Dave Wolfe found he had more time to spend with his three-and-a-half year-old daughter, Briana. "When I was on the normal shift I was always working 10-hour days and didn't have enough time on any weekday. Now I don't see her much on the days I'm working, but I make up for it on the days I'm home. I go and pick her up at preschool, watch her classes, watch ballet and gymnastics. Before the new schedule I could never do that."

At a Xerox customer service division in Dallas, Texas, researchers, led by professors Lotte Bailyn of MIT's Sloan School of Management and Deborah Kolb of Simmons College, found that employees' most pressing work–family need was for better control of their schedules. But employees, especially men, were reluctant to ask their managers for flexible arrangements. The pervasive assumption was that flexibility was a benefit available only to working mothers, even though there was no such policy. Kolb said:

> A system had developed that disempowered everybody. Our intervention was to make it clear that flextime benefits were open to all employees and then to leave it up to the work team—not the managers—to figure out how to use them. Everybody started using them—fathers, mothers, people who were not parents—and the business improved dramatically. The arrangement increased employee coverage at the service center, increased customer satisfaction, and reduced absenteeism by 30 percent.

Sandra Sullivan, president of Flex-It, a Connecticut-based consulting firm, explains the need to rethink the competitive business advantages of flexibility by making a comparison with the transition from the flying wedge to the passing game in football at the beginning of the twentieth century.

In 1905, football was a low-scoring running game. The offense consisted of a "flying wedge" in which seven players ran together into the middle of the opposition in the hope of gaining three or four yards. Then in 1906, the forward pass was legalized. Passing made it possible to gain forty yards with the flick of a wrist. During the first season, however, most teams stayed almost entirely with their conventional, tried-and-true running game. Recognizing that they were entering a new era in which the old football strategy was fast becoming obsolete, St. Louis University adapted, switching to an offense that used the forward pass extensively. That season, St. Louis University outscored their opponents 402–11. If St. Louis University followed the assumption that the forward pass must not be a good strategy because no teams utilized it, they would have had the same win–loss record as other teams. Instead they decided to learn about a new strategy and implement it to create a new era of football productivity. The same applies to flexibility. Working different hours offers a new "era" in business productivity. Organizations and supervisors can either stay with the old rules or adapt to the new style of play and train, plan, prepare, and implement.

Businesses that continue to think of flexibility as a benefit only for working mothers are creating a winning strategy at best for half the team. As we enter the twenty-first century, flexible schedules for working fathers and mothers—indeed, for all workers whenever possible—are the equivalent of the passing game in football at the beginning of the twentieth century.

Change, Don't Blame the Culture

Whether you are an employee or a manager, if your mindset is, "*They* don't allow that here," you are playing *blame the culture*. Don't wait for the company to make flexibility a formal policy, though you should certainly check to see what the relevant policies are.

Sometimes it takes a defining moment to clarify your values about work and family, as was the case with an executive who worked his way up from the manufacturing floor to one of the top twenty positions at a major U.S. pharmaceuticals company. According to one of his collegues, "About fifteen years ago, when his son fell and skinned his knee, he ran away from his dad because his dad's face was so unfamiliar. It was devastating, a real defining moment for him. He talked about what he should do with his wife. He decided to make clear to his supervisor what his priorities were—that if there was a soccer game he should be at, he would go. He attributes his subsequent success at work to that commitment; it forced him to be more efficient and to expect others to be the same." But you don't need a major problem or crisis to justify a request for more control of your time. In most cases, fathers don't want big blocks of time off, just some leeway around the edges to attend to small family matters that make a big difference.

You can apply this principle when working with customers or clients, too. I find that both working fathers and mothers get nervous when a customer requests a meeting that conflicts with scheduled time for family events. Rather than assuming that customer responsiveness means saying *yes* all the time, you can simply say, "I've got a conflict then; can we find another time that works?"

If you manage other people, remember the first corollary of "You don't ask, you don't get": Just because they're not asking doesn't mean they don't want. A vice president of a Fortune 500 company explains that on more than one occassion he has "criticized managers reporting to him for not knowing their people on a personal basis." For example, he found out that the father of a very low-level employee, a man too timid to ask for any time off, was going through surgery, he went to the employee's boss. He had no idea what was going on in the man's life. The vice president gave the boss a piece of his mind: "You need to know what's going on in people's lives enough to help them make the adjustments that are necessary."

"One of the key skills managers will need in the twenty-first century," says Perry Christensen, "is the ability to ask employees about their family needs and to respond to them when they hear about them."

Be Realistic, Not Arbitrary

Don't expect that you can rearrange schedules for all jobs. At the Calvert Group, which allows flexible schedules for virtually all employees. "Certain departments are still not able to have flextime," says Evelyne Steward, senior vice president of human resources. "Customer service employees are needed 9 to 5." NationsBank has found a lot of success with job-sharing in customer service departments, though not in places like the trading floor. "The market opens at 8:00 A.M.," says human resources director Kimberly Hains. "If you want to come in at 10:00 you can't." At DuPont, there is much less flexibility in manufacturing, where machines run twenty-four hours a day, than in corporate. And at Lotus, according to senior benefits specialist Helen Berry, "We have a whole group that is working at home. They come in one day a week for meetings. We have set them up with computers, desks, fax machines, and modems. We pay for all of that. But I couldn't do a work-at-home situation doing what I'm doing because the employees are my clients, my customers."

But being realistic does not mean being arbitrary, nor succumbing to the knee-jerk "we can't do that in our department" syndrome. Indeed, a 1990 study by Catalyst found initial resistance to flexible schedules by 41 percent of middle managers. But Barnie Olmstead, director of the San Francisco-based New Ways to Work, has designed or discovered all sorts of job restructuring arrangements that have proved to be highly successful once they were tried. "Like the lawyer who doesn't work on Mondays," says Olmstead. "He and his wife did not want their child in day care more than three days a week, so they each negotiated a four-day week. . . . [W]hen he switched jobs, he told them he didn't work Mondays because that's when he took care of his daughter. He realized he could do it, and the law firm saw he had been successful at it once before—they were hiring him because of his ability and had known nothing about his unusual schedule."

IBM's director of Workforce Diversity, Ted Childs, puts it this way: "I don't want any manager just to arbitrarily assume that a flexibility request could not fit into their workplace. I want them to at least explore it and examine it very carefully."

Tactics for Employees

With those three principles in mind, how can you actually negotiate a more flexible schedule and make it work for your business and your family? WFD's *Flexible Work Option Request* provided here gives "structure to the squishy process of handling flextime requests," according to Charles Rodgers (a principal of WFD and a designer of the request form). "Applicants answer questions that elicit descriptions about their desired work arrangements and, more important, about how their proposed schedules will benefit the company." It serves as a good worksheet for planning your request. I will refer to it as I take you through the tactics for two stages: getting buy-in and making it work.

FLEXIBLE WORK OPTION REQUEST

I. *(Employee completes this section)*

_____

NAME

_____

DATE

☐   ☐

EXEMPT   NONEXEMPT

_____

JOB TITLE

_____

DEPARTMENT

_____

MANAGER

_____

DATE REQUEST SUBMITTED TO MANAGER

Flexible Work Option Requested:

- Part time
- Job-sharing
  (EMPLOYEE MUST FIND PARTNER)
- Telecommuting

- Compressed work weeks
- Flextime
- Other

Describe your current schedule and the hours/schedule requested:

DAYS/HOURS (Current)	DAYS/HOURS (Requested)	ON-SITE (✓)	OFF-SITE (✓)
_____ SUNDAY	_____ SUNDAY		
_____ MONDAY	_____ MONDAY		
_____ TUESDAY	_____ TUESDAY		
_____ WEDNESDAY	_____ WEDNESDAY		
_____ THURSDAY	_____ THURSDAY		
_____ FRIDAY	_____ FRIDAY		
_____ SATURDAY	_____ SATURDAY		

_____

TOTAL WEEKLY HOURS

How will your proposed schedule sustain or enhance your team's ability to get the job done?

_____

_____

What potential barriers could your schedule raise with: (a) external customers, (b) internal customers, (c) coworkers, (d) your manager, and (e) others?

_____

_____

(Additional pages may be attached to this form if necessary)

How do you suggest overcoming any challenges with these groups?

_____

_____

_____

If applicable, describe any additional equipment/expense that your arrangement might require. Detail any short- or long-term cost savings that might result from your new schedule.

_____

_____

_____

What reasonable deliveries and measurements would you propose for you and your manager to assess how your performance is meeting or exceeding expectations?

_____

_____

_____

What review process with your manager do you propose for constructive monitoring and improvement of your flexible work option?

_____

_____

_____

II. *(Manager completes this section)*

Request for a Flexible Work Option ☐ approved or ☐ declined. If you declined this request, please describe why:

_____

_____

Date: _____ Manager's signature _____

Date: _____ Employee's signature _____

Effective date of Flexible Work Option *(If option is time limited or terminated.):*

_____

BEGINNING

_____

ENDING

Getting Buy-In

The first stage in arranging for a flexible schedule is to secure the buy-in of your supervisor and coworkers.

- **Make the business case.** Frame your request in terms of business needs, objectives, and expected results. Note that the *Flexible Work Options Request* does *not* ask the reason for the request. This is to lead managers to approve or deny the request strictly on business grounds. In principle, it should not matter whether you want some flexibility in your schedule to meet a family need (for example, to get your children off to school in the morning or to attend an occasional after-school event or teacher meeting) or for a personal need (for example, to take an exercise class). In reality, though, it is important for fathers to let it be known that they have family needs, if it is your ability to take care of those needs that will enable you to be more productive. Supervisors and colleagues do not need to know the details of personal situation, but it is reassuring to have some general sense of what your coworkers are up to and how they can be reached, if necessary.

- **Make your work commitment clear.** Aside from the objective business case, it can help to make the case in terms of your ability and desire to contribute to business goals. "I always give 100 percent to this company, and the arrangement I am proposing will enable me to keep doing that."

- **Enlist support of your coworkers and customers.** The *Flexible Work Options Request* asks employees to anticipate potential barriers from colleagues, customers, and others—as well as ways to overcome them. Sometimes it can be even more effective to consult with those groups in advance. According to work/family specialist Cindi Johnson, DuPont requires this type of process. She says, "We don't want to put managers in the position to say yes to you and no to me. It is not the team leader who makes the decision, the team does. They will be much more accepting of what I am doing if I sit down and include the team in the process." At BI, a Minneapolis-based company that specializes in training and performance improvement programs, associates can work out a wide range of flexible scheduling options without consulting with their managers. But no matter what the arrangement, they first have to work it out with their team members and their customers. According to Mary Etta Coursolle, vice president of human resources, "Once these two groups have said yes, there's no further red tape to go through."

- **Clarify performance standards.** Often there will be no change in performance standards when you work with more flexibility. But since you may be changing your amount of *face time* at work, it is important to clarify mutual expectations in terms of targets or standards: What are you expected to deliver, to whom, by when? Salespeople have quotas to meet. Consultants have clients to keep satisfied. Customer service representatives have customer satisfaction targets that have to be met, regardless of time on the job. If you can't measure your job by such clear standards, you can break it up into the tasks that can be accomplished as well, or perhaps even better, away from the office or during nontraditional business hours.

- **Propose a trial period.** If you think you'll meet with resistance, suggest that you try out the flexible schedule and plan to review it together after a set period of time.

Making It Work

The following tactics will help you make a flexible schedule work once you have secured buy-in from the appropriate supervisors and coworkers.

- **Let people know when you will be working.** Although your goal is to be evaluated on performance, not face time, it still helps to keep your colleagues, your boss, and your own employees informed that you are working when you leave. A simple, "I'll be finishing this up at home," is often all it takes.

- **Don't hide the fact that you're dealing with family issues.** This is one of those fuzzy issues for which there are no hard and fast rules, but one which everyone who works at home will confront. Does it really matter whether people know why you're not there? Well, it shouldn't, and they don't need to know the details of your family life. But if you want to not only meet your own needs but help foster a culture that supports other working fathers (and mothers), it can help to say, "I'm heading out to catch my kid's soccer game. I'll review all these files tonight and have my report in tomorrow."

- **Let people know how to reach you.** If you've got voice mail, learn how to change it remotely. That way you can keep clients and colleagues abreast of how and when they can reach you. And if you've got e-mail, include your e-mail address in your voice mail message. I give people the option of leaving a message or sending an e-mail to the address I give, indicating that it will be easier for me to respond by e-mail, even to set up a telephone appointment. Hewlett-Packard has a companywide Phone Extend program that can redirect phone calls so that a person can find you wherever you are. According to Jerry Cashman, Hewlett-Packard's Work Options manager, "You can dial an 800 number for someone, and you get a message saying, 'If you would like to reach Neil, press 1; if you would like to leave a message, press 2.' If you push 1, the call would be routed to wherever Neil is."

- **Create a professional work space at home.** If you will be working at home for part of the time, it's best to get a separate telephone line for work and put a business greeting on it, perhaps one similar to the voice mail at your office. You can use the same line for your fax and e-mail if those are services you use in your work. This lets you keep the work flow going without kids or other family members interrupting you or being inconvenienced by your work at home.

- **Report your progress.** Establish a regular schedule for reviewing progress with your boss or colleagues. This will help ensure that you and your boss's expectations are in sync, and that the work you do stays on track, to meet changing business priorities.
- **Flex the flex.** Be prepared to change whatever schedule you have established in order to meet an emergency business need.

Tactics for Managers

Are you a '50s father managing a bunch of '90s dads? Don't expect them to think or do what you did. Neither way is right or wrong, but they are different.

- **Focus on the strategic business issue.** By not asking or fixating on the reason for a flexibility request, you will avoid having to compare whether one father's baby is more important than another man's elderly in-laws or a single person's community service work. Focus on whether the work can get done and whether the employee can pull his or her own weight.
- **Experiment.** "People are reluctant to experiment because they don't want to be first out of the box," says Merck's Perry Christensen. "But if you track what happens, nine times out of ten you will find a positive experience."

That was certainly the case at NationsBank. In 1988, when the bank first offered the opportunity to flex, "there was a lot of hesitation from managers who wondered how we were ever going to get all the work done," said Matt Gorden, vice president of personnel. Now almost all 61,000 NationsBank employees can take advantage of Select Time. And at that level of implementation, the aggregate benefits to the enterprise start to become very apparent. LinguiSystems, a publisher of educational materials in East Moline, Illinois, with thirty-five employees, had to experiment to figure out how to extend flexibility to all workers while conforming to the Department of Labor requirement that hourly employees keep track of their time and get paid overtime beyond forty hours a week. According to Katherine Herbst of LinguiSystems, "Our hourly workers have just as many opportunities to go to the doctor or do errands; they just have to make up their hours at some point that week. They just have people cover for them while they are gone. They do not have to consider it sick time."

- **Make it visible.** Make it known that flexible scheduling options are being used by *all* employees, not just working mothers. Unless word gets around that fathers want and are using it, the myth will keep being perpetuated that this is only for mothers.

Case in point: Merck's Regulatory Affairs division, a group of over 100 employees, went onto a compressed work week for over a year, leaving it up to individuals to set their schedules. There was not a hitch in business—and neither headquarters nor the division's major customer knew that a change had been made. "It's important to communicate success stories about this," says Merck's Perry Christensen. Merck is now working to disseminate "some of the good stuff that people do but keep buried."

The United States' largest employer—the federal government—is now trying to make workplace flexibility more visible to all workers to counteract the tendency of employees to see this option as targeted to working mothers. On June 24, 1994, President Clinton announced an executive order "directing all executive departments and agencies to review their personnel practices and develop a plan of action to utilize the flexible policies already in place and, to the extent feasible, expand their ability to provide their employees . . . policies and procedures that promote active inclusion of fathers as well as mothers.

- **Help people believe it's OK** Many employees worry that participation in the flexible workplace program will make them more vulnerable in a downsizing.

"The biggest problem in making flexible scheduling work," according to Harris Bank's Vanessa Weathersby, "is changing people's attitudes. Although employees are reassured they won't be viewed negatively, they doubt whether that is a true statement. In a changing job market, employees are hesitant. So managers have to establish a level of comfort." To do that, it helps to have the active and aggressive support of the chief executive.

Ron Compton, chairman, CEO, and president of Aetna Life & Casualty Co., Hartford, has often told employees that the old rules were designed "to accommodate men whose wives were home full time." But at Aetna today, less than 10 percent of workers are part of families that have someone at home full time caring for a dependent, so "those rules just don't fit anymore." If Aetna can keep a valued person from leaving by "a little scheduling creativity," the company makes every effort do so, he says.

When NationsBank implemented companywide Select Time, CEO Hugh McColl told senior executives he would "personally waste any manager who doesn't support this program," according to NationsBanks former director of work–family programs, Karen Geiger.

When Nynex found some employees worrying about whether participation in the flexible workplace program could make them more vulnerable in a downsizing, the company implemented a proactive educational policy. According to Robyn Phillips, Nynex director of human resources, "When we find groups of employees who have an environment where flexibility can work, we discuss it with them and promote it by giving examples of success" from within the company. Ultimately, it comes down to the relationship between the employee and the supervisor, however, and not all those relationships have the optimal level of trust. The Nynex HR department tries to show that productivity and loyalty improve when flexible work arrangements are available; where successful, they can promote the program more easily.

- **Develop—but don't choke on—guidelines.** Written guidelines are important to keep the rules of the game clear and consistent for everyone involved. "But don't overdo it," says NationsBank's Kimberly Hains. "Even with 61,000 employees, we don't write a lot of policies and books." At Tom's of Maine, a company of just 65 employees, the motto is, "Let's not kill our employees with the bullets in memos. Let's just do it."

- **Conduct ongoing review and training.** WFD conducts ongoing training for employees and managers in the use of the *Flexible Work Option Request* form. In role-playing sessions, they take turns asking for and then granting or denying requests for flexible schedules. According to IBM's Ted Childs, training is important "so that managers understand the value of it and are not evaluating it in the context of what it was like twenty years ago, but rather what it is like today in today's work force."

- **Measure output, not input.** Everybody says this, but it is much harder to do than anybody says. It causes anxiety for both the employer and employee. After NationsBank acquired a lot of banks in the 1980s, it had no choice but to shift away from valuing face time. Its operations were so spread out that peolpe had to rely less on face-to-face interaction. At DuPont, Cindi Johnson says, "The manager must let go of control and trust employees to get the job done. Remember, if an employee is working at home not getting work done, work at home is not the problem; performance is the problem."

THE LONG VIEW

American business is often criticized for looking at quarterly earnings without taking a long-term perspective. The same short-term thinking can also skew our view of what it takes to change the workplace culture and what will happen if we do, especially regarding something so central to the culture as shared ideas and assumptions about the use of time.

When John Hancock Financial Services started exploring more flexible work scheduling, there was initial fear, says Kathy Hazzard, manager of Work and Family Programs. "If people could come in at 6:30 A.M., everyone would do it and then the afternoons would not be covered. But focus groups eased the fear. Really, everyone just wanted to be treated like an adult and given more control over their time." Bit by bit, as one department after another proves its success with flexible scheduling, the company is moving toward wider implementation.

While flexibility is critical, it is not a panacea.

Such increased control will *not*, it is important to note, reduce to a significant degree the immediate need that so many families have for child care. But it will reduce the pressure that so many families face in trying to get their children to and from day care. Being able to arrive a half-hour late or to leave a half-hour early from work can enable an anxious father or mother to channel energy into getting work done rather than worrying about how their family needs are letting the business down, or vice versa.

More flexible schedules will not immediately change the balance of work done by men and women within their households. But flexible schedules are the benefit more likely to be used by fathers than any other work family benefit, because they do not compromise family income. They will make it possible for mothers and fathers to decide who will be responsible for what aspects of child and family care in new and often more equitable ways.

They will enable more fathers to devote time to the need of their own children and of other children in their communities to have men coaching, mentoring, or volunteering in schools.

More flexible schedules at a few companies will not transform the workplace overnight. But in the long view, they are one of the steps that can accumulate to make it possible for your son or daughter to enter a different workplace culture twenty years from today.

Chapter 5

Managing Paternity Leave
A Smart Investment

At The Fatherhood Project, we get lots of calls from the press, but on Friday, April 26, 1996, the phones didn't stop ringing. That was the day Microsoft Chairman Bill Gates's wife, Melinda French, a former Microsoft marketing manager, delivered an eight-pound, six-ounce baby girl named Jennifer Katharine. Billionaire Bill was a father.

"Would Bill Gates take paternity leave? Should Bill Gates take paternity leave?" is what the press wanted to know. He was entitled to twelve weeks at home by both Microsoft policy and the Family and Medical Leave Act, which had become the law of the land in 1993. Even though the leave would be unpaid, most reporters thought that with a net worth then approaching $1.5 billion, Gates could afford a few weeks off.

The media, of course, was looking to Gates's behavior as part of a larger story. What would Bill Gates's decision say about the current and future state of fatherhood? If he took paternity leave, what sort of message would it send to fathers at Microsoft and across America? And if he didn't, what would that say?

According to *Information Week*, a computer trade journal, "Several Microsoft investors reportedly expressed concern that the birth of Bill Gates's daughter on April 26, 1996, might affect his leadership of the company." Not to worry. According to the story sent out by the wire services, based on a press release from Microsoft headquarters, "Dad, who was present at the birth at Bellevue's Overlake Hospital, isn't opting for paternity leave but will take 'several days off.'" At the birth of his daughter, Bill Gates did exactly what most American men still do—relied on a brief, informal arrangement rather than on the longer formal one to which he was entitled.

What do I think he should have done? The answer isn't simple.

When National Public Radio's business show, *Marketplace*, asked me what advice I would give to Gates, I couldn't help giving reporter Sarah Gardner a bit of advice first. After doing lots of interviews about paternity leave over many years, I have become wary of a journalistic syndrome I call *paternity leave preoccupation*, the alarming degree to which paternity leave usage rates are taken as an indicator of men's commitment to their families. I explained:

> Please don't turn this into one of those stories that uses paternity leave at childbirth as the *only* way to explain whether fathers are *really* participating more in their children's lives. This has got to be a very special time for him, and he should enjoy it fully; but he should realize—and the media should realize—that there are lots of years of childrearing ahead. It's going to be important for Bill Gates to be connected to his daughter everyday—on all the days that seem to blend into one another and on all the days that stand out as special. The media should be talking with Bill Gates a year from now when Jennifer is taking her first steps, three years from now when it's her first day of preschool, eight years from now when she's part of an after-school soccer league, fifteen years from now when she's going on her first date, and twenty-two years from now when she's about to take her first job out of college.

My advice was common sense, what any experienced parent would say. So why does paternity leave continue to serve as the barometer of social change for the media? For one simple and largely overlooked reason. Paternity-leave use captures and compresses—in one simple measure—the strongest of hopes and fears about whether men in America are changing.

For the hopeful, increased use of leave signals social progress, greater sharing by fathers. Optimists can take encouragement from the fact that male family-leave takers at AT&T increased 50 percent between 1993 and 1994, even though the leap was from 4 percent to 6 percent.

For the cynical, low levels of paternity leave use prove that implementing programs and policies for fathers won't make a difference because they won't use them anyway. As an article in *The Economist* put it, "[The reality is] very few take paternity leave . . . . Other than scattered spotting in California's Berkeley, north London, and a few Swedish suburbs, the New Man does not exist."

The mistake in both of these assessments is the application of a maternal standard—comparing men to women as if they *should* use their parental leave in the same way, as if the only way for a man to balance work and family is to take an extended period of time off. It's an ideologically based point of view that ignores the reality of most families' lives: On average, men still earn more than women, and many women want to physically recover and breast-feed the babies they have nurtured in their bodies for the previous nine months. If mom is breast-feeding and if dad's income is greater than hers, it makes personal and economic sense for mom to take the leave to which she's entitled and collect at least six weeks disability pay; since most paternity leave is unpaid, dad would have to forfeit his income at the very time the family is incurring additional expenses.

There's another, even more powerful fear underlying the preoccupation with paternity leave. For some, any increased use of leave by men threatens to undermine not only traditional gender roles at home, but also the work ethic that supports the United States economy.

I first discovered this fear more than twenty years ago when the California Fair Employment Practice Commission (FEPC) was preparing statewide guidelines for the elimination of sex discrimination in hiring practices. In public hearings held in 1974, when several men and women asked the FEPC to recommend paternity leave as an option equivalent to maternity leave, one of the commissioners said, quite emotionally, "Small business cannot bear the brunt of all this childbearing deal.... I've been a father and a grandfather, and I don't see why a father should have to have leave. It doesn't make sense to me. He can cripple a small business. Even a good salesman in a small business—you take him away, and you can destroy the business. I know a lot of these things aren't so politically good to be saying, but it can go to extremes and endanger the whole economy."

In 1993, almost twenty years later, this very fear surfaced when Houston Oilers' offensive tackle David Williams missed a football game against the New England Patriots so that he could be with his wife Debi during and right after the birth of their first child, Scot. Although the Oilers beat the Patriots, Williams was fined his weekly salary of $111,000 for staying by Debi's side. The story made headlines around the nation for weeks. Williams's teammates and most of the fans—even in a football-fanatic town like Houston—thought he did the right thing. His father said, "He's proved to me he is a real man," and many female columnists nominated him for Father of the Year, especially after he said, "Whatever the fine, it's money well spent. I don't regret what I've done."

But Oilers' line coach Bob Young saw it differently. Williams's paternity leave *had* endangered the business. "They ought to suspend him for a week, maybe two. Everybody wants to be with his wife. But that's like if World War II was going on and you said, 'I can't go fly. My wife's having a baby.' You have to go to work—especially when you get paid like that."

New York Times sports columnist Robert Lipsyte caught better than any other observer just how deeply the fears about paternity leave run in the American psyche: "[M]any male fans felt justifiably confused, even betrayed, by Williams's Daddy Track. Wasn't football a symbolic reconstitution of the platoon, the posse, the work gang, the factory line, where real men knew they could count on one another to cover their backs? It was a preparation for war, remember. Did anyone slip out of the Alamo on paternity leave?"

Three years later, when Jennifer Gates was born, lots of people were watching to see if Billionaire Bill would slip out of Fort Microsoft.

Is social progress being made because David Williams stayed home and sacrificed $111,000? Is the American competitive spirit safe because Bill Gates was back in his office three days after his first child was born?

These are both wrong questions. The simple fact is, more men want to take some time off at one of the defining moments of their lives: when their children are born, when their children need them for illness, or for other important reasons. Two decades of work with companies and fathers have shown me that paternity leave, when managed well by fathers and employers, is a smart investment that can benefit fathers, families, and businesses.

WHY TAKE PATERNITY LEAVE?

You *should* take some time off, even if your yearly salary is what Bill Gates earns in a nanosecond.

If it's a first child, you're about to take a quantum leap into adulthood. Give yourself the space to absorb what has just happened: You are now responsible for a totally helpless human being who needs you in order to survive and grow. No matter what she says or how calmly she behaves, your wife is just as excited and scared as you are; she needs your support.

If it's a second or even a sixth child, you're in for what continues to be one of life's most magical and joyful experiences. Give yourself the time to dwell on the miracle that has just taken place. And remember, even if it is just child number two, the work load has just quadrupled for your wife and you; she needs your support even more than with child number one.

So do your kids. For all family members, this is a major life transition. Kids need you to help them adjust to being a big brother or sister, especially if they are no longer your "one and only" child.

How much time you should take off—and when you should take it—depends on many factors: what support networks you have in place (parents, in-laws, friends, neighbors, and so on), what financial resources you have and how much the family will sacrifice financially if you take leave, what the needs are at your workplace and at your wife's, whether your wife is breast-feeding, and, most important, what you and your wife *want* to do.

You might want to take a formal extended leave for any number of reasons. In addition to getting to know your child at this very special moment, if your wife earns more than you, it might make more financial sense for you to stay home. If you want to extend the length of your child's time at home before entering child care, you might want to begin taking your leave after your wife finishes hers and is about to return to work.

In the rest of this chapter, I'll give you the full story on paternity leave: who is taking it and how they make it work, what benefits dads and companies are reaping from it, and how to make it work for you. One of the most important things to know is that you don't have to take paternity leave the way most mothers take maternity leave—in a straight block of time immediately after the birth or adoption of a child. Under federal law and many corporate policies, it is possible for dads (and moms) to create flexible approaches to parental leave that are much better at meeting the needs of both business and family.

WHY WE DON'T SEE MORE MEN TAKING LEAVE

Who takes paternity leave? Probably more dads than you realize, but they don't call it that. Much leave is taken as what I refer to as *underground leave.*

In the 1995 season premier of *NYPD Blue*, tough-guy Detective Andy Sipowicz (Dennis Franz) tells Lt. Fancy (James McDaniel) the news about his wife's pregnancy and fills out the police department's new paternity-leave request form in triplicate. But in real life, most men keep their leave underground, avoiding association with "official" policies.

Most men scrape together sick days, vacation days, and an informal discretionary day to give their families time without taking away their income. In a 1988 survey of 120 randomly chosen fathers in Massachusetts, Joseph Pleck found that 87 percent used this method to put together an average of 5.3 days off from work when a child was born. Before the Family and Medical Leave Act went into effect, a National Institutes of Mental Health study of 550 new fathers in Wisconsin, a state where either parent was allowed to take up to six weeks of unpaid leave, discovered the same pattern. Only 1 percent of fathers took three or more weeks of leave, but 98 percent of men took some time off, and, on average, men took five days by using a combination of paid vacation time, sick days, or personal days. Still, only 11 percent availed themselves of the official paternity leave policy.

Why the reluctance to use formal leave? Because whatever the policies of their companies, fathers still often feel the culture does not really endorse it, and they will hurt their careers. In Wisconsin, 63 percent of the fathers studied thought their supervisors wouldn't want them to take a long leave, and 43 percent thought they would get a negative reaction from their coworkers. And some fathers were right. In 1983, Catalyst, a New York-based research and consulting group, asked chief executives and human resource directors at 384 large companies what amount of time was "reasonable" for fathers to take off for paternity leave. For 119 companies—41 percent—the answer was "none." Shortly after Representative Patricia Schroeder introduced the Parental Leave and Disability Leave Act of 1985— which took almost a decade to become the Family and Medical Leave Act—Malcolm Forbes opined, "New daddies need paternity leave like they need a hole in the head."

Although understanding your corporate culture is important for business survival, blaming it or buying into it just keeps men's legitimate needs for paternity leave underground. And in my experience, the culture around paternity leave changes after a few pioneers take it.

Here, for example, is what happened when the first man applied for company-sponsored paternity leave at one of America's most "family-friendly" companies, as told to me by the man's boss. "I took him aside and said, as your boss I have to grant you this leave. But as you're friend, I'm advising you not to request it. Just take some vacation time if you want to be with your family. Applying for paternity leave will send the wrong message around here about your commitment to work."

The employee thanked his boss for the advice, thought it over, and returned to explain that he didn't want to sacrifice his vacation. He wasn't planning to be on vacation when he was on paternity leave—there would be plenty of work to do—so he wanted to save his real vacation for a time when he and his wife had settled in with their first child.

The upshot was that the boss ended up rethinking his own position. He realized how valuable it would have been to him to take some time when his children, now grown, were born. He realized that he was passing on the wrong legacy to his young colleague and, rather than cautioning other fathers against taking leave, began to encourage them to do it.

A similar story played out at Apple Computer, after Jim Cutler, one of the company's top 140 employees, became the first dad to use the new paternity-leave policy. Within a couple of months, three other men requested it. At Beth Israel Hospital in Boston, Massachusetts, Laura Avakian, vice president for human resources, reports the same pattern. "I remember sitting in on a meeting with male physicians around the paternity leave question. I was so conscious of how differently they were talking about it from the way women would talk about it. There was an embarrassment that their co-workers would somehow think less of them for taking the time. Now I have seen a huge shift in that attitude. Success breeds success. As one man sees another doing it, it creates an environment where it is okay. It is kind of like the first woman to get promoted to an executive job. It is a lot easier for the second and the third."

But is there no career penalty for men who choose parental

leave? To date, no research has actually addressed this issue; it has looked at career breaks only where men have lost their jobs involuntarily. For example, when Pace University researchers Joy Schneer and Frieda Reitman examined the impact of a brief period of unemployment on the careers of 38-year-old MBA graduates, they found that men who had been out of work for a few months earned, on average, 25 percent less than other men. But all of these men had been involuntarily unemployed; they had lost a job, perhaps raising eyebrows when they went to their next interview.

Paternity leave, by contrast, does not involve loss of a job and probably would not even show up on a resume as a career break. If it did, there's a big difference between saying "I was fired" and "My company was so terrific and enthusiastic about my work that I was able to take two months off when the twins were born and then get right back to work."

In 1994, when Schneer and Reitman followed up with their MBA graduates—then, on average, aged 44 and earning $100,000 a year—they found that women, but not men, took time off to care for their families. So far the best research evidence suggests not that paternity leave harms a father's career, but that fear of career harm prevents fathers from taking leave.

Until paternity leave stops being such an underground phenomenon, we probably will not have scientifically reliable information about its effects on a man's career. Fortunately, it is beginning to come aboveground, especially at the few companies that are offering paternity leave with pay. At Lotus Development Corporation, for example, here is what Gary Cormier, human resource account manager to Worldwide Sales, a group of 1,200 employees, has to say about the leave taken by Nick Camelio:

> We don't have a problem of people not being committed when they go away on parenting leave. . . . In fact, when Nick returned I gave him a promotion and salary increase. Nick was overwhelmed when his baby was born. She was waking up in the middle of the night; he was

learning how to change her. It occurred to me as I was hearing this from Nick that it was so appropriate that he was focusing on this at this time of his life, not worried about work. It must be awfully difficult for someone to ignore such an important event in his life. He came back into the job very focused on work. Nick's productivity level was very high, and I think that is a result of the paternity-leave benefit. I wouldn't have given him a promotion if I didn't see this level of commitment that was astounding. It was a real easy sell to get him more money because I had such great data from the clients that he was doing a great job.

WHAT A DIFFERENCE A PAY MAKES

The Family and Medical Leave Act (FMLA), which took effect on August 5, 1993, as the first bill signed into law by President Clinton, requires employers with fifty or more employees within a seventy-five-mile radius of the worksite to provide up to twelve weeks of unpaid leave a year for the birth or adoption of a child or for family or personal medical problems. Any employee who has worked at least 1,200 hours for a full year must be able to return to the same or a similar position, and during the leave the employer must continue to pay for benefits the employee had while working.

FMLA covers about two-thirds of the U.S. labor force in both the public and private sector, including about 49 percent of employed fathers. An explanation of your rights and answers to the most common questions about taking leave under the FMLA are included at the end of this chapter.

Under FMLA, more men are taking leave for slightly longer periods of time, but the change has not been dramatic. Informal arrangement still predominate, with about 15 percent of eligible men also taking advantage of formal paternity leave. According to the Commission on Family and Medical Leave, established by the U.S.

Congress to monitor the first two years' experience with FMLA, "Women are more likely to take most types of family leave" (58.2 percent vs. 41.8 percent) and to do so for a longer period (41 days on average for women and 33 for men). But when it comes to caring for a newborn, most employees were still off the job for less than a month; almost 80 percent of those who had to care for a seriously ill child were off the job for a week or less.

More men would take leave if they could afford to, but taking leave usually means sacrificing income. The Commission on Family and Medical Leave found that men outnumbered women almost seven to one (14.4 percent vs. 2.1 percent) when it came to needing but not taking leave to care for a newborn, adopted, or foster child. In more than two-thirds of those cases, dad felt he couldn't afford it, while in others he was afraid he would lose his job or hurt his job advancement. In still other cases he was denied the request by his employer.

Providing pay is proving to be one of the most effective ways to address two of the biggest deterrents to men's use of leave—sacrifice of family income and the fear that the culture is nonsupportive. In 1990, for example, when NationsBank decided to offer paid paternity and adoption leave, the number of men opting for it "increased tenfold," according to Virginia Stone Mackin, director of work and family programs. "I think men felt self-conscious and felt some pressure about taking it, but as they saw the environment was accepting, we saw the numbers increase." At Immunex Corp., a 750-employee firm in Seattle, fathers never asked about paternity leave; but when a five-day paid leave was implemented in 1995, ten new dads, including an adoptive father, used it right away. At Lotus Development Corp., which offers four weeks of paid leave to fathers and adoptive parents, the proportion of fathers who take leave climbed from 33 percent of leave-taking employees in 1994 to 40 percent in 1995.

In the United States, according to one recent estimate, 1 percent of fathers in either the public or private sector are eligible for some amount of paid paternity leave, compared to 3 percent of mothers in the private and 1 percent of mothers in the public sector. But in 1996, three years after the FMLA went into effect, there was an encouraging sign of change from, of all places, Wall Street. Merrill Lynch instituted a policy giving all full-time male employees the option to take a one-week paid leave within three months of the birth of a child. After receiving written requests and conducting focus groups with male employees, Merrill Lynch issued an open letter to all U.S. employees indicating that "the move comes in response to expressed employee need."

THE PAYOFF FOR BUSINESS

What about the business need to maintain productivity? Do family leaves hurt business? In its report to the U.S. Congress on the first two years experience with FMLA, the Commission on Family and Medical Leave found, by and large, "no noticeable effect on business performance." Although the commission combined leave taken for all reasons, it found an average of 90 percent of worksites reporting "no noticeable effect on productivity, profitability, and growth." It did, however, find some significant effects on employee performance: In 8.3 percent of cases, use of FMLA had a positive effect on employee career advancement (compared to a negative effect in 0.8 percent of cases and no noticeable effect in 91 percent of cases); and in 4.9 percent of cases, it had a positive effect on employee turnover (compared to a negative effect in 0.4 percent of cases and no noticeable effect in 94.7 percent).

"If I didn't get two weeks off," says Kevin Reese, a regional marketing consultant at the Calvert Group in Bethesda, Maryland, "I would not have gotten much sleep at night. It helped keep my productivity up."

The positive effect on turnover is well explained by Mark Falls, a microsystems analyst at First Union Bank, who took four weeks off when his daughter was born:

> I have never taken more than a week of vacation at a time, other than this paternity leave. From the long-term perspective, a company is doing itself a huge favor by

advocating this sort of thing. It builds loyalty. It shows good faith. You may not be here for a month, but I am not worried about the work lost this month. I am more focused on our relationship and how that is going to be improved. I would think that if I was managing people that wanted to do this, I would do it, because it would benefit me as well in the long term from a company loyalty perspective.

The ability to build loyalty—an increasingly precious value for any business to instill in both its customers and employees—is exactly why some businesses are championing paid paternity leave. Cameron Markby Hewitt, a London-based law firm, offers men the same terms as women—two weeks paid leave, one year unpaid leave, and a loyalty bonus for returning at the end of that time. Patagonia allows employees two months of paid and two months of unpaid leave and allows them to return gradually to work. Patagonia chairman Yvon Chouinard wants his employees focused. "I want them to bond with their children. If they are distracted by guilt, they can't focus." Sharon Beard, owner of a small company in Florida, Hurricane Fence, does not want the FMLA to be extended to cover small businesses like hers. But she pays paternity leave to reward loyalty. "I have given family paid leave for one of our guys. He had requested a leave. I gave him two weeks off paid. This was a worker who showed up every day, never complained, you know, gave the job his all. And you do that, you work with your employees, you value your employees."

THE PAYOFF FOR FAMILIES

Men who take paternity leave—whether paid or unpaid—almost uniformly report it as being invaluable for them and their families. Even a period of two weeks can help a dad get accustomed to the routines of caring for a baby and develop some of the skill and comfort level he needs going forward.

"I felt invested in the process from the beginning," says Paul Johnson of LinguiSystems. "You can't say you don't know how to change diapers. You are there, you gotta do it. There was real bonding going on. It was great for the whole family unit."

And it can make clear in a way that no book on child rearing can just how emotionally and physically demanding—and exciting—it is to care for a newborn. "By being hands on, seeing them continuously," says Alex Yanez, a telecommunications specialist at Patagonia, "I am learning how they react at an early age. It is fascinating to see how kids react and develop. It's like a real science by observation."

For most guys, it's a matter of settling in and helping the family consolidate, whether it's a first or subsequent child. Jonathan Zingman, an engineer for TCSI Corporation, used sick leave and vacation time right after his daughter's birth; then six weeks later he used the FMLA to stay home for two more unpaid weeks. "I don't have a dramatic story, but the leave was important because it allowed me to settle in, allowed my new daughter to settle in, allowed us to settle in as a family, and allowed my wife to recover from her surgery. The time that we spent was very much family time: doing the laundry and taking care of the kids, and that sort of thing. It was time that I was able to spend just being a father, and not the father and the engineer and all the other roles."

Joseph Robinson, a credit services officer with First Union, a bank with 40,000 employees scattered from Florida to Connecticut, saved up three weeks vacation from the previous year in order to take time off at the end of his wife's twelve-week leave; that way they could extend parental care before their daughter, Danielle, went into child care. "We wanted to have our baby as old as she possibly could be before she started day care as well as providing time for me to spend with her. I would feed her, bathe her, and take her on walks a couple of times a day." First Union's Mark Falls took a full month of leave at the end of three months the day his wife, Susan, had to go back to work so that daughter Meredith would have four full months at home before starting day care. "It kept Meredith at home for another month, and it really eased Susan's transition back into the workforce. It was for me to spend time with Meredith, but it really helped Susan get comfortable with going back to work and all of the separation anxiety that tends to go on for working mothers. Susan would call me at home a couple times a day and just ask, 'How is it going?' It was good for me, it was good for her, and we believe it was good for Meredith."

MANAGING YOUR PATERNITY LEAVE

Taking paternity leave isn't like calling in sick for a day or two, which happens unexpectedly and lasts a very short period of time. Your belly may not be showing your impending parenthood the way your wife's is, but to make leave as successful as possible it's a good idea to prepare your coworkers as much as possible. Here are some guidelines from dads who have successfully managed the three phases of paternity leave: getting ready, taking leave, and returning to work, and some guidelines from the managers who supervise them.

Getting Ready

Determine Your Eligibility

There are three ways in which you may be entitled to paternity leave. If more than one way applies, you are eligible for the benefits that are the most generous.

1. If your company has fifty or more employees within a seventy-five-mile radius, you are likely to be eligible for paternity leave under the FMLA.

2. If you are not covered by the FMLA, you may be covered by the laws of your state or the policies of your company.

3. If you are not covered by either public or private policy, you may be able to negotiate an informal arrangement with your supervisor. Just because there is no *official* policy where you

work, it does not mean you can't take a leave or shouldn't ask for it.

Ask

Just as with flexible scheduling, if "You don't ask, you don't get." According to Mark Falls of First Union, who was one of the first in his company to request a leave, "There's not a lot of precedent for it and not a lot of guys have expressed the desire to do it. But a lot of that is the fear about asking, fear of the unknown. A lot of people just assume that they would not get permission, so they don't ask."

If your request is denied but you suspect (or know) you are eligible, you may want to appeal to either your boss's boss or, if your company has one, to your human resource department. Ask if there is a designated work–family contact. But before going over your supervisor's head, communicate your intent and provide any additional supporting information. If you still need to take the issue to a higher level, present your appeal not by blaming your supervisor, but as an apparent misunderstanding, even if you know full well that your supervisor has a perfect understanding of your rights: "It is my understanding that according to [the Family and Medical Leave Act and/or state policy and/or corporate policy], I am entitled to [number of weeks] leave at the adoption or birth of a child or to care for a family member who is ill. My supervisor seems to have a different understanding. I would like your help in clarifying and resolving this situation." With this approach, you'll save some face for your supervisor and make your own return from paternity leave easier.

Plan Far Ahead

You should not wait until your wife's ninth month to ask for a leave. The more notice you can give your supervisor, the more likely you will be able to work out a plan to make sure your work gets done well while you are out. According to DuPont's Cindi Johnson, "Planning to the extent you can is the most important ingredient in making leave work."

According to analysis of the first two years' experience with the

FMLA, 67.5 percent of employers used other workers to cover the work of leave takers. So part of your planning process should be to let your teammates know about your plans and, to the extent it's within your discretion and authority, to figure out which parts of your work can be reassigned while you are out. Your supervisor will appreciate your presenting a plan, not just a problem for him or her to take care of.

At Lotus Development Corp., a female colleague on Nick Camelio's team picked up a lot of work while he was out. Then, when she was out on sabbatical, he helped her out. "The two really partnered around their leave," says Gary Cormier, who supervised them both. "That made it easy to manage."

Announce It, Don't Hide It

There is still a tendency for guys to take leave of anywhere from three days to three weeks and pretend that it is not paternity leave. That's because they are afraid the culture will not be supportive and feel it's better to be safe than sorry.

But the only way for dads to help change the culture—for themselves and for other men—is to make it very clear why they are taking family leave. That's what First Union's Joseph Robinson did. Even though Robinson used three weeks of accrued vacation to take time off when his daughter was born, he insisted that it be announced as paternity leave. "It didn't matter how I was paid. It *was* a paternity leave."

Announcing why you are on leave is quite likely to prompt very positive responses, as Mike Goodson found when he took three months' leave from his position as a human resource advisor at IBM. "The response from peers was unbelievably positive. People would stop me in the hall, men especially, and say it was great that I was doing this, and wished they had done it with their children."

Stretch It Out

The most frequent reason that fathers don't take paternity leave, aside from the reluctance to sacrifice needed family income, is that mothers are breast-feeding. In those cases, if dad is required to take all his available leave within the first month or two or even three—and lose his income to boot—he's much less likely to take advantage of it.

But dads (and moms) don't have to take their leave all in one block. The FMLA allows employees to take leave intermittently or on a reduced leave schedule for the birth of a child or the care of a newborn, newly adopted, or foster child, subject to the employer's approval of such a schedule. In the first two years of the FMLA, 11.5 percent of all leave takers took intermittent leave.

An intermittent schedule can often be customized to meet the needs of both your family and your job better than a straight block of time off. At Lotus Development Corp., Jaime Medeiros took Fridays off every week for five months instead of one month straight. That worked for his boss, who preferred not to have him out for four weeks in a row; for his wife, who had three full days of support (Friday, Saturday, and Sunday) each week while she was breast-feeding; and for Jaime, who got to see his daughter grow and develop over a much longer stretch of time. At Tom's of Maine, production worker Shawn Maquire stretched his one-month leave to two months by customizing his schedule with his boss. "I'd get up in time to be at work by 4:30 in the morning and be home by 8:30 A.M., when my wife had to leave for work. That way I got to spend the day with my daughter doing all the good stuff—feeding her, burping her, really getting to know her." Michael Berney of Montgomery County, Maryland, frontloaded his leave and then stretched it out. When his son Max was born, he took two weeks off, then a day off each week for ten weeks.

Sequence It

Another creative use of paternity leave is to take it after your wife's leave. As Joseph Robinson and Mark Falls of First Union figured out, two back-to-back leaves extend the time period before you need to arrange in-home or out-of-home care for your child.

Because the Sacramento County Sheriff's Department in California allows thirty days of leave within the first six months, Sgt.

Robert Grout was able to take his leave after his wife finished hers. "When my wife ran out of time, I became a househusband. I woke up in the middle of the night to feed, bathe, and change the baby's diapers. My wife had to get up to go to work. At that time the oldest one was not in school. I would clean the house—do the carpets, laundry, dishes."

Sequencing doesn't have to be all in one block. It may be better for you—and your company—if you are out for a week or two right after the baby is born and then take the rest of your leave at a later date. If you can afford it, take some time off while your wife is still on leave before she hands the daily care off to you for your turn.

Taking Leave

Don't Expect It to Be a Vacation

Though lots of wonderful things can happen when you're home with your child, if you romanticize the experience, you are likely to be very disappointed. "When you're with a baby, you don't get a break," says First Union's Joseph Robinson. "The only thing I was looking for by the end of the day was to look to my wife to relieve me." Mark Falls of First Union says his daughter Meredith was three-months old when he took over: "When she would nap, I would try to nap. It really was a full-time job. I would easily say that it was as tough, if not tougher than what I do at First Union. It was draining. Susan would call me at 4:15 in the afternoon and say, 'Have you gotten the dishwasher unloaded?' I would say, 'When have I had time to unload the dishwasher?' It certainly gave me a greater appreciation for what Susan had been doing for three months."

Worrying about Your Career is Normal

Even if you are legally protected, you may find yourself worrying about whether your job is safe. That's perfectly normal for fathers and mothers. When the Commission on Family and Medical Leave studied the first two years' experience with FMLA, it found that 16.1

percent of men were worried about losing their job, 17.5 percent were worried it might hurt their job advancement, and 10.7 percent were worried they might lose seniority. Women worried even more about these things: 26.3 percent about losing a job, 24.9 percent about hurting job advancement, and 14.3 percent about losing seniority. Not surprisingly, regardless of gender, workers with family income under $30,000 worried most of all—about 35 percent of all such workers.

"The biggest problem is the fear that you won't have a job when you get back," says Jaime Medeiros of Lotus. "I have never encountered it and I don't know of anyone who has personally, but I do know that it is out there. That is probably the biggest fear men have."

"It's difficult for a man to step out of his profession for a short period of time simply because nobody they know has done it before," says Patrick Flynn, an attorney with San Francisco-based Morrison & Foerster who took a three-month unpaid leave to care for his seventeen-month-old son while his wife taught sociology at Emory University in Atlanta. "It's risky and it feels uncomfortable, [but] I'd like to think that my example will make it easier for the next person."

Stay Connected While You're on Leave

Although some guys can completely let go of work while they are on leave, most find it important to stay connected to the job in some way. Joseph Robinson of First Union made regular phone calls but not because demands were being placed on him. "It was just an 'I don't want to be forgotten' kind of thing. And this is how we are doing. I brought her in one day to show everybody. Nothing more than that. More just of an update. This is how we are doing, and thanks for the time."

Mark Falls of First Union called in to touch base and made it clear to his colleagues that they could call him. "It's not like a situation where you can't talk to me, because I am not getting paid. I am coming back to work for the same company and the same job. That communication opportunity was always there."

Keeping in touch should not mean doing your job at home

while you are on paternity leave. But keeping in touch can reduce some of the normal worry about your job while you are away and make your transition back to work easier.

Returning to Work

Ease Back In

If you have stayed in touch during a relatively short leave, you shouldn't have any more problem returning to work than when you return from a long vacation. The first few days, even the first week, can be very disorienting, and then things snap back into focus.

If you are planning a long leave, it can help to return on a gradual basis. AT&T, for example, which offers up to twelve months of unpaid leave, instituted an official "ease-in" policy called the Gradual Return to Work program, which allows parents to work part-time for three months. After developing a similar program, Nynex found that employees on leave would actually return sooner if they were able to adjust their hours.

This is no more than planning the back end of your leave, just as you planned the front end. Easing back in helps you, your co-workers, and your child with your return.

Worrying about Your Child Is Normal

If you have been on anything more than a brief leave, you can expect to worry about how your child is doing without you—just as mothers do all the time. It's normal—the flip side of worrying about your career while you are with your child—and inescapable.

"When you return, take it easy on yourself," says Nick Camelio of Lotus. "I kept thinking, 'It's 10 A.M., is my baby taking a nap?'"

After John Unoski took at two-year leave from AT&T, where his wife, Jan, also works, they enrolled their daughter in day care. "I was happy to get back to working with large groups of people, but then I miss my daughter and worry a lot. I drop her off at 7 A.M. What sort of attention is she getting? You know it's pretty good, but it's not the same."

MANAGING YOUR EMPLOYEE'S PATERNITY LEAVE

If you are a manager, here are the most important factors to make paternity leave work for you and your employees:

- **Plan Ahead with Your Employee.** When you know one of your employees is about to become a father, ask if he plans to take any time off under your company's leave policy. If you don't have a leave policy, let him know you're willing to work out an informal arrangement with him around what will be a very exciting and stressful time. He may be reluctant to bring his need to your attention and it will help enormously for you to give him "permission."

- **Think Flexibly.** Don't lock yourself—or your employee—into the idea that the only way to take paternity leave is in one chunk of time right after childbirth. It might be a better fit for your work needs and his family needs to arrange a more flexible leave schedule, like those I have described in this chapter.

- **Work Out a Plan for Accessibility.** A leave is a leave, and you should respect your employee's right to be away from work, without expecting him literally to be working from home. Get the signals straight on how and when you will touch base during his leave, and how you can get in touch with him in an emergency situation.

- **Pay Attention to His Coworkers.** If work is going to be reassigned, make sure you don't just dump it on the first coworker you see. Otherwise you may breed resentment while he is gone and when he returns. If people say they can't manage the work you are assigning to them, listen carefully and then prioritize and spread the work around so the most important work gets done by people most capable of doing it efficiently.

LEAVE OVER THE LONG TERM

As important as paternity leave can be for the birth or adoption of a child, it isn't the only time in a child's life when giving dads (or moms) a chunk of time off helps them balance their work and family lives.

According to a report prepared by Dana Friedman for The Conference Board, "Children under the age of twelve average five days of sickness per year. The 1990 *National Child Care Survey* found that about half (51 percent) of employed mothers who reported that their child was sick in the last month missed work to care for that child."

Data from Sweden, which during the last three decades has experimented with different versions of parental leave to promote equality between men and women, suggest that fathers are much more likely to take advantage of leave when it is made available for sick child care *after* the first year. Under Swedish law, either parent can collect up to 75 percent of his or her income during the first year of a child's life and 75 percent of income after that while staying home with the children. Since 1974, the percentage of fathers taking advantage of leave to care for an infant has increased from 3 percent to 50 percent, but fathers still take only 10 percent of the total number of days taken by women. Critics often cite this as evidence of men's disinterest in sharing, without considering that mothers are far more likely to be home breast-feeding during the first year than afterward. After the first year, fathers' use of "temporary parental leave" jumps dramatically. Fathers take 33 percent of all leave days to care for a sick child when a caregiver is unavailable.

In addition to illness, when a child has a disability, mothers and fathers often need leave at different times. According to developmental pediatrician Anne Quinn, a child with special needs often puts considerable demands on a father's work schedule. Time issues are exacerbated.

A few American companies are beginning to recognize the need to help their working-parent employees over a longer period of time. McDonnell Douglas Corp., the country's largest defense contractor and St. Louis's largest employer with almost 41,000 local employees, allows salaried employees to request paid personal leave to care for sick children, provided they complete a portion of the work week. Chubb & Son, Inc. of the Chubb Corporation—among the largest publicly owned insurance organizations in the United States— reworked its paid time-off policy in response to employee requests for more flexibility. An employee's total number of days off, based on length of service, are all under one umbrella, leaving it up to employees to decide how to use their time—for vacation, care of sick children, school visits, care of an elderly relative, or other reasons.

When Seattle-based Boeing shifted to more flexible work schedules for a large number of its employees, it dramatically improved the daily life of engineer John Doherty, one of whose three children has an undefined neurological disorder. The unpredictability of his son's behavioral and medical episodes used to collide with John's and his wife's rigid work schedules. "The old way," he says, "was continual, repeated negotiations and stressful fights with my wife over who would leave work. A real no-win situation. Now I can say I have it covered. And I do. Flexible scheduling has been a life-saver which has reduced the overall stress levels in our lives immeasurably. For me it has been far and away the best improvement the company has made. And a good number of my colleagues agree."

Are these practices likely to become more widespread? It took almost a decade for FMLA to become law. But consider this: In the summer of 1996, after three years of experience showing its benefits to both family and business, both Republicans and Democrats in the U.S. Congress proposed legislation that would give parents the choice of getting time instead of money as a payback for overtime hours.

OPTIONS UNDER THE FAMILY AND MEDICAL LEAVE ACT OF 1993

The Family and Medical Leave Act of 1993 went into effect on August 5, 1993, for the majority of covered United States employers. The FMLA provides many employees, both male and female, options to balance their work and family lives by taking reasonable unpaid leave for several health and family reasons.

You may have wondered what leave options you are entitled to under the FMLA. You are not alone. A survey conducted for the Federal Commission on Leave found that in 1995, only 56 percent of employees had knowledge of the FMLA. I encourage you to familiarize yourself with the options for leave to which you may be entitled. Following are the key provisions of the Family and Medical Leave Act of 1993. You should consider at least two points when exploring your options under the FMLA.

- The FMLA does not supersede any state or local law that may provide you with more generous family or medical leave protection.
- The FMLA addresses your legal rights. Our research on parental leave indicates that leaves that are negotiated as a business issue, and not invoked as a legal right, are significantly more successful for all parties involved. You should consider your personal work situation when determining which approach may be appropriate or necessary for you.

This summary, like the U.S. Department of Labor fact sheet from which it drawn, is intended as a general description only and does not carry the force of legal opinion.

What Leave Am I Entitled to under the FMLA?

If you work at a covered worksite and are an eligible employee, FMLA entities you to take up to twelve weeks of unpaid, job-protected leave in a twelve-month period for specified family and medical reasons, including:

- The birth, adoption, or foster placement of a child
- The care of a spouse, parent, or child with a serious medical condition

  and/or
- The care of your own serious medical condition

As the twelve-month period, your employer may elect to use the calendar year, a fixed "twelve-month leave" or fiscal year, or a twelve-month period prior to, or after the commencement of, a leave. Leave for the birth and care of an infant or for the placement of a child in adoption or foster care must conclude within twelve months of the birth or placement.

Spouses employed by the same employer are jointly entitled to a combined total of twelve work-weeks of family leave for the birth and care of the newborn child, for placement of a child for adoption or foster care, or for the care of a parent who has a serious health condition.

Is My Workplace Covered by the FMLA?

The FMLA applies to your workplace if you work at:

- A public agency, including local, state, and federal employers and local education agencies (schools)
- A private-sector employer who employed fifty or more employees in twenty or more work weeks in the current or preceding calendar year and who is engaged in commerce or in any industry or activity affecting commerce—including joint employers and successors of covered employers

Am I an Eligible Employee for FMLA Benefits?

To be eligible for FMLA benefits, you must:

- Work for a covered employer
- Have worked for the employer for a total of twelve months
- Have worked at least 1,250 hours over the previous twelve months

  and
- Work at a location in the United States or in any territory or possession of the United States where at least fifty employees are employed by the employer within seventy-five miles.

Must I Take My FMLA Leave All at Once, or Can It Be Taken Intermittently?

Under some circumstances, you may take FMLA leave intermittently. This means that you may take leave in smaller blocks of time, or by reducing your normal weekly or daily work schedule.

If FMLA leave is for birth or placement for adoption or foster care, use of intermittent leave is subject to your employer's approval.

FMLA leave may be taken intermittently whenever it is medically necessary to the care of a seriously ill family member, or if you are seriously ill and unable to work.

How Does FMLA Work if I Have Accrued Paid Leave?

Subject to certain conditions, you *or* your employer may choose to use, or be required to use accrued *paid* leave (such as sick or vacation leave) to cover some or all of an FMLA leave.

Your employer is responsible for determining if your use of paid leave will count as FMLA leave, based on information you give. In no case may a paid leave be credited as FMLA *after* the leave has been completed.

What Is a "Serious Health Condition" for the Purposes of FMLA?

According to the FMLA, a *serious health condition* is an illness, injury, impairment, or physical or mental condition that involves:

- Any period of incapacity or treatment connected with inpatient care (that is, an overnight stay) in a hospital, hospice, or residential medical-care facility
  or
- Any period of incapacity that requires absence of more than three calendar days from work, school, or other regular daily activities that also involves continuing treatment by (or under the supervision of) a health care provider
  or
- Continuing treatment by (or under the supervision of) a health care provider for a chronic or long-term health condition that is incurable or so serious that, if not treated, would likely result in incapacity of more than three calendar days, and for prenatal care

How Does the FMLA Define "Health Care Provider"?

For the purposes of FMLA, a recognized *health care provider* can be:

- A doctor of medicine or osteopathy authorized to practice medicine or surgery by the state in which the doctor practices

  or

- A podiatrist, dentist, clinical psychologist, optometrist, or chiropractor (limited to manual manipulation of the spine to correct a subluxation as demonstrated by X ray to exist), authorized to practice and perform within the scope of his or her practice, as defined under state law

  or

- A nurse practitioner, nurse-midwife, or clinical social worker authorized to practice and perform within the scope of his or her practice, as defined under state law

  or

- A Christian Science practitioner listed with the First Church of Christ, Scientist in Boston, Massachusetts, or any health care provider recognized by the employer or the employer's group health plan benefits manager

Will My Health Care Benefits Be Maintained During FMLA Leave?

A covered employer is required to maintain group health insurance coverage for you during an FMLA leave whenever such insurance was provided before the leave was taken and on the same terms as if the employee had continued to work.

If applicable, arrangements will need to be made for you to pay your share of health insurance premiums while on leave. In some instances, your employer may recover premiums paid to maintain your health coverage, if you fail to return to work after FMLA leave.

Will My Job Be There When I Return from FMLA Leave?

Upon returning from FMLA leave, you must be restored to your original job or to an equivalent job with equivalent pay, benefits, and other terms and conditions of employment.

In addition, your use of FMLA leave cannot result in the loss of any employment benefit that you earned or were entitled to before using FMLA leave, nor can it be counted against you under a "no fault" attendance policy.

Under specified and limited circumstances where restoration to employment will cause substantial and grievous economic injury to operations, your employer may refuse to reinstate you if you are among certain highly paid *key* employees after using FMLA leave during which health coverage was maintained. In order to do so, the employer must:

- Notify you of your status as a *key* employee in response to your notice of intent to take FMLA leave
- Notify you as soon as your employer decides it will deny job restoration and explain the reasons for this decision
- Offer you a reasonable opportunity to return to work from FMLA leave after giving this notice

  and

- Make a final determination as to whether reinstatement will be denied at the end of the leave period if you then request restoration

A *key* employee is a salaried, "eligible" employee who is among the highest-paid 10 percent of employees within seventy-five miles of the work site.

Under the FMLA, When Must I Notify My Employer of My Intent to Take a Leave?

If you seek to use FMLA, you *may* be required to provide:

- Thirty-day advance notice of the need to take FMLA leave when the need is foreseeable and such notice is practical
- Medical certification supporting the need for leave due to a serious health condition affecting the employee or an immediate family member
- Second or third medical opinions (at the employer's expense) and periodic recertification

and

- Periodic reports during FMLA leave regarding your status and intent to return to work

When intermittent leave is needed to care for an immediate family member or your own illness and is for planned medical treatment, you must try to schedule treatment so as not to unduly disrupt your employer's operation.

Covered employers must post a notice approved by the secretary of the Department of Labor explaining rights and responsibilities under FMLA. An employer that willfully violates this posting requirement may be subject to a fine of up to $100 for each separate offense.

Under the FMLA, What Notification Must Covered Employers Provide Employees with Regard to the FMLA?

Covered employers must inform employees of their rights and responsibilities under FMLA, including giving specific written information on what is required of the employee and what might happen in certain circumstances, such as if the employee fails to return to work after FMLA leave.

What Is It Unlawful for My Employer to Do under FMLA?

It is unlawful for any employer to interfere with, restrain, or deny the exercise of any right provided by FMLA. It is also unlawful for an employer to discharge or discriminate against any individual for opposing any practice, or because of involvement in any proceeding, related to FMLA.

Are There Other Provisions of the FMLA of Which I Should Be Aware?

Special rules apply to employees of local educational agencies. Generally, these rules provide for FMLA leave to be taken in blocks of time when intermittent leave is needed or the leave is required near the end of a school term.

Salaried executive, administrative, and professional employees of covered employers who meet the Fair Labor Standards Act (FLSA) criteria for exemption from minimum wage and overtime (under Regulations, 29 CFR Part 541) do not lose their FLSA-exempt status by using any unpaid FMLA leave. This special exception to the "salary basis" requirements for FLSA's exemption extends only to "eligible" employees' use of leave required by FMLA.

The FMLA does not affect any other federal or state law that prohibits discrimination, nor does it supersede any state or local law that provides greater family or medical leave protection.

The FMLA does not affect an employer's obligation to provide greater leave rights under a collective bargaining agreement or employment benefit plan. The FMLA encourages employers to provide more generous leave options.

Who Enforces the FMLA?

The Wage and Hour Division investigates complaints. If violations cannot be satisfactorily resolved, the U.S. Department of Labor may bring action in court to compel compliance. Individuals may also bring a private civil action against an employer for violations.

Where Can I Go to Learn More about My Options under the FMLA?

One good place to begin is the human resource department at your workplace. It should be equipped to provide you additional information, not only on your options as insured by the FMLA, but also on organizational-specific programs and policies that might be available to assist you. You may also contact the nearest office of the Wage and Hour Division, listed in most telephone directories under U.S. Government, Department of Labor, Employment Standards Administration.

Alternatively, for further information, you may wish to consult the final rule implementing FMLA, contained in the January 6, 1995, *Federal Register.*

Part 3

Strategies for Home

Chapter 6

Connecting with Your Family

I n more than twenty-five years of leading parenting groups for working fathers and mothers, the most frequent question I have gotten from dads is, "How can I find the time for my family? With all the demands of work, it just seems like there's never enough time."

It's an increasingly common complaint, not just among fathers but among mothers—as well as among men and women who do not have children. In *The Overworked American*, Harvard economist Juliet Schor said that today's American workers are putting in more hours on the job—and less at home—than previous generations.

Not true, says University of Maryland sociologist John Robinson, who has been studying American's use of time for the last two decades. Robinson and his colleague, Ann Bostrom, argue that there is a growing gap between the perception and the reality of working hours.

What might account for this gap? According to Diane Crispell, who follows time-use trends for *American Demographics* magazine, it is because boundaries between work and the rest of life's activities are blurring into a "mixed-up work day." People work at home, work odd hours, and work around family life; they take days that mix paid work and other activities or take breaks to attend to personal business, yet report the entire period as work. The lack of clear boundaries leads people to feel that they are working all the time.

It doesn't really matter who is right in absolute terms. Most students of time use agree that some sections of the work force are working longer hours, and many Americans feel rushed during free time as well as at work. Most dads (and moms) I speak to *feel* there isn't enough time and want to know, "What can I do?"

I'm not going to advise you to "cut back", "downshift" or "simplify" your life—all trendy ideas in the popular media. Whether you can and want to do that is a matter of personal values, and it very much depends on your financial resources. I'm wary of dads who think the solution to work–family balance lies in a radical shift toward family, like an options trader in Phoenix who gave up his hundred-hour-a-week job for twenty-hour weeks to find, two years later, he was itchy for a more challenging schedule.

I'm not going to teach you how to uncover two extra hours of family time a day through "better time management." Men often learn how to manage their time better, but at the end of the day they still are not spending more time with their families. If you are in that bind, I highly recommend that you read Steven Covey's *First Things First*, which you can find in any bookstore. Covey presents the most useful approach I have found to understanding and overcoming the "urgency addiction," which can lead to working harder, smarter, and faster without ever attending to the important things we value.

Some men assume that the problem of doing too much at work can be solved by doing more at home, only to realize that their family experience is not as fulfilling as work. "The suggestion that we simply pull off a few layers of our working selves, like fusty winter clothes in early spring, not only underestimates the profound meaning of work in the lives of many men," say family therapists David Waters and J. T. Saunders. "It is often woefully ineffective." Ironically, they say, thinking that "the solution to the problem of *doing too much* at work is to *do more* at home" is "doomed to fail" unless both spouses can understand the meaning of work and home in each of their lives. To get to that point of understanding it can often help to involve a skilled psychologist or family therapist who can help a husband and wife understand "that home and work do not have to represent antagonistic forces in a struggle for his soul, that his devotion to work is not a judgment of her and family life, that her desire to have him home is not a rejection of the part of him that needs his work."

What can you do to deal with that continually nagging sense that there is never enough time for your family? In this chapter I present a different way of thinking about your family time, focusing on the importance of creating opportunities to connect with your kids in small ways on an ongoing basis. For married fathers, if you want to connect with your kids, the first place to start is by making sure you are connected with your wife or partner. The key to having a better relationship with your children often lies in spending more time—and often a different type of time—with your wife.

CAN YOU TURN DOWN EXTRA WORK?

What can you do if your corporate culture is chewing you up and loading more and more work on at the expense of your family? As downsizing leads more workers to take on the load of former colleagues, it's increasingly important to know how to turn down extra work that you can't handle without compromising your family needs.

- **Show why it wouldn't be good for the business.** "I've got so much on my plate right now, I wouldn't be able to get that done the way we need to get it done. I appreciate your asking me, but I don't want to take on something and then turn in a subpar performance."

- **Present options.** "I'll be able to take this assignment on if I give up some of the other stuff on my plate. Can we review this list of my current priorities to see what you might like me to give lower priority, or reassign to someone else?"

- **Delay.** "I can't take that project on now, but after our quarterly reviews are done next month, I'll check back with you to see if there is any way I can help."

PUT YOUR OXYGEN MASKS ON FIRST

If you have traveled on a plane, you are familiar with a standard safety drill just before takeoff. While you're settling in to read a magazine or nodding off, the flight attendant always says, "In the event of an emergency, an oxygen mask will drop from the overhead compartment. If you are traveling with children, be sure to put your oxygen mask on first."

If you routinely ignore this bit of advice, like most travelers, take a minute now and think about it. As psychotherapists Pat Hudson and Bill O'Hanlon first pointed out to me, in this announcement lies a very important lesson—no, not just about plane safety, but about staying connected with your children on a day-to-day basis.

In an airplane emergency, you will not be able to put your children's oxygen masks on unless you have put your own mask on first. At home, you will not be able to give children the oxygen—the attention—they need unless you first make sure that oxygen is flowing into your marital relationship and to you as an individual. Keeping your relationship fresh better enables you to stay connected with your kids.

Is your oxygen supply at risk? Just having children reduces the time that partners have for one another. FWI's *National Study of the Changing Workforce* found that time for a spouse declines significantly among dual-earner couples once they become parents: Couples spend fifty-one minutes less with each other on workdays and a full hour and eight minutes less with each other on off-days. Yankelovich Partners Inc. polled a nationally representative sample of 1,003 parents in May 1996 and found that "working parents may be attempting to spend more time with their children, but this appears to be at the expense of spending time with each other": 42 percent of parents are spending less time with their spouses and nearly a third of parents are reporting more tension in their relationships.

This finding agreed with an earlier study, "Processes Underlying Father Involvement in Dual-Earner and Single-Earner Families," conducted by psychologists at Pennsylvania State University and the University of Texas. Furthermore, according to University of Illinois psychologist Joseph Pleck, between 1965 and 1986, fathers increased the time they spent with children from 25 percent to 33 percent of the time that mothers spend with children.

Each time I conduct a DaddyStress/Daddy Success seminar, it becomes apparent where, for too many couples, that trade-off comes. Dads proudly tell me about the increasing amounts of time they are spending with their kids. They twist their schedules around, work ten-hour days, then come home to play games with their kids, give them their baths, help them with their homework, read them a story, and tuck them into bed.

"That is just fantastic," I say. And I mean it. "But tell me, when do you and your wife get to spend time with one another?"

Dad usually looks a little confused. "Well, not very often, I guess," is a typical response.

At one seminar a dad laughed, "Oh, we're both so tired by the time we get the kids set that we just crawl into bed, kind of look at each other, and say 'night honey.'" To which a fellow across the room shouted, "Wait a minute! You must be married to my wife!"

There's nothing wrong with being a superdad, *if* you can do it without jeopardizing your marriage. But many husbands and wives are working so hard at their jobs and at being superdads and supermoms that they forget why they got married in the first place. In managing all the details of taking care of the kids—the scheduling of who will pick up Johnny after school, who will take Sally to the soccer game, who will do this, and who the heck are we going find to cover that—they lose sense of what attracted them to one another and led them to make their commitment to each other.

In effect, these parents are trying to give their kids all the oxygen, without giving any to their relationship. The irony is that when parents' relationship suffer, kids know it and feel it.

From a lack of communication, parents are more likely to misunderstand, blame, or pick fights with one another. Kids get the fall-out. When parents don't have a space to "breathe" together—to say or show how they are feeling, away from the day-to-day fray of getting kids bathed and fed and settling sibling arguments—feelings get pent up, and kids lose, too. Kids even sense when they are getting too much attention—and their parents not enough—because they don't see their parents having enough fun.

I'll never forget one Sunday night, when my wife and I were doing some planning for the upcoming week, over a big calendar spread out on the dining room table. We were in the midst of figuring out a schedule for the week—who would pick ten-year-old Joshua up from after-school swimming on Tuesday, how was fourteen-year-old Jessica getting home from soccer practice on Wednesday, what about the parent–teacher meetings on Thursday, who was making what dinner on what days—when Josh cruised by the table, gave a quick glance, and casually said, "I'm not going to have any kids when I grow up."

"Why not?" my wife and I blurted out simultaneously, looking at each other with wide eyes. We thought having kids was one of the greatest things we had ever done and had assumed that the kids knew we felt that way.

"Too much work," said Josh. "There are too many things to think about. You're always making schedules."

Actually, Josh saw and knew only the half of it. Not only were there far more details than he knew about managing home life, but we had to go through similar planning and scheduling at our jobs, where we earned the money that made it possible for him to even participate in swimming. Nor were we about to give up our regular Sunday night planning meeting, which made it possible to navigate the week—for his dinner to appear on the table every night and for him not to be stranded at one of his after-school programs with a teacher, who also had to get home to a family, muttering angrily about Josh's parents not showing up on time. It worked for us, and it works for many couples.

But Josh was picking up on something important. We had gotten so busy that our Sunday night meeting was taking the place of the get-togethers that all couples need to keep their relationship rewarding and strong.

STRENGTHEN YOUR RELATIONSHIP
WITH YOUR SPOUSE

In my research and work with families, I have found two simple but extremely effective and reliable ways to keep relationships between partners strong, no matter how hectic or demanding the schedules. The first is by making a weekly date. The second is by creating day-to-day rituals for simply being together.

Make a Weekly Date

Remember dating? Don't laugh. Many fathers can't. The idea is to plan ahead, to set aside some special time when just the two of you can go to a movie or out to dinner or to a concert—whatever. You can even stay at home and rent a video, as long as it's *without* your children.

In my DaddyStress/Daddy Success seminars, it never fails to astonish me how many men have stopped dating their wives after they are married—and especially after they have kids. And it never fails to astonish the group when we correlate their levels of DaddyStress with whether or not they are purposefully scheduling regular dates or other "get-us-out-of-here" times with their partners. Invariably, the guys who are not making time away with their wives are feeling the highest levels of stress.

The most frequent reasons for not intentionally planning special times—many of which are understandable but not excusable—follow.

Fear of Leaving the Baby

The younger the child, the more common this excuse. At one month, even two or three, it's understandable, especially if it's a first child. It's exciting just to stay home and watch the baby, even if he or she is sleeping. You tip-toe in and out of the room, peek into the crib, and feel proud—together. But even with babies six months or a year old, I hear fathers saying, "No, we haven't gone out. The baby's not ready for a sitter." Sometimes they defer to their wives, saying, "My wife doesn't think the baby is ready for a sitter," or, getting a bit closer to what's really going on, "My wife and I don't think *we're* ready to have a sitter." Often, if their child is in day care during the week, they feel guilty about going out on a weekend evening, since they have spent so little time with their child. But they have also spent very little time with one another.

Leaving your child for an evening won't hurt your child. Not making time for a regular date—whether it's once a week or once every other week, or even once every month—will hurt your relationship. And that, in turn, can hurt your child.

If you are hard-pressed to find the right sitter, consider bartering your time with a friend or neighbor whom you know well and trust: They watch your child this Saturday night, and you watch theirs some other Saturday night. Another strategy friends used when their daughter was young was to plan their time together on a weekend afternoon to avoid the Friday and Saturday night rush on sitters. "Looking for a sitter for a Saturday afternoon was a joy," he explains, "compared to the usual crazed dash for a sitter for a Friday or Saturday night. By avoiding the 'peak nights' when the best sitters are in high demand and low supply, we had our pick."

Concern That You Can't Afford to Go Out

If you don't have the money to spend, going out to dinner and a movie may just put you under more stress, which is exactly what you don't need. Factoring in the cost of a sitter can make even a simple night out a significant expense. The strategy of bartering, mentioned earlier is one way to rein in the cost of a date. But remember, the goal of making a date is to spend time together, not necessarily to spend money together. What did you do when you were teenagers or students and didn't have money but wanted to be together? You went to the mall and window-shopped for a couple of hours. You took a long walk in the park or through some interesting part of town. You went to a coffee shop or got a soda. It may sound corny, but the simple fact is, it works.

Worry That You Don't Have Any Time

This excuse brings us full circle to where we started. But think about what it suggests: We have time for our jobs, we have time for our kids, but we just don't have time for each other. Try this experiment. Pretend I will give you $10,000 cash for every hour you and your wife could find together for yourselves next Saturday, Sunday, or whatever day you are home together. There are only two conditions: You can't have your children with you, and you can't use any of your $10,000 allotments to pay for child care. How many hours do you think you could come up with? One, two, maybe even enough for a whole afternoon or evening out? Whenever you get stuck feeling you have no time, try that little thought experiment. It won't make you rich in dollars, but the time it helps you find for each other will enrich your relationship.

There are four important guidelines to keep in mind when making your weekly date.

1. It does not qualify as a date if you include your children, no matter how much you want to be with them. If you have a weekly family outing with all the kids, that's great, but don't count it as *your* weekly date.

2. It counts as only half a date if you go out with other couples. Sure it's important to maintain your friendships, but it's equally important to preserve some time for yourselves.

3. A date should be an activity you both enjoy; sometimes what *he* thinks is a date is not what *she* thinks is a date, and vice versa. Spend some time finding some activities you will both enjoy.

4. Don't take the "weekly" part of the rule too literally. It really is a good idea to get out once a week, but if it slips to every two weeks during an especially busy time, don't worry that your relationship is going to fail.

The trick is to get started and to get into the habit. Then you're on track, especially if you are strengthening your relationship on a daily basis as well.

Create Daily Rituals for Connection

How can you strengthen your relationship on a daily basis? This comes through the second method I've found men use to stay connected to their spouses: creating daily rituals for *being* together.

I don't mean *doing* together—like doing the dishes together or cleaning the yard together or paying your bills together. All of these are valuable ways of sharing. And they can even become rituals if they are repeated on a regular basis and occur in a space or time that seems separate from the hustle and bustle of daily life. I mean times when you are not trying to accomplish anything but are making contact with one another, verbally and/or physically, when the purpose of your activity is just to *be* together. These day-to-day rituals do not typically take a long time, as you'll see from the following examples:

Got-the-Kids-Down Pause

You've spent a long day at work and feel like you've spent the equivalent of another work day trying to get the kids to sleep: half-hour argument over whether they could stay up for another half-hour to watch their favorite TV show; separate stories read to each child, the door opened a bit more because they're scared, door closed a bit more because there's too much light coming in—finally, peace. You can each turn to the extra hour of paperwork you have to finish for work or the bills you have to pay for home.

Before you start going separate ways, take some time to reconnect. Catch up on each other's day. Find out how you're each doing. The idea is to listen and to be heard, not necessarily to try to solve each other's problems. Some couples do this by having a glass of wine or cup of tea together. One couple I know has a much more luxurious ritual of taking a hot tub together every night at 10 P.M., regardless of what else is happening. Another couple who work opposite split shifts has established a 1 A.M. ritual, without which they would hardly ever see one another during the week. At 1 A.M., shortly after mom has gotten off her supermarket shift, dad wakes up so they can have breakfast together, then he catches four more hours of sleep before leaving for his shift at an automotive factory.

Neither the time nor method of coming together matters, as long as it is something that brings you together just for the point of being together.

Too-Pooped-to-Talk Connections

Some couples are so tuckered out at the end of the day that they don't want to talk to anyone. And the last things they would want to talk about is how the day went. They just want a break. Rituals for reconnecting don't have to be verbal, but it's important to be physically close. Some couples read the newspaper or a magazine after dinner, sitting together on a couch or close enough to one another in a room so that they feel that they're connected. They don't engage in a sustained or purposeful conversation; nothing more than, "Did you see this?" or "What do you think about that?" The point is simply being together. Some couples have their own version of this as they lie in bed together watching the 10 or 11 P.M. news. There's not necessarily much conversation, but there is a physical closeness. Interestingly, just being physically close can lead to the sorts of brief interchanges—no more than a few words here and there—that help people feel listened to, heard, and appreciated.

Glow-of-Television Connections

Television often gets blamed for contributing to the decline of family life. Instead of communicating within their real family, parents and children spend their time watching make-believe families on TV. But selective use of television can make for a healthy ritual for connection with your spouse. Set aside a time to watch your favorite show together. Sit close together, because physical connection is an important part of this ritual, and don't allow any phone calls or other interruptions.

Reach for the Phone

Don't rule out the telephone as an important way of staying connected. It's not the same as being together physically, but it can be very effective. Take a minute to call your spouse at work or home. It doesn't have to be every day. But it's great to get a call saying, "I was just thinking about you," or "I was just wondering how your day is going." Often you won't be able to talk at all and the call might even seem an intrusion on your work space. But you don't have to talk. It's not being able to have a detailed conversation that is important here: It's knowing that there was the attempt and the connection, however brief.

These are just a few examples of daily opportunities for connection. Whenever I do a DaddyStress/Daddy Success seminar and ask participants to reflect on the daily rituals in their lives, they are amazed to discover how much seemingly small moments of connection mean to themselves, their partners, and their relationship. They are powerful ways to strengthen your marital relationship, keeping it rich, rewarding, and fun. Take a minute to identify some of the rituals that work in your daily life, to confirm their importance, and to commit to keeping them going. Talk over with your partner some of the established rituals you each cherish, and think of some new ones you each might like to try.

STRENGTHEN YOUR RELATIONSHIP WITH YOUR KIDS

To follow my advice about strengthening your relationship with your partner you might find that you have to cut back on some of the time you are spending with your kids. As I have explained, being a superdad at the expense of your marriage can actually work to the detriment of your kids. If your relationship isn't solid and rewarding, the marriage may not only strain but end, which makes it harder for both parents to support children.

Lots of good books with advice on how to be an effective father are available at bookstores. Some provide specific advice about important topics like discipline or communicating with your kids; some offer activities to do with your kids at each stage of development; some are geared to divorced dads; and a couple explain the impact of your relationship with your own father on your relationship with your children.

Here, I want to emphasize the importance of daily connection to your kids. It's the type of interaction you have with them that keeps the relationship strong and growing.

Reaching Out to Your Kids

Go One-on-One

It's wonderful to spend time together with the whole family or with just your kids. But each child needs to feel that he or she has a unique relationship with you, too. That can come from doing something together that you don't do with your other children or doing it in a special way. Sometimes it can be a weekly ritual of going somewhere together. When my daughter was four years old, part of every Sunday morning was set aside for us to walk to the bakery to buy "her" donut. It was only a six-block trip, but we would walk slowly, looking in the store windows—especially the local toy store—to see what was different or new in the window. But the trip wasn't about buying a thirty-five-cent donut or window shopping; it was about being together; just the two of us—not with mom, not with her brother. More than twenty years later, she'll smile and claim she remembers taking those walks as vividly as the smell of her fresh donuts.

Think twice before you include other children in a ritual you have established with one child. We could have pushed my son to the bakery with us in his baby carriage, but that would have taken the focus off of the time my daughter and I had together. We found other times to take him for a stroll without carving into her bakery outing. And as my son got older, I created a special but still separate bakery ritual for him—taking him for a "black and white cookie." Of course, we did lots of things with both kids together and with my wife, but this allowed us to keep a tradition going with just enough difference for each of the kids to enjoy something unique with dad.

Hug Even When They're Big

Kids need your physical and verbal affection regularly and often—even when they squirm with embarrassment. "Whatever their age, getting a hug from dad is like touching home base," says Samuel Osherson, author of *Finding Our Fathers.*

To understand how much a hug, and expressions of affection in general, can mean to your kids, think back to how much it meant (or would have meant) to you when you were a child. A study of 300 male executives and mid-level managers found that "when managers were asked what one thing they would like to change in their relationships with their own fathers, the majority indicated they wished their fathers would have expressed emotions and feelings."

Don't get waylaid by "the sissy myth." Beginning as early as the preschool years, fathers concerned about raising "real men" often start reserving most hugs and kisses for their daughters. Mothers, whether they are aware of it or not, often buy into this same myth. But research shows that the single best predictor of masculinity in sons is actually the father's warmth and closeness.

Because daughters don't evoke the same "sissy" worries, it's usually easy for fathers to be close to them—at least until puberty. "Once girls have breasts, dads don't know what to do with their hands," says Julie Osherson, a clinical social worker from Winchester, New Hampshire. As early as age ten, your daughter may be self-conscious about her sexuality. So the little girl who once jumped into your lap is now as unsure of how to relate to you as you are to her.

The danger here is that physical and emotional distance go hand in hand. When you don't spend time with your daughter, you risk getting out of touch emotionally *and* physically. But if you get to know your daughter, you'll have a much better sense of when to give her hugs. And when she chooses boyfriends, and ultimately, a mate, she'll seek someone as appreciative and caring as you.

Families often have unstated "designated huggers." And often it's mom. Fall off your bike? Mom gives you a hug. Scrape your knee? Mom kisses it. Don't let your family rely on just one hugger. No matter how good mom is at making everything better, both of you should be sources of comfort.

Reconnect When You Get Home from Work

At my DaddyStress/Daddy Success seminars, lots of dads tell me they aren't sure how to connect with their kids when they get home from work, especially when kids get past the toddler and preschool stage of running excitedly to throw their arms around dad's knees. Instead of a screaming, "Daddy's home," it can almost seem as if everybody is too busy to notice.

It's important to enter into your children's flow, rather than expect them to enter into yours. Rather than starting a new activity, try to get in sync with whatever your kids are already doing. When he finds his nine-year-old at the computer, New York City social worker Jose Barbosa asks, "Can you show me how to do that?" His reasoning: "If I ask for help and follow my son's lead, he lets me into his world. Then I'm not forcing myself on him just because I'm home and I missed him."

To get kids to open up, avoid the standard and all-too-general, "What did you do today?" which usually generates the not-terribly-helpful, "Nothing."

Instead, ask a specific question, such as, "What toys did you and Kim play with when she was over?" To be able to ask such specific questions, of course, you have to pay attention to the details of their lives. But those are the questions with which kids and dads will connect—the details. Once they do, you'll start to get the more general information, even without asking.

Baltimore TV producer Ademola Ekulona, who is divorced, sees his youngest daughter, who is four, only two or three times a week. "I pick her up and I hold her and I usually compliment her about her hair," he says, "because she is very proud that her sisters have done her hair."

Michael Johnson, general manager of Maine Printing Company in Portland, has an extremely clever way of cutting "to the chase" and connecting with his son. Before he comes home, he calls to ask his wife what their five-year-old son, Will, is up to. When Johnson comes home, he's able to be specific. "I'll say, 'I hear you were running around with an eye patch playing pirate today.' It let's him know I have been thinking about him."

David Wasserman, who runs an audio and electronics store in New York City, doesn't get to see his eleven-year-old son until 9 P.M., after a "long retail day." He uses bedtime to reconnect. "He needs me to lie next to him. Then he says, 'How was your day, dad? I bet you were overworked and understaffed.' He's mimicking me, and it's mostly a rhetorical question, but it draws us together."

Join a Parent–Child Program

Joining a parent–child program offered by a school or other community organization can help you establish a regular time to be with your child. Tom Heck, a director of the Asheville, North Carolina, Voyagers—a seventy-year-old YMCA program formerly known as Indian Guides and Indian Princesses—relays one girl's reaction to her father's participation, "[The] undivided attention was really neat. My dad is stopping what he's doing and spending time with me."

Fathers who have participated in local offshoots of the national YMCA include Henry Winkler, Tom Hanks, and Bill Clinton. Dennis Harrish of the YMCA says, "With our society being as busy as it is, it's so easy to say, 'We'll do it later.' And you never do it. . . [With the structure of the program] there's scheduled time in which the dad spends some time alone with the child."

A programmed father–child activity is also a great way to meet other dads. In White Bear Lake, Minnesota, the community school district offers a Dad and Me program from 6 to 8 P.M. But when I visited to observe, I saw that 8 P.M. meant not a return home, but a trip to McDonald's for what has turned into a weekly ritual—dads' dinner out with the kids. Between hamburgers and catching up with the other dads, one father explained to me: "I've had several people working for me, and they always ask about my calendar: 'What's JC?' It's Julie's Class. I have everything planned around it. Next week I have an appointment with the CEO of a major customer, and I've scheduled it for Thursday, because on Tuesday we have Dad and Me."

Connecting with Your Kids at Work

Take Your Kids to Work

It can help your kids understand why you are not always available for them if they understand what it is you actually do at work. Otherwise your work remains an abstraction to them. In the past few years, the annual "Take Our Daughters to Work Day" has become quite popular, and many companies have extended it to sons as well. But there is no reason to wait until for a national event or even to limit a workplace visit to once a year. Kelvin Gunn works as the night-shift engineer at the J. W. Marriott Hotel in downtown Washington, D.C. From 11 P.M. to 7:30 A.M., he repairs anything that could possibly go wrong, from the air conditioners, TVs, and toilets in guest rooms to the generators and chillers that serve the entire hotel. Here's what happened and what it meant when Kelvin took his nine-year-old son, Kyle, to work one late summer night:

> I checked the house count and function level and what I needed to do. I didn't want there to be so much demand on me that I couldn't pay attention to him, but I wanted there to be enough so he could really see what I do. First I toured him everywhere it was possible to go in the hotel, including the storage areas that nobody knows about. We have humungous 15,000 gallon fuel tanks, eight-to-nine feet tall, and big pumps and generators we use to cool the hotel. Size seems to really impress kids!
>
> By the time the tour was over, he was ready to do something. I have a machine to do engraving for employee name tags. I showed him how to use the machine safely, and

he engraved a name for himself. That was one of the key points of the night, that he got to make something physically. He was so proud. He said, "Look dad, I'm an engineer, too." Then we worked on one of the A/C units, did a regular maintenance check of all the air handler units, and at 3:30 A.M. I took him to lunch—or breakfast—where the chef made him a double-deck hamburger and strawberry milkshake. After that, at 4 A.M., we did a walkaround, checking all the lights. I took him up on the lift we use for high places to change bulbs and asked him how he would get to a light if he didn't have a lift. I wanted him to be observant and think about how I solve problems on my job, and he was really sharp. He suggested we use a twelve-foot ladder that he saw down the hallway. By that time he was getting tired so I let him take a little break. At 6 A.M., we have to do the walk-around inspection of the hotel to make sure it is presentable. I set up the hose so he could pressure-wash some of the areas that weren't up to my standards.

Has it changed the relationship between father and son? According to Kelvin Gunn, "It brought us closer together. Now all the time he asks me if they are doing anything differently at the hotel. He wants to know about specifics, about problems and how I solve them. For me it was great. To him it was 'dad, you're the best.' Since then I have taken my eight-year-old, Kolter. I'm getting ready to take my seven-year old daughter, Kayla, and three-year-old Kolin is asking when he can go to work."

Giving your children a first-hand look at your work can have a significant impact on their career aspirations. As director of pediatric oncology at the National Institutes for Health in Bethesda, Maryland, Philip Pizzo, could never leave his beeper. With a typical work week of more than ninety hours, he rarely had time to get away with his family. So from the time his daughter, Cara, turned five, he started bringing her with him on Saturday rounds. "It wasn't work for her, it was a weekend trip with daddy," he says. "I would just introduce her as my kid. Since it's a pediatric ward, families in the hospital really liked the idea." So did Cara, who has just started her medical residency in pediatrics at Harvard Medical School.

Not all jobs, of course, are as physically glamorous or as physically accessible to children as building engineer or doctor. You might sit at a computer or talk on the phone or spend time in meetings much of the day, or you might repair underground pipe where it's too dangerous to take kids. But for most jobs, kids are curious, and there's much for them to see and learn. Simply showing them the space—taking them through the whole place—can be exciting. And it can help them connect with you and your work, just as you are trying to connect with them at home.

When You Work at Home

If you work at home, as more fathers and mothers now do, your children may think you are always available to connect with them, even when you can't. Some experts advise a rigid line between the family space and the home office, literally a closed door. I think it's important to match your home-based work–family boundaries to your own personal style of working. If you work best with totally separate boundaries with no interruptions, make that clear. But consider the case of Dan Hogan, father of three school-aged children, Matthew, Sarah, and Haley.

In 1991, after spending many years traveling away from home as a management consultant, Dan set up his own home-based "virtual" management consulting organization, the Apollo Group, in Concord, Massachusetts. The other members of his company also work from their home offices. "I know some people who work at home are rigidly strict about not being interrupted," says Dan. "I am not that way, in part, because I have the ability to return to a task quickly without being bothered about having been sidetracked. This means that my children have access to me whenever I am home, unless I am on an important phone call or have an absolute deadline. Thus when they're excited about something they have done and want to tell someone they're upset and need to talk, I am available."

Include Kids in Your Household Chores

It's not just the work you do outside the home that is interesting to kids. Until the age of ten or eleven, when they want ferociously to be off with their friends, it's cool to them to help out with the chores that to you may seem like drudgery. How much real *help* they are able to give is debatable, but the point is they *like* going to the hardware store or holding the dust pan while you sweep or washing the car. So rather than thinking of your weekend chores as time away from your kids, figure out ways to turn them into time with your kids. It may slow down how long it takes for you to finish your immediate task, but you'll be moving toward the bigger goal.

GIVE YOURSELF SOME OXYGEN

Oxygen for your marital relationship. Oxygen for your kids. What about replenishing your supply of oxygen so you have it to give to your wife and your children?

Not surprisingly, in her study of dual-earner couples, psychologist Rosalind Barnett found that one of the strongest predictors of stress among both mothers and fathers was whether they had time for themselves. So how do you find time for yourself when you are working *and* finding time for your marriage *and* finding time for your kids? Presented here are the three techniques that I have found most useful for working fathers. Fathers should customize each to their own particular needs and situation.

Create a Minivacation Zone

Blocking out a half-hour to an hour for yourself, each day or even every other day, can make a world of difference to most dads. Physical exercise, whether it's a morning run, a midday workout, or an evening walk, seem to be most effective. Spending some time on a hobby, whether it's woodworking or watching a sporting event, also works.

Create a Buffer Zone

It may be that the only time you have to yourself is when you are commuting to and from work. Despite the assumption that commuting adds stress to the workday, it can actually reduce work–family stress when you use it as a buffer between the two worlds. Instead of using your train time to read two more interoffice memos, give yourself a break and read something for fun. Some dads work their way through a good novel every week or two using this technique and feel less stressed when they get home. One man who drives to and from work found that listening to the news was an efficient way to use his time on the way home but that it was making him more stressed, not less. He switched to classical music—his own private concert—and now feels better and more relaxed when he gets home.

Create a Worry Zone

One of the biggest energy drains in our lives is worrying. At my DaddyStress/Daddy Success seminars I continually meet fathers who find themselves preoccupied with work, even while they're at home. They are supposed to be enjoying their time with the kids, but in the middle of singing "Rubber Duckie" at bath time, their minds are wandering to today's disagreement with a colleague or the proposal that's due to a client at the end of the week. Then they begin feeling guilty that they are worrying.

Advising you not to worry is a bit like advising somebody not to think of elephants. All they do after that is think of elephants. A technique that works for some dads is to create a special time period devoted exclusively to worrying. Whether you need fifteen minutes, thirty minutes, an hour, or more is up to you. The idea is to allow yourself to worry but to contain it within a defined period so it doesn't spill over and ruin your family time. By focusing on your worries in a concentrated way, you also increase the likelihood that you will hit on a workable solution or come to a resolution. The real danger of worries is when they become chronic stressors that surface and resurface.

Will there be some leakage into your family time? Of course. But give "the worry zone" a try. Many dads find it to be very effective.

SHARE THE CHILD CARE

One of the persistent tensions underlying and depleting oxygen from the relationship between busy mothers and fathers is the feeling that the arrangement for taking care of the children is not fair.

I have learned that when partners say "it's not fair," they don't mean "it's not equal." The right division is not 50–50 or any other particular number. What feels fair for one family won't feel fair for the next.

Fairness depends on an understanding of mutual expectations. Expectations that go unmet often fester and lead to frustration. Frustration quickly undermines otherwise strong relationships. But many mothers and fathers are not aware of what their mutual expectations actually are.

You can assess your family's child-care situation—and your degree of satisfaction with it—by measuring your CCQ.

You've heard of the IQ, an estimate of intelligence. Well, the CCQ, or Child Care Quotient, is a simple way of figuring out how much your partner is actually involved in child care *and* how much you expect of him or her. The CCQ is a test I invented by drawing on the research of my colleague Joseph Pleck, a psychologist from the University of Illinois who is a leading expert on how family members spend their time.

The CCQ is a gender-neutral test. Dads and moms should each take the test. What the test offers is a systematic way to think through some of the tasks involved in child care and to get a sketch of whether you are effectively communicating to find the common ground where each partner's expectations are falling near their partner's behaviors. Some couples take it together.

To determine your partner's quotient, fill out the following chart, using these directions:

1. Answer each question based on your best judgment of what your partner actually does. Leave out any items that are not appropriate to your situation. In the "What My Partner Does" column, give him or her 4 points for each task he or she performs "always," 3 points for each "frequently," 2 points for each "occasionally," 1 point for each "rarely," and 0 points for each "never."

2. Add up this column and put this number on the line next to "What My Partner Does."

3. Now go through the test questions again. This time, base your answers not on what your partner does, but on what you expect your partner to do. The second column is for these answers.

4. Add up your points in the same way and put them in the box next to "What I Expect."

5. Subtract your score from your partner's score. If what your partner actually does in the way of child care adds up to say, 14, and what you would like him or her to do adds up to 23, the CCQ is minus 9. If what your partner does adds up to 20, and what you expect adds up to 18, the CCQ is plus 2.

The highest one can get is 60 points; the lowest possible score is -60.

If your Child Care Quotient is 0, your partner is doing just as much as you expect; you've arrived at a point of low tension. If your partner's CCQ is greater than 0, your partner is actually doing more than you expect. But if your quotient is negative, you're probably dissatisfied. A CCQ of minus 4 indicates you feel mildly disgruntled; a CCQ of minus 25 suggests it's very likely that you're truly annoyed.

Because the CCQ is individualized to your situation, the test gives you and your partner a way of clarifying expectations and behaviors, which lays a strong foundation for effective communication and sharing.

If you follow the strategies presented in this chapter, you will have less of that nagging sense that there is never enough time for your family, and you will feel more connected to your children and

CHILD CARE QUOTIENT

4–ALWAYS 3–FREQUENTLY 2–OCCASIONALLY 1–RARELY 0–NEVER	WHAT MY PARTNER DOES	WHAT I EXPECT
Gets child up and dressed in morning		
Takes child to sitter, day care, or school		
Changes baby's diapers		
Takes child to doctor, dentist, etc.		
Feeds baby		
Fixes meals for child		
Picks child up from sitter, day care, or school		
Bathes child (or supervises bath)		
Stays home if child is sick		
Gets up with sick child at night		
Puts child to bed		
Attends day-care or school functions		
Sets limits or disciplines child		
Helps child with homework		
Shops for child's clothes		
Column Totals		

WHAT MY PARTNER DOES _____

MINUS WHAT I EXPECT _____

EQUALS THE CCQ _____

your wife when you are at home. But what if work takes you away from home on regular business travel? I turn next to ways to stay connected when you are traveling.

Chapter 7

Staying Connected When You're Traveling

W hen I was a kid my dad traveled a lot for business. As a sales manager for a wholesale textile company (sheets, pillowcases, mattress pads, bedspreads), he had to visit the company factory in North Carolina from our home in New York and call on key accounts from coast to coast: Sears in Chicago; Kmart in Troy, Michigan; May Company in Los Angeles; and The Bon in Seattle.

Too bad we didn't have the telecommunications and technology advances that we have now that I'm a dad. It would have reduced his need to travel so much, right?

Wrong. Contrary to popular belief, business travel has not decreased with new technology. It has increased. In his 1982 bestseller, *Megatrends,* John Naisbett accurately predicted that the advent of hightech would spawn a counter-trend demand for "high touch," face-to-face customer service. In 1994, the Travel Industry Association of America (TIA), the national nonprofit organization that represents all components of the $430 billion travel industry, recorded the highest number of business travelers ever: 38.4 million U.S. adults taking an average of 6.3 trips per year, up from the 4.7 trips per traveler taken by 33.1 million adults in 1988.

Although there are more working mothers traveling for business these days, business travel is still far more likely for working fathers. Men take 74 percent of business trips, according to the 1994 Survey of Business Travelers of the U.S. Travel Data Center, TIA's research department. TIA finds that business travelers "tend to be well-educated professional men who are married with children."

Moreover, dads' time away from home for business travel has increased since the beginning of the decade. In 1991, the average duration of a business trip was 3.2 nights; by 1994, it was up to 3.6 nights. That adds up to 22.7 nights on the road for the average business traveler per year, up from 16.8 nights just a decade earlier.

The numbers are even more startling for frequent business travelers—those who take ten or more business trips in a year. In 1994, there were 5.7 million frequent travelers, up from 5 million in 1988. Between 1989 and 1994, the average number of trips taken per frequent traveler more than doubled, growing from 14 to 28.6. Over this same period, the average number of nights spent on the road per year grew from 75.4 to 88.7, one-fourth of the calendar year!

And a new class of super-frequent business travelers has emerged, the so-called "road warriors" who represent the top 1 percent of business travelers. Achieving road warrior status requires fifty airplane flights a year and an equal number of hotel nights. Hard-core road warriors easily top these minimum levels, as did a man enshrined in the Hilton Frequent Traveler Hall of Fame for staying in more than 100 different Hilton hotels in one year. What's it like being a road warrior working father? "Their kids may not smile at them when they get home," a representative for Hyatt Hotels says, "but the front desk will."

Most likely your travel schedule falls shy of road warrior status. But if you fall somewhere between the average traveling dad and the frequent-flier dad, you are spending between three weeks and three months a year away from your family.

This travel can strain family relationships. According to a 1995 survey by Marriott and AT&T of 500 children between the ages of six and twelve, most kids want to hear more from their dads when they are on the road: Over half surveyed said they felt sad and wanted their parents to keep in touch more often when traveling. Also, your wife may not be thrilled if you've left her on her own to deal with pick-ups from day care, evening teacher meetings, and teenagers who don't want to get off the telephone.

What can make staying connected even more tricky is the fact that everyone at home assumes business travel is fun, exciting, even glamorous. Sometimes it is. But it can get old pretty fast. And it can be both exhausting and lonely.

My wife never believed that until she started doing business travel and found herself alone in a fancy hotel in Chicago at 9 P.M. on a Wednesday night. After a day of travel and meetings, she was too tired to take advantage of the hotel or city nightlife; even though the hotel room was comfortable, it just wasn't the same as being home.

Men who travel for business are even more likely to miss being home than women. A 1995 survey of 1,000 business travelers by Wyndham Hotels and Resorts found that 68 percent of men "reported feeling lonely on an extended trip" compared with 46 percent of women.

"So what can I do?" asks a participant in my DaddyStress/ Daddy Success seminar, who, like lots of dads, has to travel for his work. "My kids miss me, my wife feels abandoned, and I feel guilty about leaving. It's enough to make me want to just get away, to concentrate on work—which makes me feel more guilty."

How you handle your goings and comings—and your time on the road—has a big impact on your family's reactions to your travels. In this chapter, I present ways to stay connected to your kids and family by managing all three phases of a trip: before you go, while you're on the road, and when you return. I'll also show you how to include your kids on business trips, as more business travelers are now doing, how to energize your relationship with your wife by turning a business trip into a minivacation, and how to use nonbusiness travel as a special way to stay connected to your kids.

PREDEPARTURE POINTERS

Phase one of travel is preparing yourself—and your family—before you leave. As we saw in Chapter 6, the fit between what your wife expects and what you actually do has a big impact on your relationship. The same is true for your kids, whose ability to understand your travel will vary greatly with their age and stage of development.

Determine if This Trip is Necessary

Before you commit to a trip, consider whether you can accomplish your goals with a telephone call or a remote conference via telephone or video. It's true that these methods are not the same as a face-to-face meeting, but how sure are you that your client feels meeting in person is necessary? A prearranged hour-long telephone call—with no interruptions—can get a lot of focused work accomplished.

Equally important if you do travel, will the trade-off in your family life be worth it? Will you miss a child's musical recital or basketball game? Will you have to cancel your regular midweek "date" with your wife? Will you leave yourself so tired that when the weekend rolls around you are recuperating from your travel rather than engaging with your kids? Business travel consumes not just the time while you are away, but all the time it takes to get ready to leave and all the reentry time. When you are calculating whether a trip is worth it, be sure to figure in all the pre- and posttravel time as well.

Trim Your Travel Time

Instead of traveling the night before, consider departing very early the morning of a meeting. If you're a frequent flier, taking an average of 28.6 business trips a year, that's the equivalent of an entire month more of evenings at home. Case in point: For regular trips from New York City to Washington, D.C., I used to take the airplane shuttle service the night before. That way I was assured of arriving on time and alert for a 9 A.M. meeting the next morning. But it also meant one less night at home to help with my kids' homework or spend with my wife. I found that by getting up very early and taking a 6:30 A.M. shuttle the next morning, I could arrive on time and just as alert. I was tired at the end of the day, but I caught up on my sleep while I was on the road, instead of on my family's time.

Acknowledge Your Wife's Feelings

When you tell your wife about the trip you need to take and she says, "It's OK, I can handle it," don't automatically take her response at face value. It doesn't matter that she *knows* you have to travel as a necessary part of providing for the family. It doesn't even matter that she *wants* you to travel. Whatever she knows or wants, her work load is likely to increase when you are away, and it is also time spent apart. Even if you both take travel for granted as a normal part of your schedule, don't take your wife or her feelings for granted.

Keep Your Separation Anxiety in Check

If your child doesn't want you to travel, it can tug at your heart. But showing your own distress won't help, and it may only encourage your child to show her upset feelings even more. The same is true when you separate from your child at day care: The children who have the hardest time when their parents leave are those whose parents have the hardest time leaving. Instead, prepare your child by telling her what she most wants to hear: Although you have to travel for work, you will be coming back, and you look forward to sharing a favorite activity with her when you return.

Explain Travel in Terms Kids Can Understand

Just because you tell your kids you're traveling for business doesn't mean they have any idea why you are leaving them. The 1995 survey of 500 school-age children sponsored by Marriott's Residence Inn/ AT&T survey mentioned earlier reported that 22 percent thought their parents spent time "eating at fancy restaurants"; one child thought her father's trips consisted of "flying around and around in airplanes." James Beasley, a safety engineer who made fifty business trips a year for Intel Corporation, says his daughter, Samantha, "used to think I worked in an airplane. An airplane would go overhead, and she'd point up there and say, 'There's Daddy.'"

Explain Your Timetable in Their Terms

Children do not need to know—and probably can't understand—many of the details of your business travel. What they do most need to know is why you are leaving and when you are coming back in concrete terms that fit their sense of time, not yours. For example, it may not mean anything if you tell your four-year-old, "I'll be back on Friday night," if he doesn't yet know his days of the week. Better to connect your return to one of the week's regular events that he can understand: I'll be back after two Sesame Streets (or another favorite TV show), or I'll be back before you and I take your sister to field hockey practice on Saturday morning.

Children under three, in particular, may not understand that you are coming back at all. Start a project with them to be finished when you return. Then your wife can remind your child that you will be finishing it when you return; and when you call home, you can remind your child that you are going to finish it together. With children who are learning to count and read, you can put stickers on your kitchen calendar; each day peeled off means you are a day closer to coming home. For children ten and older, show them a map of your route—the cities and states, even countries, continents, or oceans over which you will be flying.

Show Them Where You're Going

If you have a good atlas or a home computer with access to the World Wide Web, you may be able to show your family what location you are going to and what it looks like. Instead of "Where's Waldo?" you can play your own family version of "Where's Dad?"

Be careful, however, not to romanticize the trip; make it clear that time will be spent in meetings, not vacationing. Here are a few good web sites to use to show your family where you are going:

- *Travelocity* at http://www.travelocity.com lets you zoom in on most major cities in the world and look around.

- *TravelCOM* at http://www.travelcom.es/ gives you information on many major cities around the globe. You can compare landmarks.

- *KidSmart Travel* at http://www.travel.carlson.com/kidsmart.html is a start-to-finsh guide for taking a trip with a child in mind.

- *Have Children Will Travel* at http://havechildrenwilltravel.com/ is a family-friendly newsletter for vacation and travel with everyone involved.

Establish Rituals Surrounding Your Trip

Include Children in Leave-Taking Rituals

Just as it is important to create daily rituals for staying connected, it is important to create rituals that signal your departure and imply your return. Young children can "help" you pack by figuring out different ways to squeeze socks into your suitcase; or you can let them hide a special note or surprise in your suitcase, something that you will have to find when you arrive at your destination. Children in the eight-to-ten range—typically a time when kids like to "collect" cards, stickers, or miniature play critters of all kinds—can "lend" you something from their collection to keep in your suitcase; this may actually be more meaningful to them than knowing that you are carrying their photo in your wallet. The family can have a special meal or dessert at home to signal your departure or can eat together at a kid-favorite place like McDonald's or Burger King. Or you can drive to the airport together to "wish daddy good luck."

Create a Ritual for While You're Away

Although your daily rituals for connection will be interrupted while you are away, you can create special rituals for connection while you are apart. For example, agree to think about each other at a certain time of day ("Could you feel me thinking about you at 3 P.M. when you were getting out of school?") or send a hug goodnight.

Leave a Surprise

Leave behind a special note to be put into a lunch box or under a pillow. If your child is too young to read, mom can read it, or you can leave a picture that you have drawn.

Send Mail before You Leave

If you will be taking a long trip, mail a postcard or letter *before* you leave. If you will be on an overseas trip with slow mail to your hometown, prepare some postcards to be mailed out by a colleague or friend while you are away. A piece of mail received soon after you leave is a nice pick-me-up for everybody at home.

Delay Special Family Rituals for Your Return

Some families choose to delay a celebration, such as a birthday dinner, if it falls on a day when dad has to travel. Although you do not want to completely disrupt your family's schedule because you have to travel, for many families the occasions are more special when dad is a full participant. And waiting for dad's return cuts down on hurt from missed occasions.

KEEP-IN-TOUCH TIPS

Phase two of travel is staying connected while you are away. When I was a kid, my dad had two choices: telephone or mail. Now technology has created more options, including fax, e-mail, and videotape.

If you use them in ways that fit your child's stage of development and the rhythms of your family's life, they are all excellent ways to keep in touch.

Telephone

Ask Specific Questions

If you ask, "What did you do today?" you're likely to hear, "Nothing." If you ask, "How was your day?" you'll probably hear, "OK" These answers don't tell you too much. And, as you may know from experience, they don't give you many clues on how to keep the conversation going. Start with specifics instead of generalities, and you will be much more likely to get, and keep, a conversation going. "What happened at the touch football game after school?" or "How was the math test you were worried about?" or "What did Jennifer and you do on your play date?" Of course, asking specific questions while you're on the road means that you were in touch with your child's daily life before you left. If you aren't sure what the kids did that day, talk to your wife or your child's caregiver first to find out; that will give you an idea of the specific questions to ask.

Find a "Best Time" to Call

Just because you have a few minutes to call home between flights doesn't mean your child will necessarily want to pull himself away from his favorite activity to talk with you. And don't expect your call to draw a delighted response from your wife if she is trying to get dinner on the table or three kids to bed. Try to establish a "best time" to call that will work for everybody in the family, or, given the variation in family schedules from day to day, establish which times are the best on different days of the week. That will also help establish your telephone call as a daily ritual for connection while you are away.

Make a Surprise Call

Ritual shouldn't mean rigid. Leave a surprise message on the family's telephone answering machine.

Fax

Relay Faxes from Your Office

If you will be out of the country or in a location where sending mail back home is slow, use your office fax as a relay station. Leave pre-addressed and stamped envelopes at work and then ask a colleague to forward your faxes to your family at home. Of course, if you have a fax at home, you can cut out the middleman.

Send Drawings

When it comes to staying in touch with preschoolers or kids who cannot yet write, the fax machine has a distinct advantage over e-mail: It's easy to send drawings. You can draw what something on your trip looks like, fax it home, and have it taped to the refrigerator. Conversely, your kids can fax you their scribbles or drawings of life at home. When you return you can put the faxes together in sequence and make a "book" to serve as a good starting point for discussing what happened during your trip.

Check Homework

If you have a fax machine at home, fax is a good way to help with your child's homework even though you're traveling. For example, if you usually review your daughter's math assignments or your son's compositions, have them send their work to your hotel. Then you can either call them or fax them back with suggestions or questions.

Send Surprise Greetings

If your telephone schedules don't quite mesh, faxing is a good way to send surprise greetings. If you have a fax machine at home, send a "Good Morning Greeting" while everybody is asleep.

E-Mail

Vinton Cerf, now MCI's senior vice president for Data Architecture, is often called a "Father of the Internet" for cowriting Internet Protocol (IP), the computer language that allows more than 20 million e-mail users to communicate with one another on the information superhighway. "With my travel schedule and unpredictable hours, it can be difficult to reach my kids on the phone," explains Cerf, so he relies on e-mail to "stay in touch and keep informed about what's going on in the family, regardless of where I am in the world."

Lots of traveling dads and moms are now using e-mail to stay in touch. For the first time in his nineteen years of marriage, U.S. Navy officer Timothy Cooley can stay in daily contact with his wife, Rebecca, in Portland, Maine, during his overseas deployments, exchanging notes about "frozen gutters and Boy Scout merit badges . . . the merits of letting their ten-year-old son read a Tom Clancy novel, the health of a family friend diagnosed with cancer, and the weather." The system—which runs on two old computers and a $250 software investment—can be accessed by deployed men and women at their duty stations and back home by spouses, children, and families either from home if they have a computer, from the station's Family Center, or at a local school attended by many children from military families. In the future, the base plans to buy a digital camera. Robert Hill, another Navy dad, receives e-mails from his daughter, Laura, age three, who often types "random letters onto the keyboard to him. Five months ago she signed the notes *L* but now ends them *Laura.*"

E-mail can be a powerful tool for working fathers to stay in touch with their children while traveling or even from their office when they are home. Here are tips for staying connected to your family through e-mail:

Be Spontaneous

If you have e-mail at home and a portable computer for traveling, e-mail is the easiest and least expensive way to stay in touch. It's especially handy for sending spontaneous notes or questions without writing out a whole letter.

Borrow a Computer

If you have a computer with a modem at home, you don't even need to have a laptop on the road in order to send e-mail. So many offices now have e-mail that you can easily ask the colleague or client you are visiting—or the hotel you are staying at—if you can send a message on their system. It's no different than asking if you can use their phone to make a local phone call.

Create a Travel Quiz

You can pique your children's curiosity about the world beyond their home by creating a quiz tied to your travel schedule. If you are in Chicago, for example, ask them to identify the architect who designed so many of the stunning buildings in the city. The only rules: They have to figure out not just the answer, but three ways to obtain the information without asking mom or another household relative. The idea is to encourage their capacity to learn. Did they try the encyclopedia? Did they visit or call the local library and ask for the reference desk? Did they search on-line? Did they call a local architecture firm? When they do their "investigative work," they will be doing something active—mentally active—that connects them with you.

Print Out Your E-mails

When you return, print out the e-mails sent to and from your family while you were away. Just like the "book" of faxes, they make a great way to trigger a discussion of what everybody was doing during your trip. And if you and your child save them in a file—like saving entries in a diary—they will help you both remember the day-to-day connections, long after you have forgotten a specific business trip.

Videotape

As the price of videocameras keeps dropping, and as the cameras themselves become easier to use, it becomes more feasible for families to send moving pictures to one another. This is especially handy if you are going to be away on a long trip.

{Staying Connected When You're Traveling}

Read Bedtime Stories

If you are going to be away for a very long time, video is a great way to capture at least a piece of a common family ritual. Before he left for Bosnia and the rescue of downed pilot Scott O'Grady, U.S. Marine Captain Gregory Bryant, who travels constantly, videotaped himself reading bedtime stories to three-year-old Danielle and one-year-old Jessica. The children told neighbors that their dad was gone "defending the world," but he was still very much a nightly presence in their household.

Watch Them Play/Watch Them Grow

For long trips, video works as a two-way communications tool. Have a special event like a toddler learning to walk or a ten-year-old's first soccer game videotaped for you to see.

Snail Mail

Don't get so caught up in the advantages of high-tech contact that you forget about more traditional forms of staying in touch. Even if you've got electronic mail, there is still something special about getting a handwritten note delivered in an envelope, especially if it has a unique postage stamp on it. But be prepared with a regular book of stamps in your briefcase as well, so you can easily send a postcard or letter from wherever you are.

WHAT YOUR WIFE NEEDS WHEN YOU'RE ON THE ROAD

All the tips for staying in touch with your children apply for your wife. But in addition, she may appreciate:

- **Your ear** If you call home and your wife complains or describes the problems she is having, do not—repeat, do not—offer immediate solutions. What she probably needs much more is your empathy and appreciation. After that, if she wants your advice, you can give it.

- **Your frequent flier miles** If your wife doesn't get much of a chance to get away, save up your frequent flier miles and offer them to her as a surprise. Then encourage her to visit a friend for a "getaway" weekend while you take care of the kids.

- **Your valentine** It doesn't have to be Valentine's Day to send your wife flowers. If you don't know what type of flowers she likes best, ask the florist what flowers will last the longest—it's nice to have flowers that will stay alive during your whole trip.

HOW TO TAKE THE KIDS WITH YOU

Bringing children on an occasional business trip may still be unorthodox, but it is no longer unusual. The Travel Industry Association of America reports that in 1993 about 42 million business travelers took a child with them, a 34 percent increase over the previous five years. During 1995, 15 percent of business trips—41.3 million—included children. The great majority of these trips includes dads who are either traveling with both their spouse and their children, or even sometimes alone with a child.

Professional speaker John Wayne Lee, of Crawfordville, Florida, who travels virtually every week of the year, started taking his son Jonathan with him as an infant, lest he never get to see him. At age three Jonathan earned elite status—40,000 miles—on Continental Airlines. "Maybe he's destined to become a pilot!" says his dad. According to Chris Tempesta, president of KiddieCorps, a San Diego, California-based company that supplies bonded caregivers at conferences and conventions throughout the country, the number of fathers traveling on business as a lone adult with children is small, but growing.

Some women say a man can travel on business with a child

but without a partner and be treated as a hero, but that a woman would be criticized for failing to make adequate child-care arrangements. But that's not necessarily how fathers report feeling. A male accountant who has taken his twelve-year-old son on business travel for the last four years, explains, "I think the corporate world is more understanding of a mother on business with a child." So wary is this dad of his company thinking being a dad will interfere with his work that he instructs his son never to answer the hotel room phone, just in case it's the office calling.

Bringing your child with you—whether your spouse comes along as well—can be a great adventure. If you have planned your trip well you can accomplish your business, your child can be well taken care of, and your spouse can participate in some of the professional and/or leisure activities associated with the trip. Particularly with older children, who can have fun while a parent is occupied with work, working fathers who have included children describe these trips as some of the most special times they have spent together. The following tips will help you make traveling with your child work.

Consider Your Child's Schedule

When including a child on a business trip, making some changes to your typical travel plans is likely in order to help ensure a more enjoyable trip for all. David A. Sitomer, an account manager for the Independent Telecommunications Network in Overland Park, Kansas, learned a valuable lesson the hard way. "The first time he brought his three-year-old son on a trip, Mr. Sitomer took his normal late night flight to Miami. On arrival the boy was cranky and refused to walk through the airport. He had to be carried—along with Mr. Sitomer's briefcase, carry-on bag, and suitcase. Now Mr. Sitomer books only midday business flights when he brings one of his three sons along. "You do it the first time, you're thinking the business trip," he says. "The next time I did it, I said, 'Let me schedule it around him.'" If you are crossing time zones, since it may takes children longer to adjust to new schedules, consider wearing a second watch, one set to local time and one left to your child's time, until both are in sync.

Investigate Child-Care Arrangements

"When even a handful of parents make an initial inquiry, arrangements are often made for child care. Trade associations very much want to accommodate their members," says KiddieCorp's Chris Tempesta. She advises parents always to ask, rather than assume it can't be done. Because so many of its business travel guests brought children with them, the Bonaventure Resort & Spa in Ft. Lauderdale, Florida, set up a children's advisory board comprised of fourth graders from a nearby school. So check with your hotel or corporate sponsor in advance about possible child-care arrangements. Care done right frees a working parent from worry and allows the parent to concentrate on business. Also, if a spouse is accompanying the business traveler, arranged care means he or she can spend some time with the business traveler at conference functions or can enjoy some leisure time.

Be Prepared to See the World through Your Child's Eyes

When my fourteen-year-old son, Joshua, traveled with me to Chicago, where I was to appear on the *Oprah Winfrey Show*, I discovered what made traveling with dad so special. It wasn't meeting Oprah or seeing a TV studio. Instead, it was being able to order room service from a hotel—eating dinner in what was, in effect, his bedroom. When Josh insisted on eating breakfast in our room, too, I realized that one of the greatest joys of bringing kids with you on business travel is learning what interests them.

Plan Ahead for More Trouble-Free Travel with Children

If you're planning on traveling with children on business—or at any other time—get a copy of Vicki Lansky's *Trouble-Free Travel with Children: Helpful Hints for Parents on the Go.* Among the clever tips you'll find:

- Let an active toddler jog around the airport to tire him- or herself out before boarding the plane.

- Choose [airplane] seats away from busy areas such as the galley if you are hoping your child will take a nap.

- Ask for a ground-level room in a motel to save hauling children and luggage up and down the stairs.

It is also important to be prepared with health information about your child. "When a parent drops a child off, particularly an infant, there is quite a bit of information we need to know—what is going on with sleeping, eating, diapering schedules, etc.," says KiddieCorp's Tempesta. "We have been absolutely delighted with the involvement and knowledge of the dads we see today."

Turn Business Travel into a Minivacation

You can turn the necessity of time away from your family into an opportunity for your wife and kids to join you for a weekend vacation together. If that seems a financial impossibility, consider this: Hotel rates typically drop considerably during the weekend, as does airfare if you stay over on a Saturday night. Stay alert for airline specials; you can often find amazingly low weekend round-trip fares.

For your kids, just being in a hotel may be an adventure, especially if it has a swimming pool. And if the hotel can provide quality child care—as more and more hotels now do—you and your wife can spend a day wandering around a city you've never visited, have dinner with the kids, and then go out on the town for a getaway date.

REENTRY RHYTHMS

The third phase of business travel is returning to your family. Don't expect to be able just to pick up with things as they were before you left, especially if you've been away for the better part of a week. Reunions have their own rhythms.

Clarify Expectations

Smooth reentry has a lot to do with understanding your family's expectations and feelings. You need to recognize theirs, and help them recognize yours. Since you have been away, your kids may be looking forward to a special outing; but the last thing you may want is to go out, preferring some quiet time with them at home. If you clarify what everybody expects, wants, and needs, you will be better able to figure out a reentry pattern that works best for all. For example, you may not be emotionally available when you return home. Greet everybody as enthusiastically as you can, explain that you'll need to take a short rest, but plan something special to do afterward.

Prepare for a Delayed Reaction

Even though you know they missed you, and they say they missed you, sometimes it may seem as if your wife and children are not acting like it. Happiness at having you home may be masked by anger that you have been away. Give everybody a chance to readjust, without expecting a dramatic welcome. Reestablish contact with each of your kids separately. That can mean just sitting on your child's bed for a few minutes to reconnect. After you have established contact with everybody separately, reunite with the whole family by doing something together—playing a game, watching a video, or going out for a treat.

If You Offer Presents, Don't Substitute Them for Your Presence

Buying your child a big gift every time you travel overemphasizes objects as signs of your love. But it's also fun to bring home something special, and it is affirming for kids to know you have been thinking about them and about what they would like, especially if it's a gift related to the trip.

Dan Hogan, president of the management consultancy the Apollo Group, takes pictures of the places he has been and brings them back and shares them with his children. It makes a nice gift and encourages him to take even just a few minutes to see the local attractions, which are often sacrificed when travel days get hectic.

One of my favorite sources of gifts—many inexpensive—that kids love for playing pretend is the army and navy store. You can pick up shoulder patches, lapel pins, badges, and more. Get in the habit of looking, and you'll find many army and navy stores readily accessible in downtown areas.

In a rush? Here are some on-the-fly trinkets that are always fun:

- Miniature soaps, shampoos, or lotions from your hotel—the more the better
- Tiny jars of jelly or minibottles of ketchup from your room service tray
- Flight pins from the airline
- Snow domes from the airport

SPECIAL TRAVEL TIMES—WHEN IT'S NOT BUSINESS

Travel should not always revolve around business. During the school year, long weekends are good opportunities to explore together. And summer often gives dads a chance to get away with the kids or to plan trips they'd like to take in the future. Of course, if your child is not yet in school, you have more time flexibility, but you still need to keep the outings geared to your child's age. Here are seven dad-tested travel ideas that will help you connect with your kids while having a good time. Try them out and adapt them for your own family.

Share Your Passion

Avid cyclist John Wilcockson of Boulder, Colorado, began sharing his love of bicycling with his one-year-old daughter, Emma, by strapping her into a childseat attached to the back of the bicycle built for two that he and his wife used for outings. Emma could ride a two-wheeler by the time she was four, made her first fifty-mile trip by the time she was seven, and her first week-long trip at age eight. "Cycling is about adventure," he says, "but it also gives you a great sense of independence. It's not like playing around in the street, because you're actually going somewhere, achieving something physically. Through sharing these things together she came to understand why I had this passion."

Take the Trip You Never Took with Your Dad

That's what Manhattan real-estate attorney Andrew Berkman did when he took his six-year-old son, Ben, on a Sierra Club Family Trip to the Sawtooth Mountains of Idaho. "We're essentially urban people," says Berkman. "Here we were 9,800 feet up, not in some skyscraper but at a campsite by a stream with a gorgeous panoramic view of the sky." Twenty years later, "there's a picture in our bedroom of Ben and me standing at the top of the plateau, overlooking the valley, with him barely up to my waist. We go back there now, and the valley looks the same. We change but it doesn't. I look at it all the time and find a meaning that transcends two decades, one that Ben now understands, too."

Cherish the Quiet Time

Although taking an adventurous trip together can forge lifelong bonds, don't discount the unexciting part of travel. After his divorce, the first vacation Joe Alred took with his daughter was a thousand-mile excursion from Wisconsin to the Gulf Coast, camping and fishing en route to visit family. "What really stands out," says Joe, "is the quiet times, driving or getting up from a truck in the middle of the night to go to the bathroom, not even talking to one another. We were there comfortably together. The word *together* really took on meaning."

Go with the Guys

For Jeff Waller, a chemical engineer from Racine, Wisconsin, one of the best ways to connect with his five-year-old daughter, Sarah, was on a trip with other dads and their kids. A winter weekend encampment for Indian Guides and Indian Princesses let him have one-on-one time with Sarah, and it let Sarah see him "acting like a kid with the other fathers. When she saw three guys piled on a sled, laughing all the way down the hill, she saw me having a good time with my friends, too." Often moms appreciate the time "off."

Take a Minitrip

You don't have to travel that far to get away. When Jeffrey Hill of Salt Lake City, Utah, took his first paternity leave from IBM in 1989, he had the time to begin reading up on backpacking and to take short forays—more or less long walks—with three of his children. Gradually the trips have extended for as long as a week, and backpacking has become a tradition for Hill, his wife, and their eight children. "It allows me to be with the kids without any pressure," says Hill. "When we're walking together in the outdoors, the kids just kind of open up."

No Phones, No Beepers

To give and get undivided attention—especially as your kids move into the teenage years—go somewhere without telephones, and leave behind all beepers. When his daughter, Teon, was turning thirteen, Mark Edwards of Northfield, Minnesota, took her to a retreat center in Washington's Cascade Mountain Range. "We ate meals together, worshipped together, played together, and talked about aspects of religion I had never realized she thought so much about—the nature of God, why there is evil in the world. Unlike home, where people would call me at any time, no one could reach me. Same with her. So we could really pay attention to each other."

Bring Audiocassettes

To make long trips speed by, use your car's tape deck. My wife and I taped many of our ancient (read 1960s) LPs—Peter, Paul & Mary; Joan Baez; The Weavers—so the whole family could sing together in the car. The kids loved being introduced to what we thought was "cool." Even more fun was the conversations it promoted—Did we listen to it on dates? Hear it at clubs? In movies? Which movies? Did you really dance to it? Also, hundreds of classic children's stories are now available with readings by stars such as Meryl Streep and Mel Gibson. If you don't want to purchase them, check your public library or borrow from friends.

If you follow the tips presented in this chapter, you will be able to stay better connected to your children and your wife when business travel takes you away from the family. In the next chapter, I show you how you can stay better connected to your kids and reduce your own work–family conflict—by getting involved with their schools, day care, and the other organizations where children spend so much of their daily time.

Chapter 8

Connecting through School, Day Care, and Other "Significant Others"

S ometime during the 1980s, questions about "quality time" began to predominate every seminar I did about parenting.

"Do you think spending an hour every night with my three-year-old is enough—if it's quality time?" asked an anxious mid-level manager who commuted two hours each way to and from work so that his family could live in a community with a good school system.

"Can quality time during summer and vacations offset the rest of the year?" asked a divorced factory foreman whose fourteen-year-old son lived two thousand miles away with his mother.

Debates about "quality time" started popping up in magazines and on television talk shows. Which was more important, quality or quantity? Was it even possible to have quality time without quantity? Which was more crucial for infant development? For preschoolers? For school-age kids?

On it went with psychologist pitted against psychologist, working mother against at-home mother, making many parents anxious and hypervigilant about whether they were doing things *right*.

Is quality important?

Of course. But the quality of your relationship cannot be reduced to a series of picture-perfect "Kodak Moments," however memorable or pleasurable those may be. Opportunities to connect with children, to have them truly feel our presence and understanding, occur at all sorts of unplanned times: a ten-minute drive back from a Little League game, a thirty-minute visit to the vet to take care of a sick pet, five minutes of doing the dishes together.

Is quantity important? Of course. It is naive at best, and dangerous at worst, to think that you can build connections without investing time.

But preoccupation with quality time has led parents to focus too narrowly on their relationship with a child without paying enough attention to their relationship with the "significant others" in a child's life, including teachers, child-care providers, coaches, doctors, and children's friends.

Consider for a moment how much time children actually spend with their parents during weekdays at different stages of development:

- **Preschoolers** In 1991, 54 percent of preschoolers were cared for in an organized child-care facility or in another home while their parents worked. After sleeping for about ten hours, the average three-to-five-year-old with working parents spends seven of the remaining fourteen hours out of the home in some form of child care. That's 50 percent of waking hours with a parent, and 50 percent with "someone else."
- **School-age children** After sleeping about nine hours a night, the average elementary school student spends between six and seven of the remaining hours in school. Add in another 2.5 hours or so per day for after-school activities—Brownies, Cub Scouts, 4-H, sports teams—and the average child is spending about 60 percent of his waking time away from his mother and father.
- **High-school-age children** If a teenager's sleep drops down to eight hours a night, her combined time for school, extracurricular activities, and a job goes up to at least ten hours. That's more than 60 percent of waking time away from home— without factoring in time with friends away from parents.

No matter which age you examine or what type of family you look at—dual-earner families, families with a mom working at home—the quality of your growing child's daily time is greatly related to the quality of the time the child spends with other people. But if you aren't there, what kind of influence can you have in shaping that experience?

The answer is, an extraordinary amount, and likely far more than you realize. Even if you are not physically present, you influence your child's experience by staying connected with and exerting an influence on the "significant others" with whom he or she actually spends so much time.

In this chapter I focus on how you can stay connected with the "significant others" in your child's life. I start with school, the place other than home where children spend the majority of their waking time. Once you understand the importance of your involvement in your child's education and strategies for how you can stay involved, you will be able to apply them to day care, visits to the pediatrician, and other significant settings and people in your child's life.

THE POWER OF INVOLVEMENT

Nowhere is the power of your connection with the other important adults in your child's life more clear and compelling than in your child's education. A mounting body of evidence shows that parental involvement is significantly related to children's school performance.

In 1996, Temple University psychologist Laurence Steinberg published the results of the most extensive study ever conducted of the forces in youngsters' lives that affect their interest and performance in school. Steinberg and his colleagues studied more than 20,000 teenagers and their families in an attempt to determine why American student achievement is declining and why so many students are disengaged from learning. Who or what is the culprit? Is it schools in need of restructuring? Teachers in need of retraining? Drugs? The media? The "breakdown" of the American family? And perhaps even more important, Steinberg and his colleagues sought the key factors in the lives of students who did achieve.

What they discovered was that "parents exert a profound and lasting effect on their children's achievement in school," more so than any other factor, and in ways that are not commonly recognized.

"Our findings were somewhat surprising," he explains. "The type of parental involvement that matters most is not the type of involvement that parents practice most often—checking over homework, encouraging children to do better, and overseeing the child's academic program from home. . . . Our research shows that the type of involvement that makes a real difference is the type that actually draws the parent into the school physically—attending school programs, extracurricular activities, teacher conferences, and 'back to school' nights."

Why should this type of involvement make so much difference? According to Steinberg:

> When parents take the time to attend a school function—time off from an evening activity or time off from their own jobs—they send a strong message about how important school is to them and, by extension, how important it should be to the child. When this sort of involvement occurs regularly, it reinforces the view in the child's mind that school and home are connected and that school is an integral part of the whole family's life. Attending school functions may be even more important for the message it communicates to teachers and other school personnel. Teachers cannot help but pay closer attention to students whose parents they encounter frequently at school programs, for both positive and negative reasons.

When their children have academic difficulties, Steinberg discovered, parents of successful students do not try to handle the problem themselves at home. Rather, "they mobilize the school on their child's behalf—they 'work the system.' . . . By working through the school, parents send the child the message that they have faith in the school's ability and willingness to educate the child, and this strengthens the child's belief in the efficacy of the school. Moreover, contacting the school when the child is having difficulty lets the school know that the parents are involved and that they expect the school to serve their child."

After reviewing sixty-six recent studies of family–school relationships across all grade levels, researchers Anne T. Henderson and Nancy Berla came to the same conclusion about children's learning as Steinberg: Parent involvement is the most accurate predictor of a student's achievement in school, more important than family income or demographic factors. "To those who ask whether involving parents will really make a difference, we can safely say the case is closed." The effects of involvement show up as early as preschool and continue through high school.

But research also suggests that fathers tend to be less involved with their children's school than mothers. In its 1985 study, *High School and Beyond*, the U.S. Department of Education asked students with different high school grade averages to report on the involvement of their parents. *A* students reported involvement by 92 percent of their mothers and 85 percent of their fathers; *B* students reported involvement by 89 percent of their mothers and 79 percent of their fathers. As the grade levels dropped, so did overall participation by both parents, especially by fathers.

What exactly does "parent involvement" mean? Involvement as a father is not just attending parent-teacher nights or volunteering to help with an annual school event, although these are two valuable activities. It means showing your children you care about their education through things you can do at school, changes you can push for at school, and things you can do at home.

"But my wife is already involved with my child's school," say some of the participants in my seminars. "She knows the teachers, goes to the meetings. Do I need to be there, too?"

Yes.

It is a common pattern for mom to be the "expert" in maintaining relationships with all the people outside the family who care for your child. Just as she often assumes the role of "designated hugger" inside the family, so she often assumes the role of "designated connector" outside the family. But that doesn't mean there is no room for you, or that she doesn't want to make room for you. If mom is maintaining all those connections—and working outside the home—she may be on "relationship overload" and more than willing to share them with you. And if you have not broached the subject, she may assume you aren't available or interested.

Moreover, just because mom has assumed the designated connector role does not mean that's what is best for your child. If you are involved with your child's day care or education or medical care, you will not detract or subtract from mom's involvement. Instead, you will add yours. Your child will learn that you, too, value the significant others in his or her life—that they are extensions of you when you are not there.

CONNECTING THROUGH YOUR CHILD'S SCHOOL

Being plugged in to your child's school experience—from preschool through high school and even beyond—has big benefits. According to Harvard University psychologist Samuel Osherson, " It enhances a child's self-esteem to know that what they're doing is valued by their father."

How to Connect at School

There are many ways you can contribute to your child's educational experience. Underlying them all is one simple notion: communication.

Meet the Teacher and Principal—Early

When children are in preschool and the early grades of elementary school, it reassures them to know that you know who their teacher is—not just by name, but that you have actually met the teacher. It's even better if you can meet the school principal or other person in charge, too.

Don't assume you have to wait for the first parent night to do this. If you can, arrange to drop by before or after work to introduce yourself and say hello. Let the teacher know he or she can always reach you, and find out how you can reach the teacher if you have a question. Although it's nice if you and mom can do this together, it is key that you make contact, sending an early, clear message to the teacher that your child's father is interested and serious about his or her education.

Don't Wait for Report Cards or Teacher Meetings to Confirm Problems

In 1996, a survey of parents, teachers, and students in Florida's Broward County School District, the sixth largest in the nation, confirmed that school personnel rarely hear from parents unless there is a problem. That's a typical but dangerous pattern that lets problems fester. At work, if you learned that an employee was falling behind, would you wait three or four months to give feedback?

If you sense that your child is having difficulty socially or academically, get in touch with the teacher. And if there is a family problem that might be affecting your child at school—a divorce, serious family illness, or upcoming job relocation—don't wait until report-card or parent-teacher–conference time to say, "Oh, I bet that's because of our family situation. Perhaps I should have told you."

Volunteer at School

Volunteering is a great way to get a sense of how your child spends a day at school without making him or her feel as if you are sitting there watching—which can be disconcerting for both child and teacher. You will have a chance to meet the other children in the classroom, see how your child interacts with them, and see how the teacher interacts with all of the kids. When your child mentions another child by name, you'll have a better idea of who he or she is talking about.

Particularly in the younger grades, your child gets "points" from peers for having a dad who came in, and it often adds some excitement to the classroom routine.

A great way to volunteer is to bring to school a skill or interest that you already have. Whether it's computers, cooking, or playing the guitar, the trick is to find something you like doing, then adapt it—with the teacher's help—by being a class volunteer. If you're a handyman-type, lead the preschool or elementary class in building a birdhouse or rabbit hutch. If you're a weekend gardener, get each child started on planting and caring for a seedling.

You can also bring your expertise at work to school. If you are a chemist, explain to junior high or senior high students what chemists actually do for work after they have finished memorizing the periodic tables. Show younger kids how they can shake cream into butter. The Hawthorne Elementary School in Kansas City, Kansas, has organized the "Men of Hawthorne" program to bring men of all walks of life—carpenters, truck drivers, bankers, health care workers, police officers—into the classroom to assist with activities and lead discussions with students about their work.

Visit the Classroom

Whether or not you volunteer, visiting your child's classroom can be extremely valuable. It's a great opportunity to get a bird's-eye view of what he or she is doing and insight into how the teacher teaches. Even a one-hour visit on a "normal" school day can give you far more insight than the typical, carefully orchestrated parent–teacher night, where what you mostly see is other parents.

Although it's usually more comfortable and fun to visit elementary school, I strongly recommend visiting your child's junior high and even high school, perhaps over your child's protests. When I told my eleventh-grade son that I wanted to go to school with him on parents' day, he said, "Oh, dad, that's so embarrassing. Do you have to? What is it you need to know? I'll tell you everything."

"You've been saying the classes are boring, and the school has invited parents to come in and observe. I'd like to take them up on it. I'm a taxpayer so I am paying for your schooling; why shouldn't I see what I'm paying for and what you're doing all day?"

It turned out that one mother and I were the only parents who responded to the invitation. My son's friends automatically assumed that he must have been in "huge trouble"; otherwise, why would his dad be there? Even the teachers were surprised. Most did not know that parents were allowed to visit, even on parents' day.

It turned out that visiting my son's high school classes had benefits all the way around. For all his protests—and the need to explain to his friends that he was not in "trouble"—Josh later confided that he was glad I was taking such a strong interest in him and his education. I got an inside chance to see what was so boring and to help him figure out ways to make it less so. His teachers, though a bit amazed and nervous at first that a dad would come to school, were delighted that someone was coming to appreciate their work. They also got a strong message that Josh's parents were committed and very much following his progress.

Being Involved without Missing Work

Even when work demands may seem overwhelming and prevent you from some of the most valuable ways for connection discussed here, you can still find ways to connect with your child's educational experience.

For example, walk your child to the bus stop. You'll be amazed how much kids talk spontaneously during this routine activity, which can start the day on the right foot for both of you.

At drop-offs and pick-ups, leave enough time, even five or ten minutes, to watch your child in action and to talk informally to the teacher and to other parents. You'll get an invaluable feel for how your child fits in and acts in groups (often quite different than how they interact at home or one-on-one). You'll also pick up some valuable information on what the teacher is like. Finally, by building five minutes into "pick-up time," you reduce the stress and conflict that often arises when dad arrives and child insists on lingering for five or ten minutes more.

Schedule a longer visit once a year through the fourth grade if you are unable to visit more regularly. Your child will look forward to it and never forget those days when dad came to class.

Help Your Child's School Be Father Friendly

The culture of a child's school, just like the culture of a workplace, may have an important impact on fathers' level of involvement. Most schools are so accustomed to dealing with moms that they may assume dads are unavailable or uninterested.

Bob Pasfield, a clinical social worker from Charlotte, North Carolina, explains that when his children were younger, he was responsible for them if they needed to come home in the course of the day. With five kids, that was not a rare occurrence. "We were living outside of New York City then. Marty, my wife, was commuting three hours round-trip to her job. I was working fifteen minutes from the house and ten minutes from the school. So, of course, it made sense for me to be the one to go to the school. And we wrote on the school forms: 'In case of emergencies, please contact Bob Pasfield first' and gave my office number. We listed Marty's number as well, in case there was an emergency and I was unavailable. What happened? Tracy got sick. They called Marty at work in the city. Marty, somewhat perplexed, got on the phone and, in turn, called me to get over to the school. Whenever a new nurse was hired, or the kids switched schools, the silliness started all over again."

Schools may not be aware of subtle ways in which they may actually be discouraging the involvement of dads. You can help to change the culture of your school, just like your workplace, by taking small steps such as the following, and enlisting the support of other parents, teachers, and school administrators.

Make Clear That *Parents* Means Fathers, Too

The key to getting things changed when a teacher or school says parent, but means mother, is good humor. Most educators will be embarrassed—and willing to change—once you point out habits that may be unintentional, but undeniably father unfriendly.

The next time a teacher looks only at mom when speaking at a parent-teacher conference, don't sit passively as an observer; ask her or him a pointed question to direct some attention your way. The next time a note home is addressed only to your wife, mark the envelope and salutation and send the corrected version back, with a note saying that there must have been an oversight.

If you are divorced and aren't receiving notes, write to the teacher and the principal and request to receive all notices at your address. F. Robert Maglietta, an elementary school principal at Highland Lakes Elementary in Palm Harbor, Florida, recounts the story of a fifth-grade boy who made honor roll in the school. The ecstatic child walked up to the principal and made what sounded like an unusual request: Could he have another honor roll certificate?

"I asked him why he needed two," Maglietta recalled, "and he said he wanted to mail one to his dad who lived out of state." Maglietta checked with the boy's mother, got the father's office number, and faxed over a copy of the honor roll certificate. "He was thrilled to death. He called and said, 'That brought tears to my eyes.'"

Join the School's Association for Parents and Teachers

Most schools have some form of an association for parents to help support the school through fundraising, classroom volunteering, and sponsoring school events. Often this is called PTA or PTO. Though still largely comprised of women, they are a natural vehicle for fathers to get engaged and to communicate to their children that they think school is important.

At the Lincoln Elementary School in Pompton Lakes, New Jersey, for example, John Zablocki, an executive with NBC in New York City, headed the school's safety committee for four years. He coordinated Helping Hands, the school's program of recruiting and screening volunteers to place the symbol of a hand in their front window, which symbolizes to children walking to and from school that the house is a safe place to find help if they are injured or threatened in any way. Zablocki's assignment was ideal for a parent who could not attend meetings during business hours but who could use time at night and weekends to contact parents and distribute forms.

After the first two years of involvement, when Zablocki realized he had taken on a bit more than he could manage, he and his wife,

Helene, "realized one day that we could change it—be cochairs. I was able to stay involved and contribute. We worked it this way for another two years."

Organize Dads to Volunteer

Some school administrators and dads are joining forces to recruit men to get involved. At the Fairfax-San Anselmo Children's Center in Fairfax, California, Associate Director Stan Seiderman wanted to find out why virtually all the parents who showed up for events and parent-teacher meetings were women. When he sent out a letter inviting all the fathers and father figures in the families served by his program to attend a Men's Breakfast, seventy-five men showed up, and Seiderman got his answer. "Unless I asked men specifically, took the extra effort to make it clear that fathers as well as mothers are encouraged to participate, we would get only mothers showing up," explains Seiderman.

That was in 1981. Since then, the Men's Breakfast has been held every single month, and the center has one of the highest rates of father involvement of any in the country.

Similar initiatives are cropping up all over the country, often with fathers in the lead. At the J. W. Baker Elementary School in Little Rock, Arkansas, men organized a Dads on Campus chapter to coach sports and volunteer in the classroom. In Chandler, Arizona, members of the Dads Club at the Andersen Elementary School are frequent classroom visitors and volunteers, and word of their success has prompted several nearby schools to establish their own Dads Clubs. At the El Camino Real Elementary School in Irvine, California, when a few fathers took the initiative to get involved in their children's education, they found a pent-up response from dads who were itching to do something. The call for four or five men to help fix up some shabby restrooms brought out twenty-five men and led to the formation of Camino Dads in Action, which now boasts a membership of over 125. According to Gene Bedley, former El Camino Real principal, "There is definitely a correlation between dad involvement and kids' success."

Psychologist Ronald L. Klinger recounts participating in a 7 A.M. "Donuts with Dads" event at his daughter's school in Austin, Texas. "I'm sitting there thinking this is one of the dumbest things I've ever done. My wife is back home having a real breakfast. But then I realized there were eighty guys in this room, all probably thinking the exact same thing, but they were still showing up. And that says something. Instead of having dads sit like a post, I thought, 'Let me get them for forty-five minutes and do something really useful.'" Out of that insight Klinger has gone on to organize a five-session series of fathering seminars, offered in twelve elementary schools in 1996. They proved so popular they are now being held in every elementary school in the district.

"If you build it, dads will come," to paraphrase W. P. Kinsella's *Shoeless Joe Jackson Comes to Iowa*. Working fathers are discovering that they can build it in cooperation with other dads or with school administrators.

School Involvement for Divorced Dads

At every DaddyStress seminar, several participants are divorced fathers, typically without custody. Staying involved with your child's school is inherently more difficult if you are a nonresidential parent, and even more difficult if your child's mother does not support your participation. Here are some tips for increasing your level of involvement:

- Visit or volunteer early. Explain your situation. Let the teacher see that even though you are not married, you are interested in your child's education and want to be involved.

- Make a coordinated plan for involvement with your child's mother. Discuss and try to agree on educational standards. Problems can set in when one parent expects a lower standard than the other.

- Don't make your child choose between parents. Let him or her know it is OK for the school to include both parents in school activities—or sets of parents, if there are stepfamilies.

Get Involved at Home

To stay connected with your child's school means creating a home environment that supports your child's learning at school. There are many ways to do this, including:

Reading

Read aloud to your children, not just before they can read on their own but even when they are in the later elementary school years. Don't let mom become the default designated reader. You can communicate the important value *you* put on reading far more effectively by actually reading than by talking about reading. Remember, reading does not have to be a planned or structured activity. While waiting on line at the supermarket checkout, one father encourages his daughter to hunt for words around her and sound them out. "It makes the waiting go much faster, and it is fun," he says.

Asking

Asking a generic, "What did you do in school today?" often brings the all too familiar but not very descriptive response, "Nothing." Asking specific questions—about the rabbit in your four-year-old's classroom, the sixth-grade science fair, or the tenth-grade field trip to the state capitol—opens up the chance for dialogue. Even if your child doesn't actually say that much in response, you are nurturing his or her growth. Asking your child questions about school, even questions that might have been answered in a newsletter, or by a teacher at a conference, serves an extremely valuable function: It connects you to the school as experienced by your child.

Talking Positively

Unless you talk about your child's school experience, he likely will not know how much you value it. Even if things aren't perfect at your child's school—and they never are—encourage your child with positive talk about the importance of learning and some of the good things at school.

Getting Your Child a Library Card

A first library card is a really big deal for children because it gives them a type of special power. When they go into stores with you, they can't buy any of the tempting items on the shelves unless you give them money. In the library, though, they can borrow any of the tempting books just by showing their card. Take your children often, and let them pick out lots of books.

ARE YOU "MAKING THE GRADE" IN PARENT INVOLVEMENT?

At the Frederick Douglass Elementary School in Dallas, Texas, children bring home a report card every six weeks—full of grades they have assigned their parents. Children use the card to grade parents from *A* to *F* on their school involvement in six areas. How would your children rate you? How would you rate yourself?

- Helping your child with homework
- Praising and hugging your child
- Reading to your child
- Making sure your child is prepared for school
- Furnishing school supplies
- Visiting the school and attending parent meetings

CONNECTING BEYOND THE SCHOOL

I began this chapter by drawing your attention to the wide range of "significant others" with whom your child spends time. I focused on the school as one example, a very important one. But you can adapt the approach I recommend for involvement at school to all the other significant settings in your child's life.

The Doctor's Office

Think of the doctor. Your involvement in your child's health care is good for everybody in the family. Your child will feel more protected—day-to-day and in an emergency—when you know how to take his temperature or apply a bandage. Your wife will feel less strain when you know what medicine your child is taking (the type, the dosage, and possible side effects) and how to get pills to go down. And your doctor will get an additional perspective when a problem develops. "Sometimes a father's appraisal is quite different from the mother's," says Dr. Susan Aronson, board member of the American Academy of Pediatrics, "so the doctor can get a more complete medical picture."

The best time to get involved is before your baby's birth. By interviewing the prospective pediatrician with your wife, you make clear that you plan to be an integral member of the family's health team. But if you didn't get off to such an early start, it's not too late. Here are some tips that will help you, your wife, and your doctor get you back into the loop.

Speak Up

If you haven't previously been involved in your child's medical care or if you are the only father in the waiting room, you might feel anxious when you visit the pediatrician's office. Instead of hanging back, speak up.

Introduce yourself to the office staff and to the doctor. Don't assume that they know who you are. You can say, "I'm glad I was able to make this visit today because I'm very interested. I haven't been able to come before because of my work schedule."

Don't perch behind the pediatrician's back. "Examination rooms can be crowded," says Dr. Aronson, "and if dad feels like he is playing second fiddle to mom, he might be inclined to take the corner chair." Instead, stay visible without crowding the doctor.

Be direct in asking for advice. Dr. Michael Yogman, assistant professor of pediatrics at Tufts Medical School, says doctors will appreciate your saying straight out, "Can you give me some tips on connecting with our baby?"

Rx for Good Office Visits

Here are some tips to make your trips to the doctor's office with your child more successful:

- Jot down your questions beforehand so that you won't forget them if the visit gets rushed. Be sure to bring a notebook and pencil to write down the answers.
- Take along a favorite teddy or doll for your child to play with.
- Bring an emergency snack in case it takes a long time to see the doctor.
- Talk about your pediatrician as someone who cares for children.
- Come prepared with a history of your child's illness. Your physician will diagnose as much or more from the history as from the physical exam. Key questions are: When did the illness begin? How severe is it? What are the symptoms (for example, vomiting, diarrhea)? What medications is your child taking? When did she last eat or drink? Has she had contact with others who are sick? What else have you tried to do to help your child?

Coordinate with Your Wife

It's easy for the doctor's office to get established as mom's domain. Your wife may be anxious about your taking your child to the pediatrician by yourself. Picking up on your wife's worry, your child may say she "wants mommy to go," especially if an injection is planned. Even the doctor may undermine your role by treating you like a second-class parent. "Ask your wife to call me in the morning," one pediatrician told a dad who asked for some additional information about his daughter's medical problem."

This guy's wife *did* call the doctor in the morning, to say, "Listen, doctor, anything you want to say to me about my daughter's care you can say to my husband, too. Sara has two parents who care about her." Even if your wife isn't quite that assertive, there are ways you can work together to ensure that you each have a role on the health care team:

- **Don't withdraw when your child shows a preference for mom.** It's a normal part of development for children to flip back and forth, at times wanting only mom and at times wanting only dad.

- **Develop your own style.** You do not have to mimic mom— either in playing with your child or in taking her to the doctor.

- **Plan for emergencies.** If your wife is having a hard time giving up full control of the children's health care needs, remind her that it's important for each of you to be prepared to handle an emergency when the other isn't available.

Use Your Doctor as a Resource

Your pediatrician's or family physician's responsiveness will influence your involvement in your child's health care. Take advantage of flexible hours. It's not unusual for pediatricians to have a number of evenings or Saturdays set aside to accommodate working parents, so you should be able to find a practice that fits both mom's and dad's schedule. But be reasonable about when you bring your child in. Although 8 P.M. may be best for your work schedule, it might not be the best time for the doctor to assess a child who is cranky and ready for bed.

Find a developmental pediatrician, a family doctor, or a general practitioner who can treat the entire family. Today's pediatricians are trained to help with more than colds, flu, and emergencies. Use your time with the doctor to explore your child's development and behavior and your role as parents. According to Dr. Yogman, "Having dad in my office does a lot more than help him be close to the baby. It's an opportunity for mom and dad to be close together, to share something that's ongoing and very important. It not only makes for healthier babies, but healthier marriages."

Connecting through School, Day Care, and Other "Significant Others"

There are many significant others in your child's life besides school, day care, and the pediatrician. Your child may be a member of an athletic team or club, of a scouting or 4-H group, or of a church or community organization. Apply the tips presented in this chapter to the other significant settings and people in your child's life. You will feel more connected to your child, and your child will feel more connected to you.

Conclusion

Working Fathers
Balancing the New
Work–Family Equation

B alancing the work–family equation for fathers represents one of the greatest challenges—and opportunities—of today. This book has offered a new model for thinking about dual roles and responsibilities and a set of strategies to help bridge the work–family divide. Start putting them into practice at work and at home, whether you are a father or a mother, a manager or an employee, and you will be helping yourself, your family, your business, and your community. Your success will not only help you, but serve as an example—like all those presented in this book—as other organizations and working parents struggle with the challenge.

~

In their effort to achieve excellence in strategic human resource management, commonly invoked as the business challenge of the coming decade, managers and business leaders can gain important insights from closer attention to working fathers. Deeply ingrained workplace assumptions affect both working mothers and working fathers. But as we have seen, change is possible when any member of the system—mother or father, manager or employee—begins to challenge those assumptions, to break the culture collision that stalls progress toward true family friendliness our workplaces.

Including working fathers as part of the work–family equation offers a new way to approach the issue of diversity at the workplace. Despite considerable commitments and investments, the promises of many diversity initiatives have not yet been fully realized by many companies. One commonly invoked barrier is the lack of buy-in, for the initiatives. In part, that is because proponents of diversity initiatives have had difficulty finding ways to meaningfully include white males.

Recognizing working fathers may provide a way to break the diversity logjam, to open up a new wave of discussion that can benefit all employees. A cross section of working fathers—white, African-American, Hispanic, Asian, Chicano, Asian Pacific Islander, and an array of others—is a powerful component of America's work force. Until now, their experiences have largely remained an invisible dilemma. Including them as part of the concern with diversity may open up a new wave of discussion that can benefit all employees. According to Barbara Cortright, who heads the Workforce Diversity Office of United Technologies in Hartford, Connecticut, "We're trying to get people here to think of diversity as something other than black or white. We're trying to enlighten people that it's not affirmative action—it's your personal situation."

~

Will attention to working fathers be sustained? A combination of demographic and values shifts will increase the likelihood that more and more men in Workforce 2000 will be more concerned than ever about balancing their commitments to work and family.

For example, the number of households with dual full-time working parents will increase. In 1980, 33 percent of couples consisted of a full-time employed husband and a full-time employed wife; by 1990 the number had risen to 55 percent.

The gap between what mothers and fathers contribute to household income will likely continue to close, changing the decision making about the division of labor within the home. In 1970, working wives contributed 27 percent of average family income, according to the Bureau of Labor Statistics. In 1991, wives' earnings comprised 31 percent of average family income. By 1994, wives who worked full-time were contributing 38 percent of family income. Being a mother does not seem to affect working wives' contributions to family income, except that mothers are slightly less likely than other wives to work full-time, year-round.

Furthermore, in a growing number of families, wives contribute more to the household income than husbands do. About 9 million wives in dual-earner families earned more than their spouses in 1991. Since 1987, the first year for which these data were tabulated by the Bureau of Labor Statistics, the number of wives earning more than their husbands has grown by more than a million, and their proportion has risen from less than 26 percent to more than 29 percent in 1991.

In the future the number of single father households will increase. The fastest growing type of U.S. household today is those headed by single fathers, according to projections by *American Demographics*. Their numbers are small, an estimated 1.4 million in 1995, but they may grow by 14 percent in the next five years. In fact, they are expected to be the fastest growing type of family through the year 2000.

More men will act on their shifting values. "Over the past five years, more and more the male focus groups that we traditionally hold to understand how men are thinking about women have become opportunities for men to express how they are feeling," says Marcia Brumit Kropf, vice president of research and advisory services for Catalyst. "The shift in attitudes and values is quite real and quite dramatic. Men are talking a lot about the tolls of long hours. Many managers are explaining that men, who they believe are focused on career advancement, are flat turning down relocations."

Younger men will continue the value shift begun by baby boomers. Research with younger workers suggests that the ability to have a personal life is taking on more importance and that, increasingly, employers are going to be rated on whether they acknowledge the need for work–life balance. According to FWI's *National Study of the Changing Workforce*, young workers say they are much more willing to make sacrifices in their education, careers, and jobs than in their personal and family lives. Significantly more young workers with children than workers without children were willing to make a lot of sacrifices in their education, career, and jobs for family life.

Changes in commuting patterns will enable more fathers to be involved with their children. Instead of jumping onto trains to ride into a central city, as many of their dads did, many white-collar workers today use private cars and drive from one suburban city to another. This makes it more possible and likely that they will stop at child-care centers, supermarkets, dry cleaners, and other stores along the way. Five out of six jobs created in the major metropolitan areas in the United States since 1960 have been in suburban areas.

More fathers will work at home. The return to more home-based businesses and the expanding use of telecommuting will reduce the physical boundaries between work and family. In 1996, 47.4 million people were working from home, up 29 percent from 1989, according to LINK Resources, a New York-based marketing firm. In a study on telecommuting released in 1993, the U. S. Department of Transportation estimated the number of telecommuters in the United States to be about 2 million and projected an increase to between 6.4 and 10.9 million telecommuters by the year 2000.

And a new trend will contribute to the challenge of balancing work–family issues. In the next twenty years, elder care will replace child care as the biggest dependent care issue in America. According to the Bureau of the Census, the oldest segment of the population is growing most rapidly. In 1994, an estimated 3.5 million people were aged 85 and older, representing 10 percent of the elderly in the United States. By the middle of the twenty-first century, it is projected that there will be as many people aged 85 and older as there are people aged 65 to 69.

Eight percent of workers already have adult dependent or

elder-care responsibilities. Of the workers who care for disabled spouses or older relatives or friends, 44 percent are men. Although women devote significantly more time to caregiving overall (19.9 hours per week) than men (11.8 hours per week), the "common assumption that women are far more likely to have elder-care responsibilities is erroneous." Eighteen percent of the work force expects to be providing care for an aging relative in the next five years. There are no significant differences among men and women in anticipated caregiving. Recognizing men in their roles as "working sons"—not just working fathers—will factor significantly into balancing the work–family equation in the next decade.

∾

In 1975, I wrote a book entitled *Who Will Raise the Children?* to draw attention the important role of fathers in child rearing, a topic largely neglected in discussions of the changing American family.

Some twenty years later, much public attention is being focused on the crisis of fatherlessness in American society. Indeed, at The Fatherhood Project my colleagues and I are working with communities throughout America to promote the responsibility of all men to their children. Our work has been focused on our society's mediating institutions that deal with families every day—child-care programs, schools, hospitals, religious and spiritual organizations, social service agencies—because they strongly influence the connection (or lack of connection) between fathers and their children.

Of all those institutions, none plays as important a role in a man's life as the workplace.

Who will raise the children in the twenty-first century? Mothers and fathers working inside and outside the home.

Once we have seen them both, in clearer relief, we must replace a picture that pulls us to see one, at the expense of the other, with a picture that allows us to see the whole work–family system — including children, mothers, fathers, employers, schools, and other "significant others" in our children's lives.

For different families the work–family equation will balance in different ways. Yet for *all* families, it will be a delicate balance, one that requires the interplay of men and women, companies and communities, each contributing to and benefiting from the search for workable solutions. By working together, we can meet one of the greatest challenges of the coming decade: ensuring the well-being of our children and families and the economic success of the changing American workplace.

Notes

INTRODUCTION

PAGE

6   *This "reversible figure" drawing*   Joseph Jastrow, "The Mind's Eye," *Popular Science Monthly* 54 (1899), pp. 299–312.

8   *As an increasing number of fathers*   Data on unemployed fathers are from the U.S. Department of Labor, Bureau of Labor Statistics, unpublished tables based on the March 1995 Current Population Household Survey Series.

9   *In 1995, there were just over 25 million*   Data on employed fathers are from the U.S. Department of Labor, Bureau of Labor Statistics, unpublished tables based on the March 1995 Current Population Household Survey Series.

9   *In 1994, there were over 69 million children*   Arlene F. Saluter, *Marital Status and Living Arrangements. Current Population Reports P20-484* (Washington, DC: U.S. Department of Commerce, Bureau of the Census, March 1994).

CHAPTER ONE

PAGE

15   *In the mid-1980s, when Merck & Co.*   Dana Friedman, *Linking Work-Family Issues to the Bottom Line* (New York: The Conference Board, 1991), p. 20.

Notes

15   *In 1987, when a public utility*   Joseph H. Pleck, "Are Family-Supportive Employer Policies Relevant to Men?" In Jane C. Hood, ed., *Men, Work, and Family* (Newbury Park, CA: Sage Publications, 1993). See also Cathy Trost, "Men, Too, Wrestle with Career-Family Stress, *The Wall Street Journal* (November 1, 1988), p. 33, and Joseph H. Pleck, Graham L. Staines, and L. Lang, "Conflicts Between Work and Family Life," *Monthly Labor Review* 102, No. 3 (1980), pp. 29–32.

15   *The following year, in 1988,*   Interview with Faith Wohl conducted by James A. Levine, April 1993.

15   *And in 1994, while AT&T*   B. O'Reilly, "Why grade 'A' Execs get an 'F' as Parents," *Fortune* (January 1, 1990), p. 36.

16   *The Families and Work Institute (FWI) had a unique opportunity*   Data on work–family conflict among mothers and fathers employed full time is reported in Ellen Galinsky and James T. Bond, "Work and Family: The Experiences of Mothers and Fathers in the U.S. Labor Force," in Cynthia Costello and Barbara Kivimae Krimgold, eds., *The American Woman 1996-97* (New York: W.W. Norton, 1996), p. 96. Additional data reported about work–conflict variation by family form and employment are based on special analysis conducted by James T. Bond of unpublished data from Ellen Galinsky, James T. Bond, and Dana Friedman, *National Study of the Changing Workforce* (New York: Families and Work Institute, 1993).

17   *A 1991 Gallup poll found that a majority of American men*   The Gallup Poll: Public Opinion 1990 (Wilmington, DE: Scholarly Resources, 1991).

17   *In 1992, a national survey conducted by the Roper Organization*   The Roper Organization, Inc., "Transition time for men: Will the 1990s be a 'Men's Decade'?" *The Public Pulse* 7, No. 2 (February 1992), p. 1.

17   *Two years later, in 1993, a nationally representative study*   Joseph H. Pleck, *Working Wives/Working Husbands* (Beverly Hills, CA: Sage Publications, 1985).

17   *By 1996, a Consumer Survey Center poll of men in their thirties*   Doug Levy, Karen S. Peterson, and Marilyn Elias, "Men Seek Emotional, Not Material, Success," *USA Today* (August 20, 1996), p. 8D.

18   *Does this mean that men—especially fathers—are slackening*   Special analysis of Families and Work Institute's *National Study of the Changing Workforce*, conducted by James T. Bond in 1996.

18   *This high level of simultaneous commitment*   Fernando Bartolome has been a long-time student of men's career paths. This citation is from Fer-

nando Bartolome, "The Work Alibi: When It's Harder to Go Home," *Harvard Business Review* (March-April 1983), p. 66.

18   *By 1994, when a Families and Work Institute/Whirlpool Foundation survey* Families and Work Institute, *The New Providers* (New York: Families and Work Institute, 1995).

18   *. . . according to a 1993* Parents *magazine survey* Richard Louv, "Survey: How Fathers Feel," *Parents* (December 1993), pp. 227–234.

18   *In the same year, when* Child *magazine* James A. Levine, "The 90's Father: Who Is He?" *Child* (March 1993), pp. 96–99, 146.

19   *A survey conducted for FRC* Family Research Council, *National Family Values* (Washington, DC: Family Research Council, January 1994).

19   *Although the same survey found that 58 percent* Family Research Council, *National Family Values* (Washington, DC: Family Research Council, January 1994).

19   *"[T]he questions about juggling home and family life are always asked as if there were only one sex. . . ."* Rosalind Barnett and Caryl Rivers, *She Works/He Works* (San Francisco: HarperSanFrancisco, 1996), p. 58.

19   *"[G]nawing concern about the children—such as worry over their safety or their choice of friends or about the financial burden they impose—can cause either parent to suffer stress-related problems."* Deborah Erickson, "Work and Health: Are Women and Men That Different?" *Harvard Business Review* (September/October 1995), p. 12. For a fuller exposition see Rosalind C. Barnett and Caryl Rivers, *She Works/He Works* (San Francisco: HarperSanFrancisco, 1996).

20   *"While they watched," Lamb explains* Interview with Michael E. Lamb, conducted by James A. Levine, October 1996. Lamb's research was originally published in Michael Lamb, "Qualitative Aspects of Mother-and-Father–Infant Attachment," *Infant Behavior and Development* 1 (1978), pp. 265–275.

20   *But when they controlled for a host of other variables* Kirby Deater-Deckard, Sandra Scarr, Kathleen McCartney, and Marlene Eisenberg, "Paternal Separation Anxiety: Relationships with Parenting Stress, Child-rearing Attitudes, and Maternal Anxieties," *Psychological Science.* Vol. 5, No. 6 (November 1994), pp. 341–346.

21   *. . . according to FWI's* National Study Ellen Galinsky, James T. Bond, and Dana Friedman, *National Study of the Changing Workforce* (New York: Families and Work Institute, 1993).

Notes

21   *Stress over child care,*   Ellen Galinsky and James T. Bond, "Work and Family: The Experiences of Mothers and Fathers in the U.S. Labor Force," in C. Costello and B.K. Krimgold, eds., *The American Woman 1996–97* (New York: W. W. Norton, 1996), p. 78. Interviews with Browy and Smith conducted by James A. Levine, July 1996.

21   *. . . surveyed 330 middle-class*   Jack L. Simonetti, Nick Nykodymn, Warren R. Nielsen, and Janet M. Goralske, "Counseling Employee Guilt: A Corporate Necessity," *Employee Counseling Today* 5, No. 3 (1993), pp. 17–23.

22   *"You work longer hours because of the fear. . . ."*   Uri Berliner, "Free Time Comes at a Price: More Seem Willing to Pay it," *The San Diego Union-Tribune* (June 16, 1996), p. A-1.

22   *"There's always conflict,"*   Interview with Stephen Roache conducted by Marion Lipschutz, June 1996.

22   *. . . a phenomenon documented in a 1989 book*   Arlie Hochschild with Anne Machung, *The Second Shift: Working Parents and the Revolution at Home* (New York: Viking, 1989), p. 3.

23   *. . . in a 1991 article*   Bo Emerson, "Beating a Drum for the 90s Man," *The Atlanta Journal and Constitution* (March 14, 1991), Section D, p. 1.

23   *In a 1994 article on whether*   Don Lattin, "Psychologists Dispute What Makes a Man," *San Francisco Chronicle* (August 15, 1994), p. A1.

24   *A February 1996 article in* The Arizona Republic   Linda Valez, "America's Least Wanted: In the Juvenile Crime Wars, the Secret Weapon Is Us," *The Arizona Republic* (February 18, 1996), p. H1.

24   *In a 1993 story "New Man Still a Myth,"*   "New Man Still a Myth, Labour MP" (London: Press Association Newsfile, June 9, 1993).

24   The Second Shift *was anchored*   Arlie Hochschild with Anne Machung, *The Second Shift: Working Parents and the Revolution at Home* (New York: Viking, 1989), p. 3.

24   *But Pleck noticed that Hochschild's report omitted*   Joseph H. Pleck, "Are Family-Supportive Employer Policies Relevant to Men?" in Jane C. Hood, ed., *Men, Work, and Family* (Newbury Park, CA: Sage Publications, 1993), p. 220. See also Joseph H. Pleck, "Families and Work: Small Changes with Big Implications," *Qualitative Sociology* 15, No. 4 (1992), pp. 427–432.

24   *When Pleck factored in Szalai's missing data,*   Joseph H. Pleck, "Are Family-Supportive Employer Policies Relevant to Men?" in Jane C. Hood, ed., *Men, Work, and Family* (Newbury Park, CA: Sage Publications, 1993), p. 220. See also Joseph H. Pleck, "Families and Work: Small

Changes with Big Implications," *Qualitative Sociology* 15, No. 4 (1992), pp. 427–432.

25 *Based on a thirty-five-hour work week* Data in this and the preceding paragraph are from Ellen Galinsky and James T. Bond, "Work and Family: The Experiences of Mothers and Fathers in the U.S. Labor Force," in D. Costello and B. K. Krimgold, eds., *The American Woman 1996–97* (New York: W. W. Norton, 1996), p. 84.

25 *In 1992, 96.5 percent of employed fathers* Ellen Galinsky and James T. Bond. "Work and Family: The Experiences of Mothers and Fathers in the U.S. Labor Force," in D. Costello and B. K. Krimgold, eds., *The American Woman 1996–97* (New York: W. W. Norton, 1996), p. 83.

26 *In 1960, for every hour dad put in,* Joseph Pleck, "Are Family-Supportive Employer Policies Relevant to Men?" in Jane C. Hood, ed., *Men, Work, and Family* (Newbury Park, CA: Sage Publications, 1993), pp. 219–220. Pleck estimates that "men's share of the total performed by both sexes [rose] from 20 percent in 1965 to 30 percent in 1981."

26 *When it comes to direct interaction* Joseph H. Pleck, "Paternal Involvement: Levels, Sources, and Consequences," in Michael E. Lamb, ed., *The Role of the Father in Child Development* (New York: John Wiley & Sons, 1997).

26 *With teenagers, an eleven-year study* Kathleen Mullan Harris, Frank F. Furstenburg, Jr., and Jeremy K. Marmer, "Paternal Involvement with Adolescents in Intact Families: The Influence of Fathers over the Life Course," Paper presented at the annual meetings of the American Sociological Association, August 16–20, 1996.

27 *That is exactly what Rosalind Barnett found* Rosalind Barnett and Caryl Rivers, *She Works/He Works* (SanFrancisco: HarperSanFrancisco, 1996), p. 178.

27 *"The good news," says Barnett,* Rosalind Barnett and Caryl Rivers, *She Works/He Works* (SanFrancisco: HarperSanFrancisco, 1996) p. 177.

27 *No matter how large or small their employer,* As Ellen Galinsky and James T. Bond of the Families and Work Institute point out, "It is sometimes assumed that women are more likely to work for small employers than men are, but that is not the case among employed parents. There is no significant difference between fathers and mothers with respect to the size of their employers. Overall, just under half of employed parents work for employers with fewer than fifty employees at the local worksite, and 29 percent of parents work for employers with fewer than fifty employees in the United States." See Ellen

Galinsky and James T. Bond, "Work and Family: The Experiences of Mothers and Fathers in the U.S. Labor Force," in C. Costello and B. K. Krimgold, eds., *The American Woman 1996-97* (New York: W. W. Norton, 1996), p. 85.

27 *In 1992, when the Mass Mutual Family Values Survey*   Bruskin, Goldring Research, "Mass Mutual Family Values–Fatherhood Survey," *Public Opinion Online* (Roper Center at the University of Connecticut, April 1992).

27 *One reason is that, no matter how much time*   Joseph H. Pleck, Michael E. Lamb, and James Levine first presented three dimensions of involvement—interaction, availability, and responsibility—in a series of papers in the early and mid-1980s. The latest and most comprehensive exposition of this model appears in Joseph H. Pleck, "Paternal Involvement: Levels, Sources, and Consequences," in Michael E. Lamb, ed., *The Role of the Father in Child Development* (New York: John Wiley & Sons, 1997).

27 *They are often the unpleasant chores*   Detailed explanations of the types of household chores done by men and women appear in Rosalind Barnett and Caryl Rivers, *She Works/He Works* (San Francisco: HarperSanFrancisco, 1996) and Scott Coltrane, *Family Man: Fatherhood, Housework, and Gender Equity* (New York: Oxford University Press, 1996).

27 *Still, as I listen*   Interviews with Samuel and Ruby Jordan conducted by Marion Lipschutz, 1996. Names have been changed.

29 *A female attorney writing in the New Jersey Law Journal*   "Babies and Briefs: Rhetoric Yields to Reality." *New Jersey Law Journal* (January 30, 1995), p. 25.

30 *Charles Rodgers, principal at WFD*   Interview with Charles Rodgers conducted by James A. Levine, September 1996.

30 *"Men feel that they can access only certain types. . . "*   Telephone interview with Marcia Brumit Kropf conducted by Todd L. Pittinsky, August 1996.

33 *But when translated by the popular media, thirty-seven seconds*   The thirty-seven-second figure was promulgated by the media after publication of Freda Rebelsky and Cheryl Hanks, "Fathers' Verbal Interaction with Infants in the First Three Months of Life." *Child Development* 42, No. 1 (March 1971), pp. 63–68.

33 *When the president of American Express resigns*   *The Wall Street Journal* covered the resignation of Jeffrey Stiefler, the president of American

Express, in September 1995 and then followed up in Sue Shellenbarger, "High-Powered Fathers Savor Their Decisions to Scale Back Careers," *The Wall Street Journal* (June 12, 1996), p. B-1.

33 *"Women still assume primary responsibility* Interview with Dana Friedman conducted by James A. Levine, October 1996. Also see Dana Friedman, *Linking Work-Family Issues to the Bottom Line* (New York: The Conference Board, 1991), p. 12.

CHAPTER TWO

PAGE

34 *In 1987, more than half of mothers* "Working Mothers Now the Norm," *USA Today* (1988), p. 1.

34 *When Pennsylvania State University psychologist* Jay Belsky, "The Effects of Day Care Reconsidered," *Early Childhood Research Quarterly* 3 (1988), pp. 235–272.

35 *Five years later,* Susan Chira, "Study Says Babies in Child Care Keep Secure Bonds to Mothers," *The New York Times* (April 21, 1996), p. 1.

35 *Ellen Galinsky of the Families and Work Institute* Ellen Galinsky and Judy David, *The Preschool Years* (New York: Times Books, 1988).

35 *Researchers Grace Baruch and Rosalind Barnett,* Grace Baruch, Rosalind Barnett and Caryl Rivers. *Lifeprints* (New York: McGraw-Hill, 1983).

35 *Psychologist Faye Crosby* Faye Crosby, *Juggling* (New York: The Free Press, 1991).

36 *According to Bradley Googins,* Bradley K. Googins, *Work/Family Conflicts: Private Lives—Public Responses* (New York: Auburn House, 1991), pp. 65–66.

36 *Even by 1860,* Bradley K. Googins, *Work/Family Conflicts: Private Lives—Public Responses* (New York: Auburn House, 1991), p. 76.

36 *The industrialization of America* Bradley K. Googins, *Work/Family Conflicts: Private Lives—Public Responses* (New York: Auburn House, 1991), p. 78.

37 *Enforcing the Protective Labor Law* M. Frank and R. Lipner, "History of Maternity Leave," in Edward Zigler and Merle Frank, *The Parental Leave Crisis: Toward a National Policy* (New Haven: Yale University Press, 1988), pp. 11–12.

Notes

37   *By 1912, thirty-four states*   Michele Lord, "A Short History of Parental Leave Laws," in *Parental Leave and Productivity* (New York: Families and Work Institute, 1992), p. 79.

37   *During the late 1930s,*   Urie Bronfenbrenner and Ann C. Crouter, "Work and Family through Time and Space," in S. B. Kamerman and C. D. Hayes, Eds., *Families That Work: Children in a Changing World* (Washington, DC: National Academy Press, 1982). Citation here is from Urie Bronfenbrenner, "Ecology of the Family as a Context for Human Development: Research Perspectives," *Developmental Psychology* 22, No. 6 (1986), pp. 723–742, 728.

37   *The 1958 publication*   Daniel R. Miller and Guy E. Swanson, *The Changing American Parent* (New York: John Wiley & Sons, 1958).

37   *Even in 1969, when*   Frank A. Pedersen and Kenneth S. Robson, "Father Participation in Infancy," *American Journal of Orthopsychiatry* 39, No. 3 (April 1969), pp. 467–468.

38   *According to Bronfenbrenner and Crouter*   Urie Bronfenbrenner and Ann C. Crouter, "Work and Family through Time and Space," in S. B. Kamerman and C. D. Hayes, eds., *Families That Work: Children in a Changing World* (Washington, DC: National Academy Press, 1982). Citation here is from Urie Bronfenbrenner, "Ecology of the Family as a Context for Human Development: Research Perspectives," *Developmental Psychology* 22, No. 6 (1986), pp. 723–742, 728.

38   *"For years, social scientists have focused on women in the workplace. . . ."*   Mureen Perry-Jenkins, "Men's Provider-Role Attitudes: Implications for Household Work and Marital Satisfaction, *Journal of Family Issues* 11 (June 1990), pp. 136–156.

39   *In children ages four to seventeen,*   Sue Shellenbarger, "It's the Type of Job You Have That Affects the Kids, Studies Say," *The Wall Street Journal* (July 31, 1996), p. B-1.

39   *Moreover, they find*   Sue Shellenbarger, "It's the Type of Job You Have That Affects the Kids, Studies Say," *The Wall Street Journal* (July 31, 1996), p. B-1.

39   *Research by Ohio State University psychologists*   Toby Parcel and Elizabeth Menaghan, *Parents' Jobs and Children's Lives* (New York: Aldine de Gruyter, 1994). Quotes in this paragraph are from an interview with Parcel conducted by James A. Levine, August 1996.

40   *Dads with more autonomy and control*   Karen Grimm-Thomas and Maureen Perry-Jenkins, "All in a Day's Work: Job Experiences, Self-esteem,

and Fathering in Working-class families," *Family Relations* 43, No. 2 (April 1994), pp. 174–181. See also W. Stewart and J. Barling, "Fathers' Subjective Work Experiences, Personal Well-being, Father-child relationship, and Children's Behavior," Working Paper (Kingston, Ontario: Department of Psychology, Queen's University, 1992).

40   *Dads with more autonomy and satisfaction*   Frances K. Grossman, William S. Pollack, and Ellen Golding, "Fathers and Children: Predicting the Quality and Quantity of Fathering," *Developmental Psychology* 24, No. 1 (January 1988), pp. 82–92.

41   *At six-months of age,*   F. A. Pedersen, N. Zaslow, J. Suwalsky, and R. Caine, "Parent-Infant and Husband-Wife Interactions Observed at Five Months," in F. Pederson, ed., *The Father-Infant Relationship* (New York: Praeger, 1980), pp. 65–91.

41   *At age three, premature infants*   M. W. Yogman, D. Kindlon, and F. J. Earls, "Father Involvement and Cognitive Behavioral Outcomes of Preterm Infants," *Journal of the American Academy of Child and Adolescent Psychiatry* 34 (1995), pp. 58–66.

41   *And if their fathers are involved*   Ross D. Parke, *Fathers* (Cambridge, MA: Harvard University Press, 1996).

41   *A sense of competence in daughters*   Norma Radin, "The Role of the Father in Cognitive, Academic, and Intellectual Development," in Michael E. Lamb, ed., *The Role of the Father in Child Development* (New York: John Wiley & Sons, 1981).

41   *Boys with nurturant fathers*   Norma Radin and Graeme Russell, "Increased Father Participation and Child Development Outcomes," in Michael E. Lamb and Avi Sagi, eds., *Fatherhood and Family Policy* (Hillsdale, NJ: Lawrence Erlbaum, 1983), pp. 191–218.

41   *And both boys and girls with involved fathers*   Kyle D. Pruett, *The Nurturing Father* (New York: Warner Books, 1987).

41   *In adolescence dads' involvement*   David Popenoe, *Life without Father* (New York: The Free Press, 1996) and study by Kathleen Mullan Harris, Frank F. Furstenburg, Jr., and Jeremy K. Marmer, "Paternal Involvement with Adolescents in Intact Families: The Influence of Fathers over the Life Course," Paper presented at the annual meetings of the American Sociological Association, August 16–20, 1996.

41   *Whether researchers look at cognitive development,*   Michael E. Lamb, *The Father's Role: Applied Perspectives* (New York: John Wiley & Sons, 1986).

42   *What is not so apparent,*   Michael E. Lamb, "Paternal Influences in Child Development," in G. A. Frinking, M. Jacobs, and M. Van Dongen, eds., *Changing Fatherhood* (Amsterdam: Thesis Publishers, 1995).

42   *For mothers, it was the fact of being employed*   Urie Bronfenbrenner and Ann C. Crouter, "Work and Family through Time and Space," in S. B. Kamerman and C. D. Hayes, eds., *Families That Work: Children in a Changing World* (Washington, DC: National Academy Press, 1982). Citation here is from Urie Bronfenbrenner, "Ecology of the Family as a Context for Human Development: Research Perspectives," *Developmental Psychology* 22, No. 6 (1986), pp. 723–742, 728.

42   *"There was a sociology of work. . . ."*   Rhona Rapoport, et al., *Relinking Life and Work: Toward a Better Future* (New York: The Ford Foundation, 1996).

42   *When Bradley Googins closely observed*   Bradley K. Googins, *Work/Family Conflicts: Private Lives—Public Responses* (New York: Auburn House, 1991), p. ix.

42   *In a prescient 1977*   Rosabeth Moss Kanter, *Work and Family in the United States: A Critical Review and Research Agenda* (New York: Russell Sage Foundation, 1977).

43   *A 1992 study at St. Paul Companies*   Arlene Johnson, "The Business Case for Work–Family Programs," *Journal of Accountancy* 180, No. 2 (August 1995), p. 53.

43   *Chicago-based Fel-Pro,*   Cited in Arlene Johnson, "The Business Case for Work–Family Programs," *Journal of Accountancy* 180, No. 2 (August 1995), p. 53.

43   *A study released by DuPont*   Interview with Cindi Johnson conducted by Amy Warren, August 1996.

44   *According to Mercer's Richard Federico*   Cited in J. Greenwald, "Family Benefits Breed Loyalty in Work Force," *Crain's Detroit Business* (July 1, 1996), p. 19.

44   *And they are more likely*   Arlene Johnson, "The Business Case for Work–Family Programs," *Journal of Accountancy* 180, No. 2 (August 1995), p. 53.

44   *According to the FWI's*   Arlene Johnson, "The Business Case for Work–Family Programs," *Journal of Accountancy* 180, No. 2 (August 1995), p. 53.

44   *According to a 1995 survey of 1,000 managers*   Edward Betof, MC Associates. Manchester Partners International. Philadelphia, PA (August 29, 1995).

44   *When IBM asked a group of employees*   Julie Barker, "Family Ties: Family-friendly Policies Are No Longer a Luxury—They Are a Competitive Advantage," *Sales and Marketing Management* (September 16, 1996), p. S-18.

45 *When First Tennessee National Corp.* Keith H. Hammonds, "Balancing Work and Family: Big Returns for Companies Willing to Give Family Strategies a Chance," *Business Week* (September 16, 1996), pp. 74–81.

45 *Mike Dedek, a father of three* Telephone interview with Mike Dedek conducted by Amy Warren, August 1996.

45 *Even more startling,* Arlene Johnson, "The Business Case for Work–Family Programs," *Journal of Accountacy* 180, No. 2 (August 1995), p. 53.

45 *My colleague Rosalind Barnett* Rosalind Barnett and Caryl Rivers, *She Works/He Works* (San Francisco: HarperSanFrancisco, 1996), p. 7.

45 *According to the American Medical Association* Cited in Deborah Erickson, "Work and Health: Are Women and Men that Different?" *Harvard Business Review* (Sept/Oct 1995), p. 12.

45 *Barnett found that* Rosalind Barnett and Caryl Rivers, *She Works/He Works* (San Francisco: HarperSanFrancisco, 1996), p. 7.

46 *As Senge puts it,* Peter M. Senge, *The Fifth Discipline: The Art and Practice of the Learning Organization* (New York: Doubleday Currency, 1990), p. 3.

46 *You may be surprised to learn* Peter M. Senge, *The Fifth Discipline: The Art and Practice of the Learning Organization* (New York: Doubleday Currency, 1990), p. 307.

46 *Reacting to a 1990* Fortune *cover story,* Peter M. Senge, *The Fifth Discipline: The Art and Practice of the Learning Organization* (New York: Doubleday Currency, 1990), p. 307.

47 *In a chapter from* The Fifth Discipline, Peter M. Senge, *The Fifth Discipline: The Art and Practice of the Learning Organization* (New York: Doubleday Currency, 1990), p. 307.

47 *ISenge draws on the words* Peter M. Senge, *The Fifth Discipline: The Art and Practice of the Learning Organization* (New York: Doubleday Currency, 1990), p. 311.

47 *IAs O'Brien puts it,* Peter M. Senge, *The Fifth Discipline: The Art and Practice of the Learning Organization* (New York: Doubleday Currency, 1990), pp. 310–311.

48 *According to a 1996 report of the Joint Economic Committee* Frank Gregorsky, *Women Business Owners in Post-Corporate America: A Study for the Joint Economic Committee of Congress* (Washington, DC: U.S. Congress, September 1996).

48 *And dozens of other skills* Gail B. Stout, "Change or Get Out of the Way," *Quality* 33, No. 5 (May 1994), p. 10.

49   *At MIT's Sloan School of Management,*   Rhona Rapoport, et al. *Relinking Life and Work: Toward a Better Future* (New York: The Ford Foundation, 1996), p. 11.

50   *The psychological skills*   William Pollack, "What Do Men Want? Letters to the Editor," *Harvard Business Review* 72 (March/April 1994), p. 176.

50   *Because, according to Snarey,*   Cited in Tim Donahue, "Men Can Be Devoted Dads, Have Successful Careers, Too," Gannett News Service (June 18, 1995). See also John Snarey, *How Fathers Care for the Next Generation: A Four-Decade Study* (Cambridge, MA: Harvard University Press, 1993).

50   *Peter Senge predicts that*   Peter M. Senge, *The Fifth Discipline: The Art and Practice of the Learning Organization* (New York: Doubleday Currency, 1990), pp. 311–312.

51   *Erikson says of fathers,*   Erik Erikson, *Childhood and Society* (Toronto: W. W. Norton, 1963), pp. 166–167.

51   *"What is perhaps most surprising,"*   Joseph H. Pleck, *Working Wives/Working Husbands* (Beverly Hills, CA: Sage Publications, 1985), p. 354.

51   *Snarey's longitudinal study found that*   John Snarey, *How Fathers Care for the Next Generation: A Four-Decade Study* (Cambridge, MA: Harvard University Press, 1993), p. 354.

51   *Keeping with Erik Erikson's notion*   John Snarey, *How Fathers Care for the Next Generation: A Four-Decade Study* (Cambridge, MA: Harvard University Press, 1993), p. 353.

52   *In its 1981 report,*   U.S. Commission on Civil Rights, *Child Care and Equal Opportunity for Women* (Washington, DC: Government Printing Office, 1981), p. vii.

52   *A decade later, Beyond Rhetoric,* the final report of the National Commission on Children,   National Commission on Children, *Beyond Rhetoric: A New American Agenda for Children and Families* (Washington, DC: National Commission on Children, 1991), pp. vii, 66.

52   *"This is my dream of the way the world should be,"*   "U.S. Supreme Court under Justice Ginsburg," *Work and Family Newsbrief* (Minneapolis, MN: Work and Family Connection, Inc., February 1994) citing "New Justice Lauds Law Clerk for Taking Parental Responsibility," *Minneapolis Star Tribune* (January 9, 1994).

CHAPTER THREE

PAGE

57   *As* The Wall Street Journal*'s work–family columnist,*   Sue Shellenbarger, "Lessons from the Workplace: How Corporate Policies and Attitudes Lag Behind Workers' Changing Needs," *Human Resource Management* 31, No. 3 (Fall 1992), p. 157.

58   *"This legislation was eventually repealed,*   Michele Lord, "A Short History of Parental Leave Laws," *Parental Leave and Productivity* (New York: Families and Work Institute, 1992) , p. 79.

59   *As recently as 1962,*   M. Frank and R. Lipner, "History of Maternity Leave," in Edward Zigler and Merle Frank, *The Parental Leave Crisis: Toward a National Policy* (New Haven, CT: Yale University Press, 1988).

60   *"The politically correct statement. . ."*   Charles S. Rodgers and Fran Sussner Rodgers, "The Work and Family Agenda: Not for Women Only?" *Family Resource Coalition Report,* No. 2 (1992).

64   *Analysis of FWI's* National Study   Families and Work Institute, *National Study of the Changing Workforce* (New York: Families and Work Institute, 1993).

64   *FWI's examination of "best practices"*   Dana E. Friedman, Cathy Rimsky, and Arlene A. Johnson, *College and University Reference Guide to Work–Family Programs* (New York: Families and Work Institute, 1996).

65   *Mason's experiment was so successful*   Donna Fenn, "Benefits: Long Hours for Long Weekend," *Inc.* (May 1995), p. 137.

66   *That is what Arlene Johnson learned*   Interview with Arlene Johnson conducted by James A. Levine, August 1996.

71   *One month after a speech challenging other CEOs*   Ron Compton, "Compton to Companies: Flex or Break!" *AetnaSphere* (June 13, 1994).

74   *A 1995 sampling of supervisors*   Kimberlee Vandenakker, *1995 Application to the 1995 Innovations in American Government Awards Program* (Los Angeles: Los Angeles Department of Water and Power, 1996).

76   *Customer service turnaround time*   Cited in Fran Sussner Rodgers, "The New Employer-Employee Relationship," *Human Resource Professional* (January/February 1995), pp. 16–20.

79   *Moreover, most of the fathers surveyed*   "Corporate Centers Important to Working Dads," *Employee Benefit Plan Review* 49, No. 2 (August 1994), p. 38.

Notes

86   *A ten-year study involving 20,000 students*   Laurence Steinberg, *Beyond the Classroom: Why School Reform Has Failed and What Parents Need to Do* (New York: Simon & Schuster, 1996).

86   *According to Fran Sussner Rodgers*   Interview with Fran Sussner Rodgers conducted by James A. Levine, September 1996.

87   *According to the American Medical Association,*   Cited in Josephine Marcotty, "Home with a Sick Child," *Minneapolis Star Tribune* (February 25, 1996), p. 1B.

87   *A survey of more than 1,000 working parents*   The National Report on Work and Family 9, No. 19 (Business Publishers, Inc., October 11, 1996), p. 158.

93   *These days, the media loves to tell*   Veronica Fowler, "Quality of Life Begins in the Director's Office," *The Des Moines Register* (October 23, 1994), Business Section, p. 1.

94   *In response to one of* The Washington Post's *two stories*   Virginia Hoover, "Grandstanding Congressional Dad," *Letters to the Editor, The Washington Post* (September 30, 1995), p. A-22.

CHAPTER FOUR

PAGE

96   *But the real set of work/family issues*   Ellen C. Bankert and Bradley K. Googins, "Family-friendly—Says Who?" *Across the Board* 33, No. 7 (July 1996), p. 45.

96   Culture *is defined*   David A. Nadler and Michael L. Tushman, *Strategic Organization Design: Concepts, Tools, & Processes* (New York: HarperCollins, 1988), p. 28.

100   *FWI's* National Study of the Changing Workforce *found,*   Dana Friedman, *Linking Work–Family Issues to the Bottom Line* (New York: The Conference Board, 1991), p. 18.

103   *Having to do dull, monotonous work*   Rosalind Barnett and Caryl Rivers, *She Works/He Works* (San Francisco: HarperSanFrancisco, 1996), pp. 179–188.

103   *It makes sense,*   Scott Coltrane, *Family Man* (New York: Oxford University Press, 1996).

103   *In a 1988 survey, Gallup found*   Karlyn H. Keene, Ladd and Everett Carll, "Americans at Work," *The Public Perspective* 1, No. 6 (September/October 1990), p. 82.

103   *One year later, a Roper Organization poll*   Karlyn H. Keene, Ladd and Everett Carll, "Americans at Work," *The Public Perspective* 1, No. 6 (September/October 1990), p. 82.

103   *In 1992, an American Management Association*   Sandra Sullivan and Robert Lussier, "Flexible Work Arrangements as a Management Tool," *Supervision* 56, No. 8 (August 1995), p. 14.

103   *And when FWI conducted*   Ellen Galinsky and James T. Bond, "Work and Family: The Experiences of Mothers and Fathers in the U.S. Labor Force," in Cynthia Costello and Barbara Kivimae Krimgold, eds., *The American Woman 1996-97* (New York: W. W. Norton, 1996), p. 84.

104   *They were 45 percent more likely*   Elizabeth Sheley, "Flexible Work Options," *HR Magazine* 41, No. 2. (February 1996), p. 52.

104   *Hewlett-Packard's CEO, Lew Platt,*   Genevieve Capowski, "The Joy of Flex," *Management Review* 85, No. 3 (March 1996).

105   *In 1994, after employees at Nabisco, Inc.*   Julie Barker, "Family-Friendly Policies Are No Longer a Luxury—They Are a Competitive Advantage," *Sales & Marketing Management* (September 1995), p. S18.

105   *Meanwhile, AT&T's Global Business Communications*   Genevieve Capowski, "The Joy of Flex," *Management Review* 85, No. 3 (March 1996).

106   *When flexible schedules were introduced in two federal agencies*   R. A. Winett and M. S. Neale. "Results of experimental study on flextime and family life," *Monthly Labor Review* 113, pp. 29–32.

106   *At White Plains, New York-based Nynex,*   Interview with Robyn Phillips conducted by Amy Warren, August 1996.

106   *And at CIGNA, a 1994 survey*   Elizabeth Niendorf, "Work with Flextime," *Nashville Business Journal* (October 30, 1995), p. 50.

107   *Hewitt Associates, a consulting firm*   Laura Cianci, "Inflexible Hours: Without Family Friendly Benefits, Many Employees of Small Companies Feel Trapped by Their Workplace," *The Washington Times* (April 4, 1993), p. A13, and Charlene Marmer Solomon, "Flexibility Comes Out of Flux." *Personnel Journal* 75, No. 6 (June 1996), p. 34.

107   *"When companies say, 'Oh, we have flextime , . . ."*   Genevieve Capowski, "The Joy of Flex," *Management Review* 85, No. 3 (March 1996), p. 12.

107   *But part of the problem,*   Work and Family Connection, Inc., "Personal Problems Linked to Turnover, Harmful Effect on the Job," *Work and Family Newsbrief* (Minneapolis, MN: Work and Family Connection, Inc., January 1, 1996), citing "The Impact of Mental Health on Productivity," Roper Starch Worldwide for Managed Health Network of Los Angeles.

107   *Chicago lawyer Cheryl Heisler,*   Jill Schachner Chanen, "In the Family Way," *ABA Journal* (July 1995).

109   *Similar results were produced at Merck's*   Interview with Joe Salvia conducted by James A. Levine, October 1996.

111   *In 1905, football was a low-scoring running game.*   Sandra A. Sullivan, "Flexibility as a Management Tool," *Employment Relations Today* 21, No. 4 (December 22, 1994), p. 393.

112   *On more than one occasion*   Interview with Perry Christensen conducted by James A. Levine, September 1996.

113   *Indeed, a 1990 study by Catalyst*   Julie Barker, "Family-Friendly Policies Are No Longer a Luxury—They Are a Competitive Advantage," *Sales & Marketing Management* (September 1995), p. S18.

114   *The WFD's* Flexible Work Option Request   Alessandra Bianchi, "The Strictly Business Flextime Request Form, *Inc.* (May 1995).

118   *Flexible Work Option Request*   Used by permission of Charles Rodgers, Work/Family Directions, September 1996.

118   *According to Work/Family Specialist*   Interview with Cindi Johnson conducted by Amy Warren, August 1996.

119   *According to Mary Etta Coursolle,*   Julie Barker, "Family-Friendly Policies Are No Longer a Luxury—They Are a Competitive Advantage," *Sales & Marketing Management* (September 1995), p. S18.

122   *There was not a hitch in business*   Interview with Perry Christensen conducted by James A. Levine, September 1996.

122   *On June 24, 1994, President Clinton*   William J. Clinton, *Speech to Family Re-Union IV*, June 12, 1996.

123   *Ron Compton, chairman, CEO, and president of Aetna Life & Casualty Co.,*   Michael A. Verespej, "Welcome to the New Works Pace," *Industry Week* (April 15, 1996), p. 24.

124   *Work/Family Directions conducts ongoing training* Cited in Alessandra Bianchi, "The Strictly Business Flextime Request Form," *Inc.* (May 1995).

CHAPTER FIVE

PAGE

127   *According to* Information Week,   "Busy Dad, Poor Baby," *Information Week* (May 6, 1996), p. 10.

128 *According to the story sent out by the wire services,* Yoko Kuramoto, "Latest Bill Gates-Melinda French Product Makes Debut," *The [Tacoma, Washington] News Tribune* (April 30, 1996), p. A14.

129 *Optimists can take encouragement* Data from Burke Stinson, district manager for media relations, AT&T, August 1996.

129 *As an article in* The Economist *put it,* "The End of Patriarchy," *The Economist* (May 18, 1996), p. R3.

130 *In public hearings held in 1974,* James A. Levine, *Who Will Raise the Children?* (New York: J.B. Lippincott, 1975), pp. 53–54.

130 *His father said,* Robert Lipsyte, "The Emasculation of Sports," *The New York Times Magazine* (April 2, 1995), p. 51.

130 *"They ought to suspend him for a week, . . ."* Robin Abcarian, "Football Player Fields Role as Dad like Champ," *Los Angeles Times* (October 24, 1993), p. E-1.

131 *"[M]any male fans felt justifiably confused, . . ."* Robert Lipsyte, "The Emasculation of Sports," *The New York Times Magazine* (April 2, 1995), p. 51.

133 *In the 1995 season premier* Curt Schleier, "Next on NYPD Blue—Cops in Aprons?" *The Detroit News* (October 31, 1995).

133 *In a 1988 survey of 120 randomly chosen fathers* Joseph Pleck, "Are Family–Supportive Employer Policies Relevant to Men?," in Jane C. Hood, ed., *Men, Work, and Family* (Newbury Park, CA: Sage Publications, 1993), p. 228.

133 *Still, only 11 percent* Louise Kiernan, "New Fathers Take a Pass on Unpaid Paternity Leave," *Chicago Tribune* (May 7, 1995), p. C-1. Also from interview with Janet Shibley-Hyde conducted by James A. Levine, September 1996.

133 *For 119 companies* Joseph Pleck, "Fathers and Parental Leave: A Perspective," *Parental Leave and Productivity* (New York: Families and Work Institute, 1992), pp. 17–18. (Referring to Catalyst, Inc. study.)

133 *Shortly after Representative Patricia Schroeder* Malcolm Forbes, "Fact and Comment: With All Thy Getting Get Understanding," *Forbes* (July 14, 1996), p. 17.

135 *For example, when Pace University researchers* Joy A. Schneer and Frieda Reitman, "Effects of Employment Gaps on the Careers of MBAs: More Damaging for Men Than for Women?" *Academy of Management Journal* 33, No. 2 (June 1990), pp. 391–406.

Notes

135   *In 1994, when Schneer and Reitman followed up*   Joy A. Schneer and Frieda Reitman, "The Importance of Gender in Mid-Career," *Journal of Organizational Behavior* 15, No. 3 (May 1994), pp. 199–207. Also Joy A. Schneer and Frieda Reitman, "The Impact of Gender as Managerial Careers Unfold," *Journal of Vocational Behavior* 47, No. 3. (December 1995), pp. 290–315.

136   *FMLA covers about two-thirds*   Ellen Galinsky and James T. Bond, "Work and Family: The Experiences of Mothers and Fathers in the U.S. Labor Force," in Cynthia Costello and Barbara Kivimae Krimgold, eds., *The American Woman 1996-97* (New York: W.W. Norton, 1996), p. 85. The number of fathers eligible for leave under FMLA is actually higher than the 41 percent of employed mothers, because more mothers work part-time and do not meet FMLA's requirements on number of hours served.

137   *According to the Commission on Family and Medical Leave,*   Commission on Family and Medical Leave, *A Workable Balance: Report to Congress on Family and Medical Leave Policies* (Washington, DC: U.S. Congress, 1996), pp. 95–97, 272.

137   *The Commission on Family and Medical Leave found*   Commission on Family and Medical Leave, *A Workable Balance: Report to Congress on Family and Medical Leave Policies* (Washington, DC: U.S. Congress, 1996), p. 272. The figure is 64.7 percent couldn't afford it, averaging all workers. Assuming more fathers gave this reason than mothers, even the most conservative estimates would put the figure for fathers at over two-thirds.

137   *In more than two-thirds of those cases,*   Commission on Family and Medical Leave, *A Workable Balance: Report to Congress on Family and Medical Leave Policies* (Washington, DC: U.S. Congress, 1996), p. 273.

137   *In 1990, for example, when NationsBank*   Louise Kiernan, "New Fathers Taking a Pass on Unpaid Paternity Leaves," *Chicago Tribune* (May 7, 1995), p. C-1.

137   *"I think men felt self-conscious. . . ."*   Interview with Virginia Stone Mackin conducted by Marla Winnick, August 1996.

137   *At Immunex Corp., a 750-employee firm*   Carol Smith, "Family–Friendly Companies Find That It Pays," *Seattle Post-Intelligencer* (December 8, 1995), p. C-1 and interview with Beth Fortmueller of Immunex.

137   *At Lotus Development Corp.,*   Interview with Helen Berry conducted by Amy Warren, September 1996.

138 *In the United States, according to one recent estimate,* John Cranford, "Pieces of the Package," *Congressional Quarterly Governing Magazine* (December 1993).

138 *After receiving written requests* "Merrill Debuts Paternity Pay," *Institutional Investor* 28, No. 28 (July 15, 1996), p. 7.

138 *In its report to the U.S. Congress* Commission on Family and Medical Leave, *A Workable Balance: Report to Congress on Family and Medical Leave Policies* (Washington, DC: U.S. Congress, 1996), p. xxviii.

138 *Although the commission combined* Commission on Family and Medical Leave, *A Workable Balance: Report to Congress on Family and Medical Leave Policies* (Washington, DC: U.S. Congress, 1996), p. xxviii. The range was between 86.4 and 95.8 percent.

139 *The ability to build loyalty* Rebecca Abrams, "Father of All Battles," *The Guardian* (October 25, 1995), p. T-8.

138 *"I have given family paid leave for one of our guys. . . ."* Commission on Family and Medical Leave, *A Workable Balance: Report to Congress on Family and Medical Leave Policies* (Washington, DC: U.S. Congress, 1996), p. 141.

140 *"I don't have a dramatic story, . . ."* Commission on Family and Medical Leave, *A Workable Balance: Report to Congress on Family and Medical Leave Policies* (Washington, DC: U.S. Congress, 1996), p. 152.

142 *According to analysis of the first two years'* Commission on Family and Medical Leave, *A Workable Balance: Report to Congress on Family and Medical Leave Policies* (Washington, DC: U.S. Congress, 1996).

143 *"The response from peers was unbelievably positive. . . "* Interview with Mike Goodson conducted by Keith Winnick, September 1996.

144 *In the first two years of the FMLA,* Commission on Family and Medical Leave, *A Workable Balance: Report to Congress on Family and Medical Leave Policies* (Washington, DC: U.S. Congress, 1996), p. 123.

144 *When his son Max was born,* Interview with Michael Berney conducted by Amy Warren, September 1996.

145 *When the Commission on Family and Medical Leave studied* Commission on Family and Medical Leave, *A Workable Balance: Report to Congress on Family and Medical Leave Policies* (Washington, DC: U.S. Congress, 1996), p. 299.

146 *"It's difficult for a man to step out. . . ."* Jill Schachner Chanen, "In the Family Way," *ABA Journal* (July 1995).

147 *AT&T, for example,* Interview with Tony Stiles conducted by Amy Warren, September 1996.

147 *After developing a similar program,* Interview with Robyn Phillips conducted by Amy Warren, September 1996.

147 *After John Unoski* Interview with John Unoski conducted by Marion Lipschutz, 1996.

149 *The 1990 National Child Care Survey found* Dana Friedman, *Linking Work–Family Issues to the Bottom Line* (New York: The Conference Board, 1991), P. 28.

149 *Data from Sweden* Data provided from the Swedish Social Insurance Office; translation by Linda Haas, Professor of Sociology, University of Indiana. Note also that Norway is considered a leading family-friendly country, offering generous parental-leave policies, including fifty-two weeks of maternity leave at 80 percent salary or forty-two weeks at 100 percent. Starting in 1995, Norwegians can also stretch paid parental leave over 2.5 years under a government-funded program developed by a group of trade unions and employers. In the first eight months of the program, about 1,200 parents took advantage of it—8 percent of those eligible—including 120 fathers.

149 *McDonnell Douglas Corp.,* Gianna Jacobson and Barbara Friedman, "Taking Care: Something Special," *St. Louis Business Journal* (October 1988), p. 4.

149 *Chubb & Son, Inc. of the Chubb Corporation* Evelyn Gilbert, "Insurers Are Lauded for Family-Friendly Benefits," *National Underwriter* (October 2, 1995), p. 9.

150 *When Seattle-based Boeing* Interview with John Doherty conducted by Todd L. Pittinsky, August 1996.

150 *The Family and Medical Leave Act of 1993 went into effect* FMLA became effective on August 5, 1993, for most covered and eligible employees. If a collective bargaining agreement (CBA) was in effect on that date, FMLA became effective on the expiration date of the CBA or February 5, 1994, whichever was earlier.

150 *A survey conducted for the Federal Commission on Leave* Commission on Family and Medical Leave, *A Workable Balance: Report to Congress on Family and Medical Leave Policies* (Washington, DC: U.S. Congress, 1996), Table 4-K, Appendix E.

151 *Following are the key provisions* This summary of provisions of the Family and Medical Leave Act of 1993 is adapted from Fact Sheet No. ESA 95-24, "The Family and Medical Leave Act of 1993" of the U.S. Department of Labor Program Highlights series.

CHAPTER SIX

PAGE

160   *Robinson and his colleague, Ann Bostrom,*   Diane Crispell, "Chaotic Workplace," *American Demographics* (June 1996), p. 50.

160   *What might account for this gap?*   Diane Crispell, "Chaotic Workplace," *American Demographics* (June 1996), p. 50.

162   *"The suggestion that we simply pull off a few layers. . . ."*   David Waters, and J. Terry Saunders, "I Gave at the Office," *Family Therapy Network* (March/April 1996), p. 50.

163   *FWI's* National Study of the Changing Workforce *found*   Ellen Galinsky, James T. Bond, and Dana Friedman. *National Study of the Changing Workforce* (New York: Families and Work Institute, 1993), p. 74.

163   *Yankelovich Partners Inc. polled*   Yankelovich Partners Inc., *The Impact of Workplace Changes on Families and Children* (June 1996). Prepared for Family Re-Union V: Family and Work, a Conference of the Children, Youth, and Family Consortium at the Univerity of Minnesota and Tennessee Select Committee on Children and Youth.

164   *This finding agreed with an earlier study,*   Ann C. Crouter, Maureen Perry-Jenkins, Ted L. Huston, and Susan M. McHale, "Processes Underlying Father Involvement in Dual-earner and Single-earner Families," *Developmental Psychology* 23, No. 3 (May 1987), pp. 431–440.

164   *Furthermore, according to University of Illinois psychologist*   Joseph H. Pleck, "Paternal Involvement: Levels, Sources, and Consequences," in Michael E. Lamb, ed., *The Role of the Father in Child Development* (New York: John Wiley & Sons, 1970).

173   *A study of 300 male executives and mid-level managers*   Thomas DeLong and Camille Collett DeLong, "Managers as Fathers: Hope on the Homefront," *Human Resource Management* 32, No. 3 (Fall 1992), p. 178.

175   *Michael Johnson, general manager of Maine Printing Company*   Ray Routhier, "Focus on Fatherhood," *Portland Press Herald* (June 16, 1996), p. 1G.

175   *When Johnson comes home,*   Ray Routhier, "Focus on Fatherhood," *Portland Press Herald* (June 16, 1996), p. 1G.

175   *Fathers who have participated in local offshoots*   Melissa Fletcher Stoejltje, "Daddy's Little Princess," *Houston Chronicle* (March 19, 1995), Lifestyle, p. 1.

Notes

175 *Dennis Harrish of the YMCA says,* Susan A. Cantonwine, "Indian Guides Promotes Father-Child Bond," *Dayton Daily News* (May 8, 1996), pp. Z3-6.

179 *Not surprisingly, in her study of dual-earner couples,* Rosalind Barnett and Caryl Rivers, *She Works/He Works* (SanFrancisco: HarperSanFrancisco, 1996).

CHAPTER SEVEN

185 *In 1994, the Travel Industry Association of America* Travel Industry Association of America, *The 1994 Survey of Business Travelers* (Washington, DC: Travel Industry Association of America U.S. Travel Data Center, 1995).

186 *TIA finds that business travelers* "Business Travel. More Travelers, More Trips," *PR Newswire* (October 17, 1995).

186 *In 1991, the average duration* Travel Industry Association of America, *The 1994 Survey of Business Travelers* (Washington, DC: Travel Industry Association of America U.S. Travel Data Center, 1995).

186 *And a new class of super-frequent business travelers* Leslie Wayne, "If It's Tuesday, This Must Be Family," *The New York Times* (May 14, 1995), p. 1.

186 *Hard-core road warriors* Leslie Wayne, "If It's Tuesday, This Must Be Family," *The New York Times* (May 14, 1995), p. 1.

186 *Their kids may not smile at them* Leslie Wayne, "If It's Tuesday, This Must Be Family," *The New York Times* (May 14, 1995), p. 1.

186 *According to a 1995 survey* Kristin Jackson, "Traveling Parents," *The Orlando Sentinel* (January 21, 1996), p. L2.

187 *A 1995 survey of 1,000 business travelers* Jay Clarke, "Tips and Tales from the Female Business Traveler," *Pittsburgh Post-Gazette* (June 16, 1996), p. F-6.

189 *The Marriott/ATT&T survey mentioned* "Inn-Credible Ways to Stay in Touch," *PR Newswire* (June 19, 1996).

190 *James Beasley, a safety engineer* Leslie Wayne, "If It's Tuesday, This Must Be Family," *The New York Times* (May 14, 1995), p. 1.

195 *"With my travel schedule and unpredictable hours, . . .* "MC: Don't Rely on Snail-Mail this Father's Day," *PR Newswire* (June 15, 1994).

195   *For the first time in his nineteen years of marriage,*   Eric Blom, "Maine Military Families Bridge Miles with E-Mail," *Portland Press Herald* (August 5, 1996), p. 1A.

195   *The system—which runs on two old computers*   Eric Blom, "Maine Military Families Bridge Miles with E-Mail," *Portland Press Herald* (August 5, 1996), p. 1A.

195   *Robert Hill, another Navy dad*   Eric Blom, "Maine Military Families Bridge Miles with E-Mail," *Portland Press Herald* (August 5, 1996), p. 1A.

197   *The children told neighbors*   Interview with Captain Gregory Bryant for *Family Man,* PBS film produced by James A. Levine, 1996.

198   *The Travel Industry Association of America reports*   Travel Industry Association of America, *The 1994 Survey of Business Travelers* (Washington, DC: Travel Industry Association of America U.S. Travel Data Center, 1995).

199   *A male accountant who has taken*   Bonnie Miller Rubin, "Parents' Business Trips Becoming Family Outings," *Chicago Tribune* (June 27, 1996), p. 1.

199   *The first time he brought his three-year-old son*   Anna D. Wilde, "It's a New Generation of Business Traveler," *The New York Times* (November 12, 1995), Section 3, p. 1.

200   *Because so many of its business travel guests*   Bonnie Miller Rubin, "Parents' Business Trips Becoming Family Outings," *Chicago Tribune* (June 27, 1996), p. 1.

CHAPTER EIGHT

PAGE

208   *Preschoolers: In 1991, 54 percent*   Lynne M. Casper, Mary Hawkins, and Martin O'Connell, *Who's Minding the Kids?* Current Population Reports, P70-36. (Washington, DC: U.S. Department of Commerce, Bureau of the Census, 1991).

209   *In 1996, Temple University psychologist Laurence Steinberg*   Laurence Steinberg, *Beyond the Classroom: Why School Reform Has Failed and What Parents Need to Do* (New York: Simon & Schuster, 1996), p. 13.

210   *What they discovered was*   Laurence Steinberg, *Beyond the Classroom: Why School Reform Has Failed and What Parents Need to Do* (New York: Simon & Schuster, 1996), p. 102.

Notes

210 *"Our findings were somewhat surprising"* Laurence Steinberg, *Beyond the Classroom: Why School Reform Has Failed and What Parents Need to Do* (New York: Simon & Schuster, 1996), p. 125.

210 *According to Steinberg* Laurence Steinberg, *Beyond the Classroom: Why School Reform Has Failed and What Parents Need to Do* (New York: Simon & Schuster, 1996), p. 126.

210 *Rather, "they mobilize the school. . . ."* Laurence Steinberg, *Beyond the Classroom: Why School Reform Has Failed and What Parents Need to Do* (New York: Simon & Schuster, 1996), p. 127.

211 *"To those who ask whether involving parents. . . ."* Ann T. Henderson and Nancy Berla, *A New Generation of Evidence: The Family Is Critical to Student Achievement* (Washington, DC: National Committee for Citizens in Education, 1994).

211 *In its 1985 study,* High School and Beyond, Dennis P. Doyle and Terry W. Hartle, "Better Schools Begin at Home," *The Record* (June 11, 1985).

213 *In 1996, a survey of parents, teachers, and students* Ledyard King, "Parents Get 'Incomplete' in School Poll," *Fort Lauderdale Sun-Sentinel* (June 18, 1996), p. 1B.

214 *The Hawthorne Elementary School* Laura Scott, "Positive Role Models," *The Kansas City Star* (December 11, 1995), p. B4.

217 *"I asked him why he needed two,"* John A. Cutter, "Family's New Face," *St. Petersburg Times* (October 25, 1993), p. 1D.

218 *At the J.W. Baker Elementary School* Cynthia Howell, "Education Column," *Arkansas Democrat-Gazette* (January 21, 1996), p. 1B.

218 *In Chandler, Arizona, members* E.J. Anderson, "Fathers Aid School with Own Club," *The Arizona Republic/The Phoenix Gazette* (September 20, 1995), p. 1.

218 *According to Gene Bedley* Shelby Grad, "A Trend Grows in Irvine: Dads Help Out at School," *Los Angeles Times* (June 22, 1996), p. A-1.

221 *At the Frederick Douglass Elementary School* Larry Bleiberg, "Parenting from A to F," *The Dallas Morning News* (December 25, 1994), p. 33A.

CONCLUSION

PAGE

229 *In 1980, 33 percent of couples* Deborah Erickson, "Work and Family: Are Women and Men That Different?" *Harvard Business Review* (Sept/Oct 1995), p. 13.

229   *In 1991, wives' earnings comprised*   "Female Breadwinners," *The Number News* 13, No. 11 (November 1993), p. 6.

229   *Being a mother does not seem*   Susan Kraft, "Why Wives Earn Less Than Husbands," *American Demographics* (January 1994), p. 16.

229   *Since 1987, the first year for which*   Howard V. Hayghe, "Working Wives' Contributions to Family Incomes," *Monthly Labor Review* 116, No. 8 (August 1993), pp. 39-42.

229   *Their numbers are small, an estimated 1.4 million in 1995,*   Tim Cavanaugh, "The Amazing Shrinking (and Expanding) House," *American Demographics* (November 1995), p. 13.

230   *Significantly more young workers*   Ellen Galinsky, James T. Bond, and Dana Friedman, *National Study of the Changing Workforce* (New York: Families and Work Institute, 1993), p. 99. See also Arlene Johnson, "The Business Case for Work–Family Programs, "*Journal of Accountacy* 180, No. 2 (August 1995), p. 53.

230   *Five out of six jobs*   Richard L. Forstal, "Going to Town," *American Demographics* (May 1993), p. 42.

230   *In 1976, 47.4 million people*   Barri Bronston, "Homework," *The Times-Picayune* (September 16, 1996), p. C-1.

230   *In a study on telecommuting*   William G. Deming, "Work at Home: Data from the CPS," *Monthly Labor Review* 117, No. 2 (February 1994), p. 14.

231   *By the middle of the twenty-first century, it is projected*   Bureau of the Census. *65+ in the United States.* U.S. Bureau of the Census, Current Population Reports, Special Studies, pp. 23–190 (Washington, DC: U.S. Government Printing Office, 1996).

231   *Although women devote significantly more time*   Ellen Galinsky, James T. Bond, and Dana E. Friedman, *The Changing Workforce: Highlights of the National Study*, No. 1 (New York: Families and Work Institute, 1993), p. 58.

For Further Information

DADDYSTRESS®/DADDY SUCCESS PROGRAMS

These programs are for executives, managers, and employees in a variety of organizational settings.

- Seminars for working parents and managers on balancing work and family life
- Consultations and briefings on creating a more father- and family-friendly workplace
- Presentations on a wide variety of aspects of fatherhood

THE FATHERHOOD PROJECT®

The Fatherhood Project is a national research and education project that is examining the future of fatherhood and ways to support men's involvement in childrearing. It was founded in 1981 at the Bank Street College of Education in New York City under the overall direction of James A. Levine and the codirection of Dr. Michael Lamb and Dr. Joseph H. Pleck. It was relocated in 1989 to the Families and Work Institute and now operates under the direction of James A. Levine and Edward W. Pitt. Current components include:

- **The Father-Friendly Business** an ongoing examination of how workplace policies and culture can support men's involvement in family life

- **National Practitioner's Network** helping to launch a national network of community-based practitioners designed to facilitate and promote local activities that support fathers and strengthen family support of children

- **The Male Involvement Project** a national training initiative that channels the expertise of Head Start and other community-based early childhood programs that have already been successful at increasing male involvement to others who share the same goal

- **Publications** a series of practical guidebooks including *New Expections: Community Strategies for Responsible Fatherhood* and *Getting Men Involved: Strategies for Early Childhood Programs*

FAMILIES AND WORK INSTITUTE

The Families and Work Institute is a national, nonprofit research, strategic planning, and consulting organization that conducts policy and worksite research on the changing work force and changing family/personal lives. FWI:

- Identifies the emerging issues for all workers—considering the entire life cycle, from prenatal and child care to elder care, and all levels of employees, from managers to assembly-line workers

- Benchmarks work–life solutions across all sectors of society—business, education, community, and government

- Evaluates the impact of solutions on employees, their families, and employers' productivity

For Further Information

FWI's research staff have backgrounds in public policy, child development, business, women's career mobility, fatherhood issues, and community development. Funding for the Families and Work Institute comes from the country's major foundations and corporations.

For more information or to order publications, please contact Families and Work Institute at the following address:

Families and Work Institute
330 Seventh Avenue, 14th Floor
New York, NY 10001

Telephone: (212) 465-2044
Fax: (212) 465-8637

Web Sites:
http://www.fatherhoodproject.org
http://www.familiesandwork.org

To contact the authors, please use the following e-mail addresses:

LevineJA@aol.com
tpittinsky@hbs.edu

Index

Index

Index

F

face time, 74–75, 96, 102, 119, 124
Fair Labor Standards Act, 156–157
Fairfax-San Anselmo Children's
 Center (Fairfax, CA), 218
Falanga, Ed, 78
Falls, Mark, 138–39, 140, 142, 144,
 145, 146
Families and Work Institute (FWI),
 2, 18, 33, 43, 97, 259–60. *See
 also National Study of the
 Changing Workforce*
Family and Medical Leave Act of
 1993 (FMLA)
 key employees, 155
 passage of, 127, 133
 provisions, 136–38, 141, 144,
 150–57
Family Research Council (FRC),
 18–19
family(ies), 32–33, 48–50. *See also*
 work–family conflict
father friendly. *See also* workplace,
 family friendly
Fatherhood Project, The, 8, 127,
 258–59
fathers. *See also* working fathers
 child development and, 37–42,
 45, 50
 defined, 16n
 as economic providers, 14, 18, 21,
 125
 importance of, 35–36
 roles of, 14
"Father's Participation in Infant
 Care" (article), 37
fax, 121, 192, 194

Federico, Richard, 44
Fel-Pro (company), 43
Fifth Discipline, The (book), 46, 47
Finding Our Fathers (book), 173
First Tennessee Bank, 75
First Tennessee National Corp., 45
First Things First (book), 161
First Union Bank (Charlotte, NC),
 75, 138, 140, 142
Fletcher, Larry, 80–81
Flex-It (company), 110
flexible scheduling
 employees, tactics for, 114–21
 getting buy-in, 118–19
 importance/benefits of, 69,
 71–72, 75, 102–6
 long-term impact, 125–26
 making it work, 119–21
 managers, tactics for, 121–24
 men, use by, 106–8
 negotiating, 114–19
 paid time-off, 149–50
 principles of, 108–14
 realistic expectations for, 113–14
 strategies for increasing, 108–24
Flexible Work Option Request,
 114–17, 118, 124
Flores, Oscar, 73
Flynn, Patrick, 146
FMLA. *See* Family and Medical
 Leave Act of 1993 (FMLA)
focus groups, 2–3, 66–68, 70, 109,
 229
for-profit sector, 64
Forbes, Malcolm, 133
Ford (company), 46
Ford Foundation, 2

Index

Index

Saunders, J.T., 161
S. C. Johnson & Son, Inc., 63–64, 68, 84
scheduling, flexible. *See* flexible scheduling
Schneer, Joy, 135
schools
  classroom visits, 214–15
  community service in, 213–14, 218–19
  father-friendly, 216–19
  involvement in, 86–87, 150, 209–16, 219–21
  joining PTO/PTAs, 217–18
Schor, Juliet, 160
Schroeder, Patricia, 133
Second Shift, The (book), 23, 24–25, 32, 33
"second shift" metaphor, 22–28, 33, 125
Seiderman, Stan, 218
Seitchik, Adam, 87
seminars. *See* parent education
Senge, Peter, 46, 47, 51
separation anxiety, 21, 141, 189
service sector, 49
Shellenbarger, Sue, 57
sick children, care of. *See* child care
sick leave, 140. *See* also Family and Medical Leave (FMLA) Act
Simonetti, Jack, 21
single parents, 21, 48, 49, 229
Sitomer, David A., 199
sitters. *See* child care
small businesses, 81, 130
Smith, Alan, 21
Snarey, John, 50

Sotsky, Les, 61
spouses. *See* marriage
St. Paul Companies, 43
Stein, Marjorie, 106
Steinberg, Laurence, 85, 209, 210, 211
Steward, Evelyne, 91, 113
Stewart, Steve, 78–79
Stillwell, Henry, 107–108
Stinson, Burke, 70, 100
Streep, Meryl, 206
stress, 19–21, 45, 101, 103, 179. *See also* work–family conflict
Sullivan, Sandra, 110
supervisors. *See* managers/supervisors
surveys and polls
  business travel, 189–90
  flexible scheduling, 103
  paternity leave, 133
  working fathers, 17–19, 28, 69
  work–family conflict, 15–16
Szalai, Alexander, 23, 24

T
"Take Our Daughters to Work Day," 176
task forces, work–family issues, 68–69
Tatum, Johnny, 91
Taylor, Brian B. and Jacquelyn, 88–89
TCSI Corporation, 140
teachers. *See* schools
teams, work, 75–78, 119
teenagers. *See* children
telecommuting. *See* home offices

Index